TREKKING AND CLIMBING IN THE
INDIAN
HIMALAYA

HARISH KAPADIA

Climbing consultant: VICTOR SAUNDERS

First published in 2001 by
New Holland Publishers (UK) Ltd
London · Cape Town · Sydney · Auckland

Garfield House, 86–88 Edgware Road, London W2 2EA, UK

80 McKenzie Street, Cape Town 8001, South Africa

14 Aquatic Drive, Frenchs Forest, NSW 2086, Australia

218 Lake Road, Northcote, Auckland, New Zealand

2 4 6 8 10 9 7 5 3 1

Distributed in India by
India Book Distributors (Bombay) Ltd
1007/1008, Arcadia, 195 Nariman Point
Bombay (Mumbai) 400 021
Post Box 11619, India

INDIA BOOK DISTRIBUTORS (BOMBAY) LTD.

ISBN 1 85974 670 5

Publishing Manager: Jo Hemmings
Series Editor: Kate Michell
Editor: Sara Harper
Design: Alan Marshall
Cartography: William Smuts
Production: Joan Woodroffe

Reproduction by Modern Age Repro Co. Ltd, Hong Kong
Printed and bound in Singapore by
Kyodo Printing Co (Singapore) Pte Ltd

The author and publisher have made every effort to ensure that
the information in this book was correct when the book went to
press; they accept no responsibility for any loss, injury or incon-
venience sustained by any person using this book.

Front cover: At the foot of Hansbeshan, Kinnaur (Trek 14).
Back cover: the author. *Cover spine:* On Kush Kalyan ridge
(Trek 11). *Title page:* Camp at Purne village, Zanskar (Trek
22). *This spread:* Climbing to Chhamser Kangri, Ladakh
(Trek 24). *Opposite contents page:* Siniolchu, 'the most
beautiful peak in the world'. Sikkim (Trek 1). *Contents page
top:* Camp above Tola, view of Nanda Devi, Kumaun (Trek
4); *middle top:* Procession of goddess Gangotri, Garhwal
(Trek 10); *middle bottom:* Kurgiak nala, Zanskar (Trek 22);
bottom: Garhwali lady, Garhwal (Trek 9).

CONTENTS

ABOUT THIS BOOK

Covering the Indian Himalaya from east to west, this book is divided into four regional chapters: Sikkim Himalaya, Kumaun and Garhwal, Himachal Pradesh, and Zanskar–Ladakh. Each regional chapter gives in-depth coverage of a number of recommended trekking routes plus selected climbing peaks that can be accessed during the course of the treks.

Like the trekking routes themselves, the peaks featured range in difficulty (from an easy scramble to a moderately technical climb) but mostly fall well within the horizon of any properly equipped and experienced party. They are presented as a natural highpoint of trekking in a high-altitude region.

Three introductory sections precede the regional chapters. An opening chapter provides a brief snapshot of the Indian Himalaya, its geography, people and culture. The second chapter provides all the practical advice you should need on arrival in the country and for travel by motorised transport as far as the trailhead; while the third covers all the practicalities thereafter – the logistics of setting off on trek and the possible extra requirements that may be involved in climbing peaks en route.

Regional directories at the end of each regional chapter consolidate the general advice given in the introductory sections with specific listings information.

Appendices on protecting the Himalaya, minimal impact trekking, mountain photography, and health and safety for trekkers complete the book.

LEGEND

———	Highway	✈	International airport
———	Provincial road	✕	Airport/airstrip
————	Secondary road	▲	Temple
··········	Track	ᴧ	Camp site
————	Trek route	⌒	Cave
▪▪ ▪▪▪ ▪▪	International boundary	*Shingo La*	Mountain pass
············	Railway	Nanda Devi ▲ 7816m (25644ft)	Peak in metres (feet)
☐ DELHI	City	*Duwo Glacier*	Glacier
◉ CHANDAGARH	Major town	dam, river	Water features
◎ Joshimath	Town		Altitude contour (4000m/13125ft on trek maps)
○ Karu	Village		Ridge
		ZANSKAR RANGE	Mountain range
		❶➤	Trek number

Trek Essentials boxes summarize each trek, including approximate number of days required, means of access to the start and finish, highest elevations reached, trekking style involved and official restrictions, if any. Also mentioned are notable variations on the route.

Top-class **mapping** pinpoints the route of each trek, with ridge lines, selected altitude contours, glaciers, passes and nearest roads included. Also illustrated in fainter dotted lines are alternative trails.

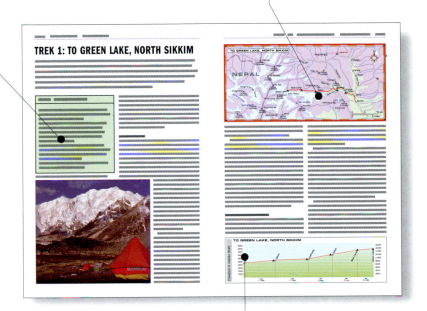

Strip maps illustrate the elevation profile of each trek, including key passes and village spot heights, as well as walking times.
(NB Strip maps are illustrative and not designed for cross-reference between treks.)

Climb Essentials boxes summarize the characteristics of each climbing route, including summit height, principal camps and grade of climb.

Specially sourced **topo photographs** show the general approach route to each climbing peak, with the route clearly marked in red.

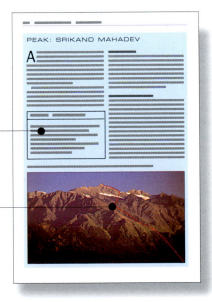

1

INTRODUCTION TO THE INDIAN HIMALAYA

Among the light I am the radiant sun
Among the stars I am the moon
Among the lakes I am the ocean
Among the mountains I am Kailash
Among the immovable I am the Himalaya

(Lord Krishna, *The Bhagavad-Gita*)

The Himalayan chain is spread southeast to northwest across the Asian continent. What is called the 'Indian Himalaya' is that part of the Himalayan chain which lies within Indian territory. In the east, the Indian Himalaya originates from a knot between Burma, China and India. The chain continues to the borders of Bhutan. Beyond that lies Sikkim, home to many peaks including the world's third highest, Kangchenjunga. The Himalayan range west of Sikkim forms part of Nepal, until you reach the borders of Kumaun and Garhwal. From here the Indian Himalayan chain continues without a break through Kinnaur, Spiti, Ladakh and lastly East Karakoram.

Khardung village in the Nubra Valley on the Leh–Khalsar road with the Arganglas group in the background.

The Baspa River flows past Chhitkul village, Kinnaur.

THE LAND

The Himalayan mountain range separates the Indian subcontinent from the Tibetan plateau. Strictly speaking, the Himalaya should be defined as the chain contained between the Tsangpo, Brahmaputra and Indus rivers, but informally the Karakoram and the Hindu Kush are often included as part of the chain.

HISTORY

In many ways the history of India is directly linked with the Himalayan Range. It was here that the Indus Valley civilization, one of the earliest organized cultures, flourished along the banks of the River Indus between 2500–1500BC. The migration of the Aryans, tribal herdsmen who later became farmers, occurred around 1500BC. Hindu religion took shape with the Aryans, and nature worship emerged as a dominant force. The Himalayan Range was revered as the abode of the gods and many of its mountains were worshipped as divine and cosmic images of gods. A pilgrimage to these holy sites became a tradition amongst the Hindus.

As the Mauryan and Gupta dynasties flourished, Hindu culture and heritage spread from northern India to the tip of the south. A caste system was established which has remained an integral part of Indian life to this day. In time, however, an important change to the religious scene occurred with the emergence of Buddhism, from the 5th century BC, which spread from the foothills of the Himalaya to Tibet, China and beyond – and continues to dominate these regions to this day. To halt the spread of Buddhism and revive the Hindu religion, the Indian guru Shankracharya made a tour of the whole of India, including the Himalaya, and established numerous temples.

Muslim raids on the north culminated with the establishment of the sultanate of Delhi in the 12th century under which much of India was unified. A later Muslim invasion in the 16th century established the Mogul empire. The Mogul emperor Akbar (1556–1605) introduced various land reforms and forms of local administration. Architecture reached its peak during his reign. The cultural heritage of India thus came to be shaped by not just two, but three main religions.

For many years the high Himalayan passes continued to be the gateway to India, with a trickle of European scholars and explorers coming in. However, with the opening of new sea routes in the 17th century, Dutch, Portuguese, British and French traders came to India. This heralded the decline of the Mogul empire. The British East India Company established political supremacy and gradually shifted power to the British government.

India remained under British colonial rule until 1947. While it suffered economically, the country nevertheless gained a new administrative structure for its government, newly organized laws and communications, and an intricate network of railways throughout the country. During this period major explorations were undertaken in the Himalaya for purposes of trade, survey and defence. It was in fact the beginning of systematic trekking and exploration of the range.

On gaining independence in 1947, India was split in two – India and Pakistan. This division led to a long-running dispute over the region of Kashmir, which continues to be a sore point between the two nations today.

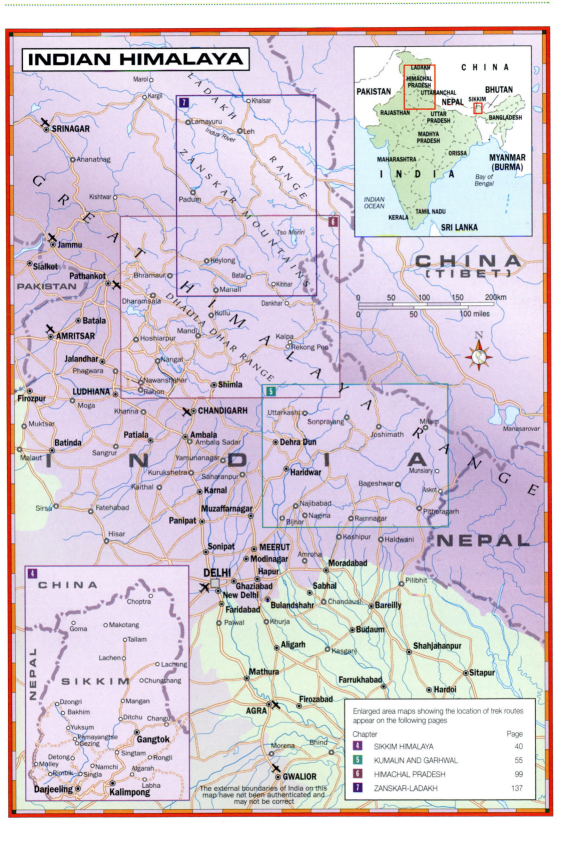

INDIAN HIMALAYA

Enlarged area maps showing the location of trek routes appear on the following pages

The external boundaries of India on this map have not been authenticated and may not be correct

Since independence India has followed democratic traditions, but has also faced four outbreaks of war, each involving action in the Himalayan Range. The first was with China in 1962, in Arunachal Pradesh and Ladakh. The following three wars were with Pakistan: in 1965 conflict erupted in the ranges near Kargil; 1971 witnessed the formation of Bangladesh and violence along the Shyok Valley in Ladakh; and in 1999 fighting broke out in the heights over Kargil. The Himalayan Range continues to play a significant role in the geopolitical landscape of India today.

EXPLORATION OF THE HIMALAYA

The Indians have always looked up to the Himalaya as the 'abode of snow', which is literally what the name means. In the Hindu scriptures spiritual tranquillity is associated with the Himalaya and there are many shrines in these mountains. Locals also crossed the range for trade, but the exploration and climbing that we know today started with the arrival of the British.

A major concern of 19th-century British foreign policy (known as the 'Great Game') was to reduce Russian influence in the area. Explorers were sent into the range to gain geographical information and intelligence about the strength of Russia's forces. One of the most notable explorers at this time was Francis Younghusband, who led an expedition across Sikkim to reach Lhasa in 1904. Soon explorers were followed by British army surveyors who systematically drew maps of each area. This resulted in the discovery in Nepal of the highest peak in the world, Everest, during the years 1849–1855. Then came the climbers.

One of the better-known early expeditions was that of Hugh Ruttledge, who explored Kumaun in 1929. In 1905 and 1907 Arnold Mumm and Charles Bruce spent five months in Garhwal and climbed several peaks. Trisul 7120m (23360ft) was climbed in 1907 by Dr Tom Longstaff and it remained the highest climbed peak in the world for several years.

The Himalayan Club was formed in 1928 to assist mountaineering expeditions. During the 1930s Frank Smythe, Eric Shipton and HW Tilman evolved a new style of climbing and exploration, typified by travelling lightly, often with just a Sherpa or two. Frank Smythe reached the summit of Kamet (7756m/25447ft) in 1931 to break the record. He was soon overtaken by the classic climb of Nanda Devi (7816m/25644ft) in 1936.

After World War II and Indian independence in 1947, there were serious doubts about whether mountaineering would continue to flourish. Some of the British climbers who stayed on, such as Jack Gibson and John Martyn, enthused Indians into climbing and the sport continued. One of their colleagues, Gurdial Singh, climbed Trisul in 1951, the first peak to be climbed by an Indian on an Indian expedition. In 1953 Everest was climbed and one of the summitters, Tensing, was an Indian national. To celebrate this particular event a mountaineering institute was established in Darjeeling which has since trained many Indians. Now three such institutes operate to full capacity and further contribute to the growth of the sport. In 1958 the Indian Mountaineering Foundation was established and authorised by the government to deal with the bureaucratic aspects of mountaineering in the Himalaya.

REGION BY REGION

Broadly speaking the Indian Himalaya consists of the following regions: Arunachal Pradesh; Sikkim; Kumaun; Garhwal; Kinnaur; Spiti; Kullu; Lahaul; Kishtwar; Kashmir; Zanskar; Ladakh; and Eastern Karakoram.

Kinnauri architecture with the Charang Ghati Pass in the background.

Arunachal Pradesh

Also known as the Assam Himalaya, much of this area, stretching from Gori Chen in the east to Namcha Barwa, is still to be explored. Due to government restrictions, not many mountaineers have been allowed to visit the area. There are several high peaks, such as Gyala Peri (7150m/23460ft), Kangto (7090m/23260ft) and Nyegi Kangsang (6983m/22910ft), few of which have been climbed from the Indian side, and some such as Nyegi Kangsang are still unscaled. Some peaks have been approached from Tibet and climbed from the north. The only peak that has been regularly climbed from the Indian side is Gori Chen (6858m/22501ft).

Kinnauris celebrating the festival of Phulej or the arrival of the flowering season.

FM Bailey and HT Morshead were the first explorers here (around 1912), followed by F Kindon-Ward in 1939. HW Tilman also visited this area in the same year and wrote his report *Assam Himalaya Unvisited*. The book by FM Bailey, *No Passport to Tibet*, is an excellent reference.

The slopes of the Assam Himalaya witnessed the full fury of the war with China in 1962 and the area was closed to civilians for many years. Now, previously restricted areas are open to visitors and joint expeditions (with Indian members) are allowed.

Sikkim Himalaya

Sikkim shares a mountainous border with Nepal in the west and with China in the north and east. It became an Indian State in 1975. All the early expeditions to Tibet before World War II, including Francis Younghusband's famous expedition in 1904, passed through Sikkim on their way to attempt Everest.

Doug Freshfield was one of the early mountaineers to visit this area, in 1899. His book *Round Kangchenjunga* is a classic record of all the areas in north Sikkim. In west Sikkim, Kabru (7338m/24076ft) was climbed in 1935 by CR Cook. Kokthang and Rathong were climbed much later, in 1964. Even now, some peaks have not been climbed from the Sikkim side, though ascents have been made from Nepal.

Northern Sikkim consists of the Zemu Glacier Valley from which rises the third highest mountain in the world, Kangchenjunga (8586m/28170ft). Paul Bauer and his German team repeatedly attempted to climb it via its eastern approaches before World War II. Ultimately, the Indian Army team was successful in doing so in 1977, and there have been several subsequent repeat ascents. Other tempting peaks around Kangchenjunga include Simvu (6812m/22350ft) and Siniolchu (6877m/22563ft).

Further north is Pyramid Peak, the most recent 7000m (22967ft) peak to be climbed by the Himalayan Association of Japan (HAJ) in 1993. In the vicinity are Jongsang and Chorten Nyima. Pauhunri, with the pinnacle of Donkhya Ri, is one of the chief attractions on the eastern side.

Kumaun

Kumaun lies to the west of Nepal and consists of three valleys. The area is generally confused with Garhwal but, in fact, Garhwal was a part of Kumaun until partitioned by the British and renamed.

SIKKIM IN BLOOM

Sikkim became an Indian State in 1976 and we were amongst the earliest trekkers there. On our trip to the Green Lake, my companion Zerksis Boga and I went across high passes to the Lhonak Valley. At one point, as we neared Thangu, Boga suddenly sat down near a bridge. The slope before us was covered with yellow rhododendrons in bloom. I took one photo then he firmly stopped me: 'No more photos please. This beauty must belong only to memories', he said.

The first valley, in the east, is the Darma Ganga Valley. At its head are several peaks above 6000m (19686ft), some of them technically difficult to climb. Sangthang and Lalla We in the east can be approached from here but the area is still out-of-bounds to foreign climbers.

The Milam Glacier Valley is the central valley in the Kumaun. On its eastern branch, the Kalabaland Glacier is an excellent climbing area. Chiring We (6559m/21520ft) rises from the Kalabaland Glacier in the north and has been climbed only once (in 1979 by an Indian team). To the south rises Suitilla (6373m/20910ft), a formidable and difficult peak. The Panch Chuli group lies in the southeast – it has five different peaks which were summitted with great difficulty from the east and the west. At the head of the Milam Glacier are the attractive peaks Hardeol (7151m/23462ft) and Tirsuli (7074m/23210ft). Nanda Devi East has been climbed from this valley.

The western valley of Kumaun is the Pindari, flanked by the peaks of Panwali Dwar (6663m/21861ft) and Nanda Khat. This area is popular with climbers. The Sunderdhunga Valley branches off from the Pindari and leads to the southern foot of the Nanda Devi Sanctuary.

The area from where the Rishi ganga River starts is the famous Nanda Devi Sanctuary, the centrepiece of the Kumaun–Garhwal region. Until 1934 the gorge of the Rishi ganga was the least-known part of the Himalaya. The Nanda Devi Range is a long one, about 120km (75 miles) in circumference, having many peaks above 6000m (19686ft), and with approximately 380km^2 (147 sq miles) of ice and snow. The Nanda Devi Peak (7816m/25644ft) is considered to be the most beautiful peak in the Indian Himalaya. It was climbed in 1936 by Tilman and Odell and the ridge between these peaks was crossed by an Indo-Japanese expedition in 1976.

Other noteworthy peaks on the rim of the Sanctuary are Changabang (6864m/22520ft), Rishi Pahar (6992m/22940ft) and Bethartoli Himal (6352m/20841ft). The northernmost peak of the Inner Sanctuary, Changabang, was climbed in 1974 by the Indo-British team led by Chris Bonington. Four days later, an Indian team climbed Devtoli (6788m/22271ft), at the Inner Sanctuary's southernmost tip. Despite many successful climbs, there are still several unscaled peaks here, particularly in the northern part of the Sanctuary.

To preserve the fragile ecosystem, this area is now closed to mountaineers. Only one army expedition has been allowed access during the last 15 years and it is not known when and whether anyone will be permitted to climb here again. However the peaks on the rim of the Nanda Devi Sanctuary can be climbed by approaching them from the side valleys outside the core area.

Garhwal

Garhwal lies in the centre of the Indian Himalaya. In the Hindu scriptures spiritual tranquillity is always associated with these snowy mountains and there are numerous popular Hindu shrines located in Garhwal. The earliest recorded travel in the Himalaya is that of the Indian guru Adi Shankracharya, who crossed Mana Pass from Badrinath to Guge district in Tibet in 800. Jesuit priests from Europe – Antonio de Andrade and Manuel Marques – crossed Mana Pass to Guge in Tsaparang province in Tibet in 1624. In more recent times mountaineers have been visiting and climbing in this area for many years.

North Garhwal consists of peaks such as Kamet (7756m/25447ft) and Mukut Parvat (7242m/23761ft). Many other high peaks here

Garhwal's spectacular Bhilangana Valley.

have not been climbed. Large glaciers such as the Bhagirath Kharak and the Arwa valleys have several peaks, including the Chaukhamba group, Kunaling and the Arwa Tower. The Hindu temple of Badrinath also attracts many pilgrims.

A large number of glaciers edge their way into the Gangotri region from all sides. Many mountaineering parties have visited this area since it was opened to foreigners about two decades ago. The famous peaks here are Thalay Sagar (6904m/22652ft), Bhrigupanth (6772m/22219ft), Shivling and Satopanth. At the head of the main Gangotri Glacier rise the peaks of Chaukhamba. Its Peaks I (7138m/23420ft), II (7068m/23190ft), III (6974m/22882ft) and IV (6854m/22488ft) have proved a challenge for the best climbers. Kedarnath Peak (6940m/22770ft), on the southern divide of the Gangotri Glacier, has also been climbed from its southern approach, which is more difficult. The Gangotri temple is a popular pilgrim destination.

Another landmark in Garhwal is Kamet, which stands tall over the Saraswati Valley. Kamet Peak was attempted several times and finally in 1931 Frank Smythe and Eric Shipton reached the summit. RL Holdsworth, who was with them, famously smoked a pipe on the summit.

Towards the north is the Jadh Ganga Valley, surveyed by JB Auden in 1939. It was visited again in 1990 when Trimukhi Parvat East was climbed. The next year an army team climbed the main peak.

The valleys to the extreme west of the Garhwal have some lovely peaks, where many students and mountaineers have trained. The Swargarohini group can be difficult, although Bandarpunch West (6102m/20021ft) and Bandarpunch (6316m/20722ft) have been climbed a couple of times. This area is very convenient for a quick trip from Delhi.

Kinnaur

Beyond Garhwal the Himalayan Range takes a northwesterly turn, entering what is loosely called the western Himalaya. Immediately to the north are the valleys of Kinnaur, forming part of Himachal Pradesh. Recent bureaucratic changes have allowed visitors unrestricted entry to the area west of the national highway. Peaks such as Jorkanden (6473m/21238ft), Manirang (6593m/21632ft) and several others are now easily accessible.

Around the eastern valleys of Baspa, Tirung and Leo Pargial (6791m/22282ft) rise many peaks above 6000m (19686ft). Marco Pallis climbed Leo Pargial in 1933 and wrote a wonderful book about the experience, *Peaks and Lamas*. Kinnaur's architecture, people and customs are further attractions.

Lamas surveying the terraced fields of Ladakh from the roof of Spituk Monastery.

Spiti

Spiti is the most barren trans-Himalayan area, first brought to the knowledge of mountaineers by Jimmy Roberts in 1939 and later by two expeditions of Sir Peter Holmes, in 1955 and 1956, to the remote western valleys of Ratang and Pin.

In the east, the high peak of Gya (6794m/22291ft) was long a prized goal, attempted from the Lingti Valley in the west and from Chumar in the north. Its north and third peak were soon climbed, but the main peak continued to defy mountaineers. A team from the Indian Mountaineering Foundation ascended it in 1999, only to find a piton and a flag already on the summit. Despite poor reporting and poor photographs, earlier army climbers appeared to have reached the summit in 1998. The controversial Shilla (6132m/20119ft) also stands proudly above this valley.

In the west stretch the Ratang, Gyundi and Khamengar valleys. Khangla Tarbo (6315m/20718ft) is one of the better known peaks. No permits are required and approaches from the north are free of any restrictions.

Kullu

The lovely dales of Kullu are a major attraction for those who prefer to climb difficult but low peaks. Since the days when General Charles Bruce passed from the Dhauladhar to Kullu and went across Rohtang, several climbers have visited these valleys. Bob Pettigrew is credited with several climbs and explorations in these ranges from 1965 to 1970. The south Parvati area has peaks such as Dibibokri Pyramid, Papsura, and Parvati (6127m/21013ft). This area is also open to all climbers. With peaks such as Mukarbeh and Indrasan (6221m/20411ft), traditional local customs, and a strikingly different culture, Kullu has a lot to offer amateur and professional climbers.

Lahaul

The area north of the famous Rohtang Pass consists of the valleys of Lahaul. Lahaul is generally spoken of in the same breath as Spiti because administratively they are linked, having a common district headquarters at Keylong in Lahaul.

Around the Bara Shigri Glacier rise the peaks of Kullu Pumori (6553m/21500ft) and Shigri Parbat (6626m/21740ft). To the north the Chandra Bhaga group (CB group) has the Minar (6172m/20250ft) and Akela Killa (6005m/19702ft) peaks, all known by numbers and around the same height. Phabrang (6172m/20250ft) and Mulkila (6517m/21383ft) are the chief attractions on the west side. Reasonable roads lead to nearly all the valleys and the approaches are easy and hassle-free. The Manali–Leh highway crosses the centre of Lahaul, and other roads lead to the eastern and western valleys. These roads have reduced the approach time and Lahaul is an excellent destination for trekkers.

Kishtwar

This is the area west of Lahaul along the Chandra bhaga River, which is known as the Chenab when it enters Kishtwar. Due to current political troubles and turmoil, it is not easy to reach here and a thorough knowledge of prevalent conditions is a prerequisite. To climbers, it offers highly challenging and difficult peaks such as Brammah I (6416m/21051ft), Brammah II (6425m/21080ft), Sickle Moon (6574m/21569ft) and Hagshu (6300m/20670ft).

Kashmir

The valley of Kashmir has been known for centuries for its beauty. In ancient times caravans passed through and more recently, trekkers and campers have flocked here. Early climbers attempted the small peaks in the south, such as Kolahoi (5425m/17800ft) and Haramukh (5143m/16874ft). A large area around Sonamarg was visited by British climbers. *The Climbers Guide to Sonamarg*, published by the Himalayan Club, is an excellent reference book. However since 1989 the area has been politically unstable.

Zanskar

The barren valleys of Zanskar, south of Ladakh, were once inaccessible, but now a road runs through Zanskar's centre. Hundreds of trekkers cross to Padum in central Zanskar and proceed to Leh in Ladakh. This is rapidly becoming one of the world's most popular trails, and is easily approached from Kargil in the west. En route is the area's star attraction, Phuktal monastery, built high up, almost inside a cave. The Hungarian scholar Csoma de Koros stayed here for many years.

Zanskaris are a hardy lot and brave the cruel winters there, although cut off from all sides. As the summer approaches they traditionally follow a route along the Zanskar River to Nimo. On this route, called 'Tchaddar', they are now sometimes joined by trekkers.

For professional climbers are the high peaks of Nun (7135m/23410ft), Kun (7135m/23410ft), Z I (6181m/20280ft) and Z II (6175m/20260ft). Kun was climbed in 1913 while the first ascent of Nun was made by Bernard Pierre's team in 1953.

Ladakh

Ladakh used to be called 'Little Tibet'. Caravans passed through Leh on the way to and from central Asia. Traders came from all directions: Tibetans from the east, people from Kullu in the south, Muslims from Balti valleys in the west and caravans from Central Asia in the north. Today, despite the influx of plane-loads of tourists, it has not lost any of its charms. There are many places suitable for trekkers and mountaineers and almost all of Ladakh's valleys are open to foreigners. The blue

---

FESTIVALS

Some of the major festivals in India include the Republic Day Celebrations (26 January); Holi, the festival of colours celebrating the end of winter (February–March); Phool Walon Ki Sair (October) and Diwali, the festival of lights (October–November). Local festivals are held in almost all Himalayan areas and their times differ every year according to the Hindu calendar. Buddhist and Muslim festivals are also held regularly.

waters of Tso Moriri, the wide barren landscapes and the nomads (Changpas) are just some of the area's other attractions.

The southeastern valley of Rupshu has several peaks: the highest of them, Lungser Kangri (6666m/21870ft), was climbed by an Indian expedition in 1995. Three of the others, Pologongka, Kula and Chhamser Kangri were climbed in quick succession by mountaineers of various nationalities. However, many peaks, including Chakula, have yet to be climbed.

Trekking with pack mules through the dry, barren landscape of Ladakh.

Eastern Karakoram

Behind the town of Leh the Khardung Range runs eastwards from the confluence of the Shyok and Indus rivers until it meets the Pangong Range. To the north of both these ranges lies the East Karakoram, which has some of the highest peaks in the Indian Himalaya.

One of the highest roads in the world crosses Khardung La to enter the Shyok Valley. From the pass, Saser Kangri II can be seen to advantage. Its west peak was climbed by a team of Indian and Japanese climbers in 1985 while the east peak, at the same height (7518m/24665ft), remains unclimbed. The Saser group was explored by Jimmy Roberts in 1946, and its main peaks have all been climbed, with the exception of what Roberts called 'Plateau Peak' (7287m/23907ft). Ascents have been attempted on Saser Kangri I from both the eastern and western approaches and it has a long record of climbs. Saser Kangri III was once climbed by an Indian team coming from the east.

Another group is that of Rimo Muztagh, which contains the famous central Asian trade route over the Karakoram Pass. From the Nubra Valley a feeder 'silk route' leads to the Karakoram Pass. Here stands Mamostong Kangri, first climbed in 1984, and Aq Tash, a stupendous rocky pyramid, first climbed by an Indo-Japanese team in 1993. Three peaks of the Chong Kumdan group, including the main peak at 7071m (23199ft), were climbed in 1991 along with several others. Chong Kumdan was famous for the natural dam it created when the advancing Chong Kumdan Glacier blocked the Shyok river during winter. With the advent of summer the river would swell up, causing the dam to burst, and resulting in floods and havoc for several hundred kilometres downstream. The last such dam was formed in 1928 and since then, mercifully, the glacier has been in retreat.

The Siachen Glacier area contains some of the highest peaks in the Indian Himalaya. The earliest recorded exploration here was in 1821. Dr TG Longstaff visited the glacier in 1910, followed by the Bullock–Workman expeditions in 1911 and 1912. In 1930 and 1935 Italian and Dutch expeditions climbed here. After this, the area was not visited for many years until the 1970s, when different teams, mainly Japanese, crossed over from Bilafond La onto the Siachen Glacier and climbed peaks such as Teram Kangri I (7462m/24483ft). The Japanese mountaineers were very active in this region, and climbed many difficult peaks. Then, once more, the area was closed to all for several years.

In 1984, members of a Japanese expedition, the first foreign mountaineers to be allowed into this area from the Indian side, climbed Mamostong Kangri I. The following year an Indo-British team climbed Rimo III and a few other peaks in the Terong Valley. Some peaks on the Siachen Glacier have been climbed by the Indian Army. There are still several unexplored peaks in the Siachen Muztagh, such as Saltoro Kangri I and II.

The valleys of the Eastern Karakoram are open to joint ventures by Indian and foreign mountaineers. Permits for climbing are available for many peaks.

PEOPLE

The vast Himalayan Range contains many villages and a fairly large population. Villages are found not only in lower regions, but also in more deserted and higher areas, especially in the western parts. Each region forms almost its own ethnic group, with a unique culture, language, dress-code and festivals. Kinnaur has some 23 dialects, and people from different villages have to speak Hindi to communicate with each other. With schools and increased interaction with the plains of India, some of these traditions are changing. However, there is still so much variety remaining that a wonderful article in *The Himalayan Journal* (Volume 54: *'Pahari Topi*, Where did you get that hat?') comes to mind, describing the different hats worn by people of the Himalaya. There are many!

Sikkim has several ethnic groups, starting with the native Lepchas. Large numbers of Nepalis have settled in the region, while nearby Darjeeling is home to the Indian Sherpas. People in Sikkim are mainly Buddhist and as such their traditions include hoisting a prayer flag on each building to celebrate Loser (generally held in February) as their new year. They have also built several notable large monasteries.

Kumaun and **Garhwal** are ethnically similar to one another, though a Kumauni would not like to be called a Garhwali. Both share a strong tradition of service in the Indian army in the regiments of the same names. These people are Hindus and worship at important temples such as Badrinath and Kedarnath.

Traditional musicians outside a Hindu temple in Kinnaur.

Some of the Hindus of Kumaun traded with Tibet across the high passes – with the Tibetan caravans descending in turn to their valleys. This interaction led to numerous intermarriages and the assimilation of each other's traditions. The resulting group was classifed by the British as Bhotias. They are Hindu by religion but follow many of the Buddhist traditions of Tibet. Today there are many Bhotian settlements in Kumaun, celebrating Dusherra for example, the Hindu festival of harvest, and Diwali, the Hindu new year.

To the west, the **Kinnauris** trace their lineage to the Kinner Desh ('Land of Kinnaur') of ancient scriptures. They have indigenous architecture and festivals, such as the festival of Phulej to celebrate the arrival of the flowering season. Most of them are Buddhists. Similarly **Spitians** and **Lahaulis** have several tribal traditions, and used to have many connections with Tibetans.

The Hindus of **Kullu** and **Kangra** follow the worshipping of different goddesses. These idols are taken in a procession on the day of Dusherra to Kullu where a major festival is held (generally in October). Farmers by tradition, they were formerly ruled by Hindu *rajas*.

To the west of these areas is the Muslim population of **Kishtwar** and **Kashmir**, extending as far as Kargil in Ladakh. People here follow various Muslim sects. The Muslims of Kashmir coexisted peacefully with the Hindu Pandits of the valley until recently.

The northernmost parts of the Indian Himalaya, the **Ladakh** areas, are mostly Buddhist and follow traditions and religious practices similar to those of western Tibet. Large monasteries have been built by Buddhist gurus over the centuries. As Ladakhis were by tradition traders, many ethnic groups can be observed in an evening stroll around the streets of Leh. You may meet a local Ladakhi Buddhist, a Hindu trader from Lahaul or Kullu, a local Muslim settled here from central Asia or Kashmir or even a representative of a small Christian settlement left over from the days of the Moravian Church. All now freely interact with Indians from the plains and western tourists.

The writer Norman Mailer reportedly rebuked President JF Kennedy after the Bay of Pigs fiasco. He said, 'you invaded a country without understanding its music.' It could similarly be argued that a trip to the Indian Himalaya will be much more enjoyable if you appreciate its rich cultural history and diverse ethnicity.

CLIMATE

The Indian Himalaya is spread across almost the entire subcontinent, and the weather varies dramatically in each region. The seasons generally follow a pattern from east to west. Winter and monsoons will arrive in Sikkim first and then move westwards to Ladakh.

Winter is severe all over the Himalaya, especially in the higher reaches. In winter in areas in the west, such as Zanskar and Ladakh, temperatures can go down to −40°C (−104°F). With heavy snowfall all the passes become blocked and villages are isolated. Except on select routes by well-equipped parties it is difficult to trek at this time. Winter generally arrives by early December but sometimes there is no snowfall till early January. Most areas will remain snowbound till late April. Sometimes for lower areas of the Himalaya this is a good time to trek, with very clear distant views and deserted valleys.

Summer is the best time to trek and climb. This is known as the 'pre-monsoon' season. March and April for Sikkim, May and June for Garhwal–Kumaun, are all suitable for trekking and climbing, although there will be more snow and some haze during this period. It is a warm season in higher areas.

Monsoons arrive in Sikkim by mid-May and in central areas by late June. The first showers are heavy and the entire region is enveloped in thick fog. Views of peaks are near impossible but can be dramatic when any peak is visible. Roadblocks are common. This is the best season for flowers and studying flora. The Valley of Flowers is best

A smiling Kumauni girl from this ethnically diverse region.

botanically in August, although for views it is best in June.

Autumn is called the 'post-monsoon' season. The rains withdraw again going westwards. By late September the weather is improving and allows excellent views and conditions until mid-November. During this period you can get clear views of the ranges and, except for local disturbances, the weather remains clear.

There is one exception to this general weather pattern – the Trans-Himalayan areas. These areas mostly lie beyond the reach of the monsoon. From western Garhwal the Himalaya Range turns sharply north. The farther you go, the less will be the effect of the monsoon. Thus the areas of Kinnaur and Spiti have clear weather from May to November. Zanskar and Ladakh are open from early June to early October when the winter sets in. However, as a result of global warming these weather patterns are changing and the glaciers are melting at an alarming rate.

WHEN TO GO

The following are generally the best periods to trek and climb. However, local storms, daily weather patterns and global disturbances can bring rains at any time.

Sikkim	March–April, October–November
Kumaun	April–June, September–November
Garhwal	May–June, October–November
Kinnaur	June–November
Spiti	June–November
Kullu–Kangra	May–June, October–November
Lahaul	July–October
Zanskar	July–October
Ladakh	June–October

2

ARRIVING IN

THE INDIAN HIMALAYA

Once you've lived with the mountains
You will return
You will come back
To touch the trees and grass
And climb once more the windswept
Mountain pass

(Ruskin Bond)

India is a vast country with the Himalayan Range forming its northern boundary. Its climate and geography are complex, so when considering your trip you need to plan carefully where to go, when to go and what your budget is. The initial experience of India – the heat, the noise and the street life, the vibrant colours and the multitudes of people – may bewilder and exhaust the first-time visitor, but the country and its people are friendly and hospitable. Once you have spent some time here everything will fall into place, and you will be amply rewarded with your first glimpse of the Himalayan peaks, one of the most spectacular mountain ranges in the world.

Trekkers at Korzok Village in the Rupshu district of Ladakh with the Mentok Range rising up in the background.

TRAVELLING TO INDIA

Delhi is the gateway for most trips to the Indian Himalaya. Daily scheduled international air connections to Delhi are operated by the world's major airlines, and there are numerous internal flights linking Delhi to the rest of India. For treks out of Darjeeling visitors can either fly to Delhi then fly or travel by train or road to Darjeeling or Gangtok.

There are various road entry points to India. The classic overland route to India from Europe is through the Middle East, via Turkey, Iran and Pakistan. There are regular bus services between Delhi and Kathmandu in Nepal, and it is also possible to travel overland through Southeast Asia.

Visas

All foreign nationals (including Commonwealth citizens) require a valid passport, and an appropriate visa (entry, transit or tourist), obtained from Indian embassies and consulates overseas.

Tourist visas are usually valid for six months from the date of issue. However, if you wish to prolong your stay in India, you may apply for a visa extension at the Foreigners' Registration Office in Delhi, Srinagar or Darjeeling, or at the office of the Superintendent of Police in all State and District capitals (in Leh or Manali, for example). The Foreigners' Registration Office in Delhi is located at Hans Bhavan, Tilak Bridge, New Delhi (tel 331-9498, 331-8179).

Certain places, such as Sikkim, the Andaman Islands and Lakshadweep, require special permits, and you will need an 'X' visa for climbing peaks and mountaineering (see page 38).

If you plan to visit a neighbouring country such as Nepal and then re-enter India, you should obtain a double/multiple entry visa.

Health Regulations

A valid yellow fever certificate is mandatory for anyone who has been, even in transit, in Africa or South America or Papua New Guinea in the six days prior to arrival in India. The certificate becomes valid 10 days after vaccination and in its absence a person will be quarantined for a period of up to 6 days. India no longer requires immunisation against smallpox and cholera.

Customs Clearance

On arrival pass through immigration and customs: if you have nothing to declare walk through the green channel.

The usual duty-free allowance for passengers (above 12 years of age) of 200 cigarettes (or 50 cigars or 250g tobacco) and liquor and wines up to 32oz (1 litre) applies.

You are permitted to bring in numerous articles for your personal use, including cameras with five rolls of film, a reasonable quantity of jewellery, one pair of binoculars, one portable musical instrument, one radio set, one tape recorder, one portable typewriter, a laptop computer and professional equipment on the condition that you take them back with you when leaving India. (High-value goods will be entered on a Tourist Baggage Export Form to ensure they are exported.) Drugs and narcotics and the import of firearms are prohibited. There are duty-free shops at the airport both in the Arrival and Departure lounges.

Export Regulations

For gold, silverware and other jewellery of high value or large quantity, an export certificate should be obtained from the vendor and declared to the customs authorities in advance of travel.

There are restrictions on the export of antiquities and art objects more than 100 years old. In case of doubt, consult the Director of Antiquities, Archaeological Survey of India, Janapath (tel 301-7220). Export of most wildlife products is prohibited and strictly regulated; therefore avoid buying anything made of ivory, reptile skin, fur, musk, tortoise shells and any part of wild animals.

Departure Tax

Check if your travel agent has paid your departure tax of Rs 500 for all international departures and Rs 150 to all neighbouring countries. If not you must set aside the required amount in Indian rupees and pay it before you check in.

Time Difference

There is only one Indian Standard Time (IST) for the whole country. In winter (end October to end March) IST is 5 hours ahead of GMT; 9 hours ahead of American Eastern Standard Time; and 5

DOMESTIC AIRLINES

Indian Airlines: PTI Bldg, Sansad Marg, tel 371-9168/0369. 24hrs booking at Safdarjung Airport, tel (reservations) 462-0566/2220, 463-1335/7

Jet Airways: Jetair Hse, 13, Connaught Circus, Yusuf Sarai, tel 651-7443, 685-3700, 651-9551

Sahara India: GF Amba Deep Bldg, KG Marg, tel 332-6851/335-2771, Airport: 566-5234/5879

hours behind Australian Eastern Standard Time. In summer (end March to end October), IST is 4 hours ahead of GMT; 10 hours ahead of American Eastern Standard Time; and 4 hours behind Australian Eastern Standard Time.

MONEY
Currency

The Indian rupee is divided into 100 paise. The currency is available in denominations of Rs 1,000, 500, 100, 50, 20, 10 and 5 as well as coins of Rs 5, 2, 1 and of 50, 25 paise. You are not

Rail-cars, once used by British Viceroys, are still in use today on the Kalka and Shimla Hill Railway.

allowed to bring Indian currency into or take it out of the country. You may bring in an unlimited amount of foreign currency or traveller's cheques, but anything above US$ 10,000 (or US$ 2500 if in cash) must be declared on arrival.

Credit Cards

Diners Club, Mastercard, American Express and Visa are among the widely accepted credit cards.

Banks and Exchange

The State Bank of India and associated banks have branches near most starting points of treks. Indian rupee traveller's cheques are accepted by these banks. However, they will NOT cash foreign

traveller's cheques or foreign currency, and credit cards are not acceptable. Therefore make sure you carry sufficient Indian currency for the trek. Take enough small denomination notes, as obtaining change may be a problem.

Tipping

Waiters and doormen expect a tip, and in restaurants anything between 5% to 10% on the final bill is the norm. In some restaurants and hotels a 10% service charge is included in the bill. When paying by credit card the tip may be added to the final total before signing. On a trek, porters, muleteers, caretakers at rest houses and taxi drivers expect a tip. A nominal sum may be given depending on the ser-

EMBASSIES AND CONSULATES IN NEW DELHI

Australia: 1/50-G Shantipath, ND 21, tel 688-8223, 687-2035, fax 688-5199, 687-4126, (Public Affairs) 688-2732

Bangladesh: 56 Ring Road, Lajpat Nagar III, ND 24, tel 683-4668, 683-9209/4065, fax 6839-237

Bhutan: Chandragupta Marg. Chanakyapuri, ND 21, tel 688 - 9230/9807/09, fax 687-6710

Canada: 7/8 Shantipath, ND 21, tel 687-6500, fax 687-6579

China: 50-D Shantipath, ND 21, tel 687-1585/86/87

Denmark: 11, Aurangazeb Rd, ND 11, tel 301-0900/002, tlx 31-66160 AMDK IN, fax 301-0961

France: 2/50-E Shantipath, ND 21, tel 611-8790, fax 687-2305

Germany: 6/50-G Shantipath, ND 21, tel 687-1831, 687-1891, tlx 31-72177, fax 687-3117, 687-7623

Italy: 50-E Chandragupt Marg, ND 21, tel 611-4355/53, fax 687-3889

Nepal: Barakhamba Road, ND 1, tel 332-8191, 332-9218, tlx 31-66283 NEMB IN, fax 332-6857

Netherlands: 6/50-F Shantipath, ND 21, tel 688-4951/54, fax 688-4956

New Zealand: 50-N Nyaya Marg, ND 21, tel 688-3170, fax 687-2317

Pakistan: 2/50-G Shantipath, ND 21, tel 467-6004/ 467-8467, tlx 31-65270 PARP IN, fax 687-2339

Sri Lanka: 27 Kautilya Marg, ND 21, tel 301-0201, 301-0202, tlx 63435 SLHC IN, fax 301-5295

Switzerland: Nyaya Marg, ND 21, tel 687-8372, tlx 3172350 AMCH IN, fax 687-3093

United Kingdom: Shantipath, ND 21, tel 687-2161, tlx 31-65125, fax 687-2882

USA: Shantipath, ND 21, tel 419-8000, fax 419-0017

REGIONAL TRAVEL

Sikkim: Travel by train to New Jalpaiguri station from Delhi or Calcutta. Fly from Delhi or Calcutta to Bagdogra airport. Take buses or taxis to Darjeeling and Gangtok.

Kumaun: Take a night train from Delhi to reach Kathgodam early in the morning. Road transport is available to Munsiary, Bageshwar and all other destinations.

Garhwal: For most areas of Garhwal take the night train to Haridwar or Dehra Dun. Taxis and buses (from Rishikesh) go to Joshimath, Kedarnath, Gangotri and Sankhri and other starting points for treks.

Kinnaur/Spiti: Reach Chandigarh or Kalka by night train. Take the small-gauge train to Shimla or a direct bus or taxi to Rekong Peo (headquarters for Kinnaur) or Kaja (headquarters for Spiti).

Kullu/Manali: Fly to Bhuntar from Delhi then bus or taxi to Kullu (9km) and Manali (41km). Or take a direct bus/taxi from Delhi to Kullu/Manali (12 hours). Alternatively, travel by train to Chandigarh/Kalka and take a bus or taxi to Kullu/Manali (8 hours). When passes are open you can take another bus/taxi to Spiti, Darcha and Leh from Manali.

Dhauladhar: Travel by night train to reach Pathankot early in the morning. Regular buses and taxis will take you to Dharamsala.

Ladakh: Daily flights connect Leh with Delhi, Chandigarh, Srinagar and Jammu. It takes at least 4 days to reach Leh via Manali (the Manali–Leh highway is generally open July to October). At present it is not advisable to travel on the Srinagar to Leh road.

vice provided. If porters are discharged during a trek, they expect half-pay for the return journey. No tips are required for village hospitality and some people may be offended if you offer them money.

Trekkers enjoying the chai shop experience in Leh, Ladakh.

TRANSPORT

Most trekkers and climbers embark from Delhi for their destinations in the Himalaya. A long trip may be required to reach the trek starting point.

Taxis

Taxis are available for almost all destinations in the Himalaya. Public taxis are easy to spot, being painted black and yellow; some air-conditioned 'cool cabs' are silver and blue. They are all metered, though you will usually pay an updated fare which is shown on the tariff card. Night-time rates are higher. A moderate fee is charged for transporting luggage.

There are taxis at the airport to take you to the city. A pre-paid taxi service facility is available: contact the Pre-Paid Taxi booth at the arrival building. Some airports have three categories of prepaid service: 'limousine', 'luxury' and 'ordinary'.

Buses

There is a local bus from the airport into Delhi. Inexpensive day or night buses run from Delhi to most destinations in the Himalaya, or you could take a train to the end of the line and then continue by bus. Express buses make few stops and most have air-conditioning, reclining seats and videos. Generally buses depart early in the morning (most buses leave from the interstate bus terminal at Kahmir Gate). It is advisable to avoid night travel on hill roads in crowded buses, as on the winding roads accidents sometimes happen.

Air Travel

Indian Airlines (the government-run national carrier) operates flights from Delhi to other Indian cities and internal flights are available to a few trekking areas such as the Kullu Valley and Ladakh. There is also a growing number of private airlines.

Foreigners buying air tickets in India must do so in foreign currency, paying the 'dollar rate' either in traveller's' cheques, credit cards, or cash (requiring an encashment certificate). There are no penalties for cancellations or failure to turn up but if you lose your ticket Indian Airlines will not replace it so guard it carefully.

Special Air Fares

Indian Airlines has special fares that give unlimited travel across India or within a specific region for a certain amount of time. There is also a youth fare for tourists aged between 12–30, which allows a 25% discount.

Air Travel Tips

If you do not have a confirmed booking, go to the airport and be persistent in checking your position on the waiting list.

Batteries should be stowed in your check-in luggage rather than in your hand luggage.

Mark every piece of cabin/hand baggage you carry on to the aircraft with the small tags available from the check-in desk.

Train

India has one of the largest railway networks in the world, with excellent train connections. A vast network of computer reservation systems link major stations. It is possible to book railway tickets 60 days in advance and even from abroad. Bear in mind that berths on express trains may be booked several weeks in advance

In Delhi, where most tourists and trekkers destined for the Himalaya arrive, contact the Northern Railway Computerised Reservation Office and Enquiry at IRCA building (near New Delhi Railway station, Pahadganj), tel 334-8787. Authorised agents can also reserve railway tickets. Beware of touts who may approach you to reserve tickets.

There is a tourist quota on many trains and a special reservation can be made on production of passport and payment in foreign currency. Call the International Tourist Bureau (1st Floor, New Delhi Railway Station, Paharganj side, tel 374-4164, 334-6804, fax 334-3050) between 7.30 am and 5 pm for advice and bookings.

Consider buying an Indrail pass, which allows tourists (foreigners as well as Indians resident abroad) to travel from 7 to 90 days across India's vast rail network without any additional reservation fees or sleeper charges. Reservations, however, must be made well in advance, and are available from the tourist section at Indian Railway booking offices in most cities. Fares range from US $135

TOURIST OFFICES

Government of India Tourist Office, 88 Janpath, tel 332-0005/0266/0008; (Domestic Airport) 566-5296, (International Airport) 569-1171

Delhi Tourism Development Corporation, N Block, Connaught Place, tel 331-4229. Central Reservation Office: Coffee Home I Annexe, Emporium Complex, Baba Kharak Singh Marg, tel 336-5358/3607

Regional Tourist offices in New Delhi

Himachal Pradesh, Chandralok Building, 36 Janpath, tel 332-5320, 332-4764

Jammu and Kashmir, Kanishka Shopping Plaza, 19 Ashok Road, tel 334-5373

Sikkim, 14 Panchsheel Marg, Chanakyapuri, tel 611-5346

Uttar Pradesh, Chandralok Building, 36 Janpath, tel 332-2251, 371-1296

The busy Manali–Leh Highway is one of the few roads to climb through the high mountain passes into Ladakh.

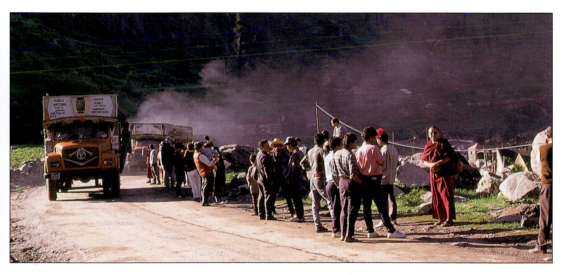

BASIC NEW DELHI ACCOMMODATION

Trekker's Dormitory, The Indian Mountaineering Foundation, Benito Juarez Road, nr South Delhi University, Dhaula Kuan, Anand Niketan, tel 467-1211, fax 688-3412
e-mail: indmount@vsnl.com

YMCA Tourist Hostel, 1 Jaisingh Road, nr Connaught Place tel 336-1915, 336-1847, fax 374-6032, 374-6035
e-mail: ymcath@ndf.vsnl.net.in

YWCA Blue Triangle Family Hostel, Ashoka Road, Connaught Place, tel 336-0133, 336-5014, fax 336-0202

YWCA Tourist Hostel, Parliament Street, nr Connaught Place, tel 336-1561

Ashok Yatri Niwas, Ashok Road, Near Connaught Place, tel 334-4511

Rail Yatri Niwas, Ajmeri Gate, New Delhi Railway Station (for railway passengers)

International Youth Hostel, 5, Nyaya Marg, Chanakyapuri, tel 611-6285, 410-1246

upwards according to the class of accommodation and period of validity. Also check out the Circular Journey Tickets.

COMMUNICATIONS

Local, interstate and international calls can be made with ease in any part of India. STD/ISD call booths with direct interstate and international dialling are widely available. Hill areas and some major hill towns have direct dialling – their codes are in the information directory for each region.

Many telecom centres offer telecommunications facilities including fax. Fax facilities are available at the main post offices. Cities have multi-media telecom centres with desk-top video conferencing, high-speed transfer and other facilities. Cybercafés for e-mails are available in cities and towns and are fast spreading to the smaller towns in the Himalayan foothills.

Postal Services

Nothing can compare with a letter from home, especially after a long trek. Postal services are available in most of the hill areas. By a vast and amazing network the post reaches the most remote villages in the Himalaya, though it takes a little longer than usual. If you wish to receive mail, cities and towns will have a poste restante facility in the main post office. When trekking, mail can be kept for three weeks if addressed to c/o the Post Master of the last or the first post office on the trail. However allow at least three weeks for the mail to reach its destination in the remote Himalayan post offices.

In major cities and towns, special 'speed post' is available for a faster delivery of time-bound mail including registered letters and parcels within 24 to 72 hours. Facilities include a money-back guarantee in case of delay. An international speed post service delivers international mail within 72 hours.

OPENING HOURS

Shops, banks and post offices generally open at 10 am. Banks generally close down for business at 2 pm and post offices at 5 pm. Most shops are open till 5 pm. Government offices work from 10 am to 6 pm, five days a week (Monday to Friday).

ELECTRICITY

The electric current is 220–240 volts AC. Many hotels will provide transformers/adaptors to enable visitors to use their appliances.

ACCOMMODATION

India has an extensive range of accommodation. You can stay here both comfortably and very economically according to Western standards. All the major towns and cities have high-quality hotels, offering a full range of personal and business facilities. In addition to private hotels, the various State Tourism Development Corporations offer accommodation at most tourist centres. There are holiday homes and Rest Houses in the foothills of the Himalaya and at major starting and end-points of treks. Details are given in the Regional Directories for different areas.

A suggested list of hostels and dormitories in New Delhi is given separately (see box).

FOOD AND DRINK

Indian cuisine is varied and spicy. Food is generally cooked fresh, especially in small eating places, since cold storage facilities are hard to come by.

Vegetarian food is readily available and the most popular vegetarian dish, the *thali,* is served on a large steel plate with four or five small bowls in it. Meat *thalis* are also available. The term *sabzi* describes all cooked vegetables – for example, *aloo subzi* are spiced potatoes. Lentils and legumes are known as *dal*. Breads such as *roti, chapati, parathi, naan* or *puri* and rice (*bhat*) usually accompany a meal, along with pickles, chutney and papadums.

Samosas are deep-fried triangular puffed pastry, stuffed with meat or vegetables; *pakoras* are deep-fried vegetable dumplings.

The central open ground in Chamba Town. To the right is the Old Palace and below it are several temples.

Drink

Most varieties of international brands of soft drinks are available in towns and cities. Remember to take any cans, bottles or cartons to the nearest town.

Alcoholic drinks are freely available in the Himalayan states. Check about 'dry days' when no alcoholic drinks can be served, purchased or consumed. In certain public places such as temples, railways and buses it is prohibited to consume alcoholic drinks.

Water

Only drink bottled water bought from a reliable source. Before travelling make sure that you have enough for your entire journey. Tap water or water served in smaller restaurants is unsafe to drink. Add an iodine-based water purifier to water from streams and rivers, particularly if the trail passes near a village. While camping, enquire about specific points from where drinking water can be obtained.

HINDI LANGUAGE

The following are some Hindi words and phrases that may be useful for trekkers visiting the Indian Himalaya:

Aaj	Today	Ghoda	Horse	Mantra	Buddhist	Subah	Morning
Bada	Big	Gompa	Monastery		incantation	Tsampa	Roasted millet flour
Bail	Bullock	Haan	Yes	Mataji	Mother	Ye keedhar	Where is this?
Bhaiya	Brother	Kangri	Snow mountain	Momo	Tibetan stuffed	hai	
Bharal	Blue sheep	Kiang	Tibetan wild ass		steamed dumplings	NUMBERS	
Chalo	Let's go	Kitna paisa	How much money?	Nahee	No	Ek	One
Chorten	Buddhist monument	huaa		Nala	Small stream	Do	Two
Chota	Small	Krupaya	Please	Namaste	Hello, Good	Teen	Three
Dava	Medicine	Lama	Buddhist monk		morning, etc	Char	Four
Din	Day	Maaf	Excuse me	Paise	Money	Panch	Five
Dhaba	Local eating place	keejiye		Peetaji	Father	Chhe	Six
Dukan	Shop	Mahina	Month	Phu	River	Saat	Seven
Gaav	Village	Mandir	Temple	Raat	Night	Aath	Eight
Gai	Cow	Mani	Stones engraved	Ri	Mountain	Nau	Nine
Ghat	Steps on river bank		with prayers	Sham	Evening	Dass	Ten

3
TREKKING AND CLIMBING IN
THE INDIAN HIMALAYA

Above all, do not lose your desire to walk; everyday I walk myself into a state of well-being and walk away from illness; I have walked myself into my best thoughts. Thus if one just keeps on walking, everything will be all right.

(Kierkegaard)

Indians have trekked in the Himalayan range for trade, religion and defence for many centuries but the idea of trekking for pleasure developed much later. The sheer vastness of the Indian Himalayan range and the difficulties of reaching the starting points initially deterred trekkers, but once facilities and transport routes to the areas were developed more and more people enjoyed the hills for pleasure. Today the Indian Himalaya is visited by thousands of trekkers, both foreigners and Indians, who come to experience the mountains, interact with the locals, and appreciate the flora and fauna and the clean air. To obtain maximum pleasure from your trek, plan well ahead.

The Bhagirathi group of peaks are visible on the horizon as trekkers approach Gaumukh on the Gangotri Glacier.

THE ART OF TREKKING

The love of nature and the pursuit of the unknown have eternally drawn man to leave the comfort and security of his home and venture beyond the blue range on the horizon and to discover new valleys, forests, rivers and high mountains

Trekking is undoubtedly of value to physical fitness but its aim is not to produce athletes. It is an activity which should develop real love for the mountain regions and appreciation of their grandeur. Trekking leads to a closer interest in plants, trees, birds and animals, indeed in all forms of nature study. It inculcates the virtue of sacrifice, the value of physical exertion, sometimes to the limit of endurance, and, above all, the spirit of comradeship. A sense of adventure adds excitement towards attaining your goal.

Trekking is an art that can be learnt at any age. It does not demand great strength or immense wealth but merely a desire and willingness to take the rough with the smooth. Once initiated, you soon learn to minimise your needs, but you must never compromise with safety. A good trekker knows his own minimum requirements, and carries his entire home on his back: bed, kitchen and other essentials, but to achieve a sense of freedom he must give up certain comforts. Trekking instils qualities of self-reliance, personal fitness and a willingness to help.

Walking

You will first need to learn the art of enjoying long walks. The main consideration is the conservation of energy. The walk should be comfortable and acquire a certain pace and rhythm, a swing that comes naturally. Everyone has to discover the pace that suits him the best. Avoid breathlessness by reducing the pace: keep going for a certain amount of time, say an hour and half, then rest for ten minutes. You will reach your destination in reasonable time and what is more, be fresh enough to attend to your needs at the camping place. The movement of your feet should be precise. Set the whole foot on the ground for greater balance, which helps conserve energy and muscular effort. On steeper slopes move sideways in a zigzag manner to reduce the effort required and to avoid breathlessness. Another way of achieving the same result is to take smaller vertical steps wherever possible. Bend forward a little while climbing uphill. On descent, the effort may appear less, but there is a greater, jerking movement that tires the knees and the toes, which you can reduce by correct placement of the foot and gentler shift of body weights to the next downward step. Land on your heels if the ground is soft.

BASIC TREKKING EQUIPMENT
Footwear

Correct footwear is essential on long walks for the comfort and protection of your feet, without which the enjoyment of a trek will be ruined. Correct footwear shields the foot from sharp objects and supports the ankle for greater balance in movement. A walking shoe should combine a sturdy rubber sole and a flexible upper, preferably of strong canvas or soft leather covering up to the ankle. A pair of well-fitting socks will prevent internal chafing, which causes blisters. The shoes should not be too tight – ideally, the shoe will be felt as part of the foot and yet allow some free movement of the toes. Toe-nails should be cut short.

Sound footwear is a priority. Before going on long treks get used to the new shoes by wearing them on shorter walks to break them in.

Three principal factors determine what items a trekker may need on a trek: the weather, the terrain or region and the duration of the trek.

IMPORTANT ADDRESSES

The **Indian Mountaineering Foundation** (IMF), which is responsible for all climbing expeditions and the rescue of trekkers, can be contacted through:
The Director, The Indian Mountaineering Foundation, Benito Juarez Road, New Delhi 110021 (their complex is near the South Delhi University Complex, near Dhaula Kuan), tel 467-1211/7935/1572, fax: 688-3412,
e-mail: indmount@del2.vsnl.net.in
website: www.indmount.com

The **Himalayan Club** is an international body which has published the *Himalayan Journal* since 1928 (an essential reference for trekkers and climbers). The Club has two major libraries in Bombay and Delhi and holds regular lectures and illustrated talks by visiting trekkers and climbers. The Club welcomes visiting trekkers and climbers. For participation, information and help contact:
either Hon. Secretary, The Himalayan Club, PO Box 1905, Bombay 400 001, tel 261-2461, (Secretary Mr Muni) 644-1682/643-6637, e-mail: munico@vsnl.com
website: www.Himalayanclub.com
or Mr Mandip Soin, Hon. Local Secretary for Delhi, G-66, East of Kailash, New Delhi 110 065, tel 691-2641, fax 684-6403, e-mail: ibex@nde.vsnl.net.in

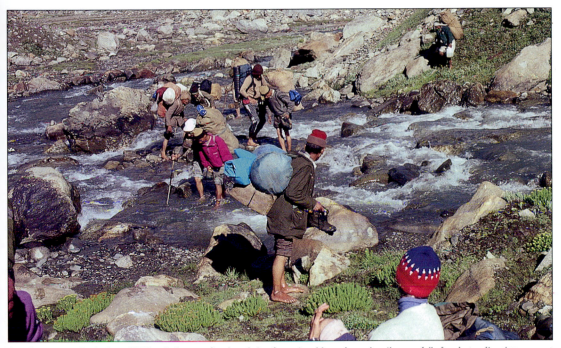

Crossing streams in the Parvati Valley, Kullu, can often be a balancing act and hazardous when they are full of spring melt-water.

Clothing

On a short trek it is a good policy not to carry more than one item of each type of clothing that you might require to protect against wind, cold, rain, and sun. Such clothing should be light but durable.

On a weekend trek you will find shelter at the end of the path at a village, in a school or a temple. During fine weather you may camp under the open sky near a stream or a water point. A ground sheet and a sleeping bag would be ideal in the open where there is a likelihood of low temperature or a cool breeze. In the absence of a sleeping bag, an additional woollen sweater, a balaclava and a woollen blanket will do. Improvised sleeping bags made from woollen blankets are worth taking with you to prevent cold seeping through air gaps.

Rucksack

The size and type of a rucksack will depend on the bulk and the weight you have to carry for a given trek. A weekend outing will seldom require more than a small rucksack, enough to carry a lunch box, water bottle and a roll of ground sheet and cover. A longer trek away from habitation would

TREKKING/CLIMBING TOUR OPERATORS

The following operators are registered with the IMF:
Rimo Expeditions, B-5/6, No 4320, Vasant Kunj, New Delhi 110 070, tel 689-8734, fax 689-8710, e-mail: rimo@vsnl.com, website: www.atrav.com/rimo
Himalayan Run & Trek Pvt Ltd, 5-D, Pocket 'A' Group II, 35-D, Dilshad Garden, New Delhi 110 095, tel 228- 5805, 247-2700, fax 247-2800, e-mail: hrtpl@del2.vsnl.net.in/cspandey@vsnl.com
Ibex Expeditions, G 66 East of Kailash, New Delhi 110 065, tel 691-2641, fax 684-6403, e-mail: ibex@nde.vsnl.net.in
Shikhar Travels, 209, Competent House, F-14, Middle Circle, Connaught Place, New Delhi 110 001, tel 331-2666, fax 332-3660

Rucksack Tours Pvt Ltd, B-412, Som Datt Chambers I, 5 Bhikaji Cama Place, New Delhi 110 066, tel 617-3717, 618-3696, fax 619-4377, e-mail: rani@nde.vsnl.net.in, website: www.rucksacktours.com
Trans-Himalayan Expeditions Pvt Ltd, H-6/B Hauz Khas, New Delhi 110 016, tel 685-0468, fax 685-0469, e-mail: realms.thim@gems.vsnl.net.in
Kangchenjunga Treks & Tours, 1, DB Giri Road, Darjeeling 734 101, West Bengal, tel 56408, fax 53058.
Himali Travel Specialists, Sharma Lee, 30, DB Giri Road, PO Box 52, GPO; Darjeeling 734 101, West Bengal, tel 55672/52741, fax 54487, e-mail: himalits@cal.vsnl.net.in

involve more items to carry and consequently, greater weight. Shoulder straps should be broad and padded underneath, and a loaded rucksack that pulls backwards is of poor design. The modern backpack is designed to fit the shape of the spine with a lower support spreading the weight on the upper part of the hips. It is amazing how much more you can comfortably carry in a well-designed rucksack and a good rucksack will ultimately affect your enjoyment of the trek.

Food
Walking and climbing quickly consumes energy and body fluid, which must be carefully replenished at proper intervals. Always have a good breakfast before the start of a march. If consumed energy is not renewed, exhaustion may result. During longer halts take greater fluid intake. A water bottle is a must for each trekker and should be kept filled with clean water at every opportunity.

Food for a longer trek will involve cooking at least one meal a day. A folding kerosene stove or a gas stove is useful for snacks or for preparing tea or coffee. In the absence of a stove, dry wood can be used for fuel. Food items should be easy to carry. Light aluminium vessels or pans are required along with other cooking utensils.

Accessories
A trekker may need to carry a few more items such as a compass, books, maps, a knife, torch, first-aid kit, pieces of string, candles, a box of matches, toilet paper and objects related to interest such as photography, bird-watching or botany. Rock climbing enthusiasts will take many more items.

Goats surround a camp in the Shaone Gad, Kinnaur.

TREKKING STYLES
The Indian Himalayan range is divided into several very different regions (see Chapter 1). Unlike Nepal, very few treks can be undertaken in India without complete arrangements for food and tents. Only a few places offer lodging and food. Everywhere else you will have to carry supplies.

Most of the villages have no supplies to sell, especially after the winter months or in the rains when roads are blocked. However, at many starting points basic rations/groceries, utensils and other small requirements may be available.

You can ask a trekking agent to organize your trek for you but you will need to discuss in detail everything you require. Make sure that you deal only with recommended agents (see page 31).

Porters and Mules
If the trek is self-organized you will have to arrange porters or mules (on some trails) at the starting points. There are no fixed rates and they vary in different areas. You must make everything clear before hiring them: loads to be carried, whether you will give them food and shelter or they will arrange their own, and the return wages. The accident or death of a porter or mule must be reported to the nearest authorities. Compensation will be expected to be paid depending on the circumstances of the accident.

TREKKING PRACTICALITIES
Trekking is best enjoyed with an early morning start. A normal day's march may cover a distance of 12 to 20km (8–12 miles), which should be achieved by early afternoon, allowing some time for a lunch break on the way. The march should not leave the trekker completely exhausted at the end as the whole purpose of enjoyment would be lost. When planning the route and the stages on a trek, do not let the trek merely be a long trudge from morning to evening. Allow for time to relax and absorb the feel of the place at the end of the march.

Companions
With all the material wealth that a man may possess, he is poorer if he is without the warmth of human companionship. Man is in search of peace and quiet joy in the wilderness, yet it adds a new dimension to share these pursuits with a few

like-minded companions. More often than not a spirit of comradeship pervades the whole effort during the trek, and a good companion will help you overcome unforeseen difficulties. However, it is best to enjoy trekking in a small group rather than in a crowd. Adjustments and understanding are easier in a small group and lead to a lasting bond after the common pursuit in the mountain region is over. Sharing a long journey through mountains with a few companions reveals sides of human personalities that safety and comfort of civilization often conceals, Faced with the hardships of the mountain trek, a person's true self is exposed and the trip may indeed be a voyage of self-discovery.

Tired trekkers enjoying a well earned rest by prayer flags on Shinkun La, Zanskar.

Planning

One of the delights of trekking is the planning of a trek long before you set out, spending time poring over maps for information on alternative treks and gathering details for available resources.

Finally, the trek is selected, the details worked out, materials collected and the journey embarked upon. However, situations inevitably arise to alter the best-laid schemes, including many factors beyond your control. Yet things do work out somehow and the trek is completed after enduring the wind, the cold and the rain, through remote valleys, over passes and hilltops. If you are a keen observer, you will not fail to notice the flight of the birds that soar high above in the deep blue sky, or the delightful flowers blooming on the mountainsides. The cool mountain air refreshes the body and stimulates the senses.

EQUIPMENT

Clothing (including worn)		Camping items and utensils			Watch		Additional items for
1	Wide-brimmed hat, cloth/felt	1	Half-pint mug, enamel/	2	Combs		high-altitude trails
1	Balaclava/ski hat		stainless steel	1	Toothbrush	1	Thermal shirt
1	Scarf, woollen/silk	1	Deep plate	1	Toothpaste	1	Thermal long pants (longjohns)
2	T-shirt	2	Teaspoons	1	Soap	1	Gloves, woollen
2	Long-sleeved shirts	1	Flat box/tin	1	Torch with extra batteries/bulbs	2	Thick stockings
2	Fleece jacket/warm jumper	1	Water bottle, large, metal	1	Penknife	1	Headband, woollen
1	Fleece trousers	1	Thermos flask, small	1	Dozen thick candles	1	Altimeter
1	Trekking pants (trousers)	1	Cotton bed sheet	6	Boxes of matches	1	Weather thermometer
1	Pajamas	1	Air pillow	1	Writing pad, envelopes,		
1	Shorts	1	Kit bag with plastic liner		stamps, postcards		Climbing equipment
2	Socks, thin	1	Rucksack	2	Ballpoint pens	1	Set windproof jacket and trousers
2	Socks, thick	1	Sleeping bag	1	Small sewing kit	1	Pair leather/feather gloves
2	Handkerchiefs	1	Foam mattress	1	Personal first-aid kit	1	Duvet jacket
1	Trekking shoes (walking shoes)			1	Sunburn cream, Nivea or	1	Snow gaiters
1	Light trainers		Other articles		Vaseline; sun-block	1	Climbing shoes
1	Sandals	1	Towel, medium size			1	Crampons
1	Waterproof jacket	1	Ski pole (for walking)		Special items	1	Ice-axe
2	Underwear, cotton	1	Folding umbrella	1	Camera, films and accessories	1	Harness
1	Swimming costume	2	Boxes toilet paper	1	Binoculars, plant and bird books	1	Rope
2	Sunglasses	1	Extra spectacles, if worn	1	Map and compass	1	Set climbing 'gear'

Mules crossing a snow-filled valley floor en route to Milam, Kumaun.

ships that were encountered. This lingering memory is one of the greatest delights of trekking.

When trekking and mountain climbing, people often find a philosophy of life. If you do, you and the mountains will be inseparable throughout your life, and you will always respond to their call, for you have fallen under their spell.

RESCUE

There is no organised rescue system in place in the Indian Himalaya. In case of an emergency, contact the nearest village, police post, Indo-Tibet Border Police post or the army post. In each area there are government officials – a District Commissioner, a District Magistrate and their deputies, the Assistant District Magistrate and the *Tehsildar* (Local Officer), who will give assistance to rescue and help trekkers.

To arrange a helicopter, contact the Indian Mountaineering Foundation (for climbing teams) or your embassy in New Delhi. Full charges will have

Reward

The reward begins when accomplishment ends: the arduous effort is followed by a warm spreading aftermath, in which physical pleasure becomes a transcending happiness. On your return home, you will look back with deep satisfaction on a dream accomplished, forgetting the hazards or the hard-

PERSONAL FIRST-AID KIT

Commercial trekking groups will usually carry a full expedition medical kit. If you are travelling independently you may want to base your own kit on the following list (refer to the bibliography for more advice). NB While many of the items listed require a prescription in Europe and America, all are available over the counter at pharmacies in Asia at far less cost. Note that some of them are strong medications, the administration of which in inappropriate circumstances could have serious consequences. Familiarize yourself with current medical practice before carrying them in the hills.

Insect repellent (Repel 100 or Jungle Formula)
Antiseptic cream (Bruladine)
Sun cream and lip salve
Throat lozenges
Deep Heat or Tiger Balm
Anti diarrhoearal (Diacalm or Immodium)
Anti protozoan (Flagyl or Tineba – for treating giardiasis)
Antibiotics (choose broad-spectrum antibiotics for treating a variety of infections – carry a course of each)
Mild analgesics (Aspirin/Paracetamol for headaches, etc – NOT Codein-based painkillers, as these suppress the breathing function and are not advisable at altitude)

Strong analgesics (Co-Proxamol/Ponstan/Temgesic – use with care)
Anti-inflammatories (Nurofen or diclofenac sodium – stomach irritant)
Eye drops (Optrex or Murine)
Plasters and moleskin/blister kit (Compede is recommended)
Bandages and safety pins
Re-hydrant salts (ORS – carry several sachets)
Dextrose/glucose tablets
Multi-vitamin tablets
Iodine-based water purification tablets or a small bottle of tincture of iodine with a dropper (chlorine-based water purifiers are not suitable)
Povidone iodine (for cleaning wounds)
Zinc oxide tape
Crepe bandages and safety pins
Butterfly (paper) sutures or Steri-Strips
Cotton wool/swabs
Melolin dressings
Clinical thermometer
Scissors

to be paid for the helicopter and arrangements must be made in advance with your embassy before you start from Delhi.

ADMINISTRATION AND BUREAUCRACY

As you travel to the foothills of the range and reach the starting points, the local administration takes charge of all official matters. For any permits, or emergency, rescue, helicopter or law and order problems you should contact them.

Each area is divided into different districts. The District Magistrate or District Commissioner heads the area and his offices are situated at the head-quarters of the district. Under him are the ADM (Assistant District Magistrate) and *Tehsildar* and local police stations. These authorities will issue papers and permits if required in an area and will be responsible for your safety.

The Indo-Tibet Border Police are situated at many locations and may check your permits where required. The army is also located at many places. In an emergency of any kind any of the above can be contacted for help.

Bureaucracy and Permissions

Many trekkers and climbers have complained about the problems of bureaucracy and rules for climbing in the Indian Himalaya. Indian bureaucracy has been described as an elephant that moves slowly, which is strong and eats lots of paper. This is a legacy of the British administration but it helps if you understand how this elephant operates. The Himalayan areas are classified into several segments, each controlled by the different states in which they lie. Initial permission is granted by the government in Delhi and then forwarded to the respective states. The Indian Mountaineering Foundation (IMF) is the central coordinating body but it must be appreciated that the IMF cannot on its own give clearance to any foreign expedition. They merely forward papers to the Ministry of Defence and Ministry of Home Affairs.

The reason for these restrictions is because the Himalaya are not only a mountaineer's paradise but also a chain that defends the country from its hostile neighbours. At least four major wars have been fought in this area and hence the need for security. Along with the international border, which no one is allowed to approach, there is a parallel line drawn on the map, which is called the 'inner line'. This was originally established by the British to prevent anyone from crossing into Tibet. It runs parallel to the border with Tibet at a distance of 20 to 40km (10–25 miles) from it. Certain areas were

A trekker contemplates Aq Tash peak in Ladakh.

completely banned to visitors and it was only in 1974 that Ladakh was 'opened'; in 1993, areas in Spiti, Kinnaur and South Parvati were opened. In the designated open areas any foreigner can climb after obtaining a clearance, which is generally granted. If foreigners wish to climb within the inner line areas either a joint expedition with Indians has to be organized or a special permission obtained. All this takes time.

Inner Line Locations

It helps if you know the locations of the inner line so that you can plan your trip in order to avoid any restrictions. In general, foreign expeditions are not allowed to go across the inner line and Indian nationals have to have special permission. The position of the inner line and the rules concerning access change from time to time. However, large areas of India are open for climbing and trekking, and almost all areas are open to joint expeditions with Indian nationals. At present the general layout of the inner line is as follows:

Arunachal Pradesh

Almost the whole of this area is entirely within the inner line.

INDIAN HIMALAYA ONLINE

Websites of general interest
www.indmount.com (official site of the Indian Mountaineering Foundation)
www.himalayanclub (official site of the Himalayan Club)
www.indus-intl.com (for books on mountaineering and trekking in India)

Sikkim websites
http://sikkim.nic.in
www.sikkiminfo.com
see www.india-tourism.de

Kashmir and Ladakh websites
http://jammukashmir.nic.in

Himachal Pradesh websites
http://himachal.nic.in/
http://himachaltourism.nic.in/
www.himachalguide.com

Kumaun and Garhwal (Uttar Pradesh) websites
www.up-tourism.com/

Arunachal Pradesh websites
see www.india-tourism.de

Others
www.indiatravelog.com/trekking
http://travel.indiamart.com/mountaineering-trekking
www.shubhyatra.com

Sikkim

The northern areas are within the inner line, but recently many parties have been allowed to climb there with permission. Special rules apply.

Kumaun

(A) Eastern Kumaun (Darma Valley): Indian mountaineers are now allowed entry.
(B) Central Kumaun: The areas are open to the Milam Glacier and Milam village. This gives mountaineers access to the Kalabaland Glacier, lower Milam Glacier and Nanda Devi East. Several high and unclimbed peaks are available here.
(C) The Nanda Devi Sanctuary is closed for environmental reasons.

(D) Western Kumaun: The Pindari and the Sunderdhunga Valley areas have no restrictions.

Garhwal

(A) Northern valleys: The areas north of Badrinath and around Kamet are still closed to visitors and are within the inner line. Some joint expeditions have been allowed here.
(B) Major parts of central Garhwal, such as Dunagiri, Uja Tirche, and Panpatia Bank, are open.
(C) The western Garhwal area is totally open. Here lies the Gangotri group, and the peaks in the Bandarpunch valleys.

Kinnaur

The Satluj River cuts almost through the centre of Kinnaur. Areas to the west and north of this river have recently been opened to all without any restrictions. Anyone can travel on the Hindustan–Tibet road. The eastern valleys are selectively and partially open. As in the Baspa Valley, you can travel to Chhitkul across the Charang Ghati. In the Tirung Valley, Charang can be visited. Peaks such as Phawrarang, Jorkanden of the Kailash Range and others are now available for climbing.

Spiti

The western part of Spiti, west of the Spiti River, consists of many large valleys which are now open to outsiders. Foreigners travelling in this area have to be in a group of at least four persons and a permit is required between Jangi and Sumdo on the Hindustan–Tibet road. You can travel to Spiti from Manali without permits when the roads are open.

Kullu

The entire Kullu area including Manikaran, Dibibokri and Tos Nala is now free of restrictions.

Lahaul

The entire area is open for trekking and climbing.

Kishtwar and Kashmir

Although the area is declared open, because of the recent political situation in Kashmir, climbing is restricted to certain routes only. The areas are best avoided until the situation improves.

Zanskar

Fully open without any restrictions.

Ladakh

(A) The eastern parts of Ladakh, such as Pangong Lake, are open with permits for visitors.

(B) The south-eastern areas of Rupshu are open for free travel. These new peak and trekking possibilities include Lungser Kangri, Chhamser Kangri and Kula. However you will need a formal permit obtainable from Leh to visit the area.

Eastern Karakoram

(A) Once forbidden, the Nubra Valley up to Sasoma is open to foreigners (in groups of four) with permits which are granted easily. Visits to the Saser Kangri West base camp and to several monasteries are possible.

(B) Towards the west, trekkers and tourists are allowed free access to Diskit and Hunder villages. They can trek south across the Khardung Range.

(C) Other areas such as the Siachen Glacier and Rimo require permits and are highly restricted. Foreigners or Indians are not allowed there except after official clearance which is difficult to obtain.

CLIMBING IN THE INDIAN HIMALAYA

Amongst the Himalayan nations, on the whole, only Indians climb mountains for pleasure. The Nepalese and the Sherpas join expeditions for financial reasons. Pakistan has few mountaineers (but some very proficient individuals). In India nearly 100 Indian expeditions and trekking teams visit the Himalaya every year. Thousands more visit the range as pilgrims or tourists.

In general there are two broad types of Indian expeditions to the Himalaya. The larger expeditions are organized and wholly funded by government agencies, such as the army, the Indo-Tibet Border Police or individuals selected by the Indian Mountaineering Foundation. The many small Indian expeditions are organized by private enthusiasts. They climb because 'it is there' and, despite meagre financial resources, non-availability of good equipment and other difficulties, they have achieved much and contributed to the knowledge and exploration of the range.

About 60 foreign expeditions arrive in India each year bound for the Himalayan Range. The majority of foreign climbers come from Europe, the USA, Japan and Korea. There have also been several joint ventures in the Himalaya consisting of Indian nationals and foreign members.

Climbing Formalities

Trekking in the Indian Himalaya, in the so-called 'open areas', does not require any special permission, except in certain districts as mentioned above (see page 35). However there are elaborate rules for climbing any peak. There is no distinction between a peak to be climbed by a trekker or an expedition party. The same set of rules applies for the import of equipment, travel, search and rescue, and other matters applicable to trekking.

Any foreigner wishing to climb a peak in the Indian Himalaya needs to obtain prior permission from the Indian government (at least 90 days before their arrival in India) and pay relevant charges through the offices of the IMF in New Delhi.

Applicants must ascertain from the IMF the availability of the peak during the period they wish to climb. As soon as a proposal is received from

(see page 35)

BOOKSHOPS

There are several bookshops in New Delhi which stock books on trekking, mountaineering and allied subjects. They include:

The Bookworm, B-29 Connaught Place, tel 332-2260
Bahri & Sons, Opp. Main Gate, Khan Market, tel 469-4610, 461-8637, fax 687-3570
ED Galgotia & Sons, 17-B, Connaught Place, tel 332-2876, 375-5150
English Book Store, 17L Connaught Circus, tel 332-9126, 372-2031, fax 332-1731
Survey of India, Map Sales Office, Janapath Barracks, Janapath Lane
TBI Publishers, 46, Housing Society, South Extension Part I, tel 463-2903

A temple complex in the shadow of the mountains at Bharmor, Himachal Pradesh.

PEAK FEES

Once a peak has been provisionally booked by the Indian Mountaineering Foundation, the leader should send handling charges and the application to the IMF, at the following rates:

Below 6500m: US$1500 for a party of 12 persons.
6501-7000m: US$2000 for a party of 12 persons. (Additional flat fee of US$400 for up to 4 extra persons.)
Nun-Kun (Kashmir): US$3000 for a party of 12 persons. (Additional flat fee of US$400 for up to 4 extra persons.)
Peaks in restricted areas (any height): US$4000 for a party of maximum 8 persons.
Peaks in Eastern Karakoram: US$4000 (Only joint expeditions are permitted to climb, with an Indian national as leader for a party not exceeding 8 foreign members. In joint expeditions, out of a maximum 16 members, 8 have to be Indians.)
Four trekking peaks: US$300 for a party of 12 persons. (Additional flat fee of US$100 for up to 4 extra persons.)
Other charges: US$400 will be charged from each expedition as an environmental levy (non-refundable). US$500 is to be paid for cost of the liaison officer's equipment. Special charges and rules apply for climbing in Sikkim. Contact the IMF for details.

the expedition team, the IMF books the peak(s) provisionally, subject to its availability, on a first come, first served basis. The team will then be allotted a registration number which must be quoted in all future correspondence. The expedition team should nominate two or three alternative peaks, in order of priority, in their proposal. The IMF will ask the Indian government for permission to climb when they have the application form along with full particulars and documents.

Trekking across glaciers to Saser La in Ladakh.

All expeditions, including joint expeditions, are allowed a maximum of sixteen climbing members. Expeditions are not allowed to take trekking parties or film crews as additional members, in order to protect the Himalayan environment. The minimum number of people on an expedition is two.

Fifteen days are generally allocated to travel from base camp to the peak and back. This period may be increased or decreased by the IMF depending upon the difficulty of a particular peak. If an expedition wishes to attempt additional peaks for which permission has not already been obtained, requests can be made in writing to the liaison officer accompanying the expedition (see below), who may allow such an attempt, provided that the peak is not being climbed by other expeditions. The handling charges payable will be 50 per cent of the normal fee per peak, which will have to be paid to the IMF before the expedition team returns to its country of origin.

A detailed report on an official form must be submitted to the IMF (with photographs and route map) after the expedition is over. The report should include details of how many porters were recruited, from where, and what payment was made per day, per head and whether there were any recruitment difficulties or with nationals as a whole. If the expedition team subsequently publishes a book or makes a film about the expedition, a copy must be submitted to the IMF.

'X' Mountaineering Visa

All team members require 'X' mountaineering visas endorsed on their passports from the Indian Embassy in their country BEFORE arrival in India, once the expedition has been cleared (normally one month before the date of commencement). Tourist/entry visas cannot be converted to 'X' visas in India.

Liaison Officer

Every foreign expedition has to be accompanied by an Indian liaison officer appointed by the IMF, irrespective of whether the peak lies in the restricted or in the open area. The liaison officer, who will be a mountaineer, is to be treated as a member of the expedition. He (or she) will be provided with equipment/clothing by the IMF, for which the expedition team has to pay US$500, along with booking fees.

Expedition Planning

Expedition teams are required to stay in New Delhi for one working day on their arrival and departure for briefing/debriefing respectively and to complete other formalities at the IMF headquarters.

On arrival at the last district or sub-division of Garhwal, Kumaun, Himachal Pradesh, Jammu and Kashmir, Sikkim and Arunachal Pradesh, the team leader and the liaison officer must report to the District Magistrate/Deputy Commissioner or the sub-divisional officer and Superintendent of Police and the army's information headquarters.

Insurance Cover

Expedition members must have insurance cover for accidents and ground/helicopter search and rescue. A copy of the insurance policy must be given to the IMF during the briefing in New Delhi.

Mountaineering Equipment

Mountaineering equipment brought by a foreign expedition team to India is exempt from customs duty based on the IMF's authorisation. These items must not be sold or given to anyone and, except for stores consumed or articles lost or left behind on the mountains, must be re-exported by the expedition leader.

MAPPING

Several maps of the Indian Himalaya produced by the Survey of India and other sources are available for trekkers and mountaineers. The following maps may be useful for different areas:

Sikkim

State Map of Sikkim, Survey of India, 1:150,000
Sikkim, Swiss Foundation for Alpine Research, 1:150,000
NG-45-3 and *NG-45-7*, AMS Map Series, 1:250,000

Kumaun–Garhwal

Kumaun Hills, Survey of India, 1:250,000
Badri to Kedar, Survey of India, 1:250,000
Gangotri to Yamnotri, Survey of India, 1:250,000
Indian Himalaya Sheets 7 and *8*, Leomann Sketch Maps, 1:250,000
Garhwal East and *Garhwal West*, Swiss Foundation For Alpine Research, 1:150,000
NH-44-5, NH-44-6, NH-44-9, NH-44-10, AMS Map series, 1:250,000

Himachal Pradesh

Shimla Hills, Survey of India, 1:250,000

The Chhika Forest en route to the Hampta Pass in the Kullu Valley.

Kullu Valley, Survey of India, 1:250,000
Sheet 53/E, Survey of India, 1:250,000
(all 16 sheets of this series are available on a scale of 1:50,000)
Indian Himalaya Sheets 4, 5 and *6*, Leomann Sketch Maps, 1:250,000
NH-44-1, NH-43-4, NI-43-7, NI-43-12 , NI-43-13, NI-43-16, AMS Map series, 1:250,000

Ladakh–Zanskar–East Karakoram

Jammu and Kashmir State: Sheets 1 and 2, Survey of India, 1:250,000
Indian Himalaya Sheets 1, 2 and 3, Leomann Sketch Maps, 1:250,000
NI-44-9, NI-44-13, NI-44-5, NI-43-4, NI-43-6, NI-43-8, NI-43-11, AMS Map series, 1:250,000

TREKKING PEAKS

The official trekking peaks of the Indian Himalaya are:

Peak (height)	Longitude	Latitude
Stok Kangri (6153m/20188ft)	77 28'	33 59'
Ladakhi (5345m/17537ft)	77 03'	32 22'
Friendship (5289m/17353ft)	77 12'	32 23'
Hanuman (6070m/199916ft)	79 50'	30 28

4
SIKKIM
HIMALAYA

Each morning the sun's serene rays cast a magical glow on the majestic Kangchenjunga, as it slowly spreads across Denzong – valley of Rice. Many flowers are born to bloom unseen in the lush forests and mountain air of Sikkim.

(Sikkimese quote)

Sikkim Himalaya is one of the more physically accessible sections of the Himalaya for trekkers and climbers, easily reached within four days from Calcutta. Much of Sikkim remains off-limits but the areas that are open more than compensate. The western valleys, particularly the Singalila Ridge bordering Nepal in the west, are great tourist attractions. The northern valleys, where visiting restrictions are likely to be lifted, are full of slopes covered with multi-coloured blooming rhododendrons.

The last of the steam engines in Darjeeling, now a World Heritage Railway.

Exhibits in the popular Himalayan Mountaineering Institute Museum.

Sikkim is also associated with the Himalayan Mountaineering Institute in Darjeeling, West Bengal. The Institute was established after the successful attempt on Everest in 1953, and has made a major contribution to the training of Indian mountaineers and trekkers. Darjeeling was also the home of Sherpa Tensing (see box, page 52), in whose honour there is a statue and a museum in the Institute.

While trekking you will come across reminders of this region's history. Pre-World War II expeditions attempting Everest from the northern approaches passed through Sikkim, and many famous names were registered in the rest house log-books. Calcutta was the headquarters of the British Raj, and the Himalayan Club built a hut at the foot of the Sebu La pass, which allowed trekkers to go across from Lachen to Lachung valleys without carrying a tent or much food. The hut is now in ruins, but you can still imagine the echoes of the British memsahibs ordering their servants to fetch tea.

The Kangchenjunga is the prime attraction of Sikkim Himalaya. You can admire its beauty from many places: while sipping tea in a Darjeeling restaurant, from the top of Tiger Hill, or while trekking to Sandakphu, Guicha La or Green Lake. In the 1930s, Paul Bauer and his German team repeatedly attempted this peak from the Sikkim side but were defeated by the northeast spur. At last, in 1977, an Indian army team reached the summit from the Sikkim side. The Kangchenjunga rises steeply from the Zemu glacier – too steeply even for the setting sun to be visible after late afternoon. Doug Freshfield, who was here in 1899, wrote about the eastern sunset, which is a wonderfully unique phenomenon. The steep rise of the Kangchenjunga blocks the western horizon and the sun disappears behind it; early in the afternoon, dark shadows gather over the glacier. The east, up to Bhutan, remains brightly lit for a long time with its changing colours, creating a unique illusion.

Sikkim is always alluring, be it because of the Darjeeling Hill Railway, now declared a World Heritage Project, the sprawling tea estates, the Himalayan Mountaineering Institute, the Sherpas, or Kangchenjunga itself.

In the records of exploration and climbing in Sikkim, the names of Sir Joseph Hooker, the great botanist explorer, Douglas Freshfield and Dr AM Kellas (eminent climbers of their day) stand out. They first alerted western eyes to the beauty of the area and to the trekking and climbing opportunities in the late 19th century.

HIMALAYAN MOUNTAINEERING INSTITUTE

Darjeeling played an important part in the history of attempts on Everest – all the pre-World War II expeditions passed through here on their way to Tibet. It is also the home of the legendary Sherpa Tensing Norgay. When Tensing reached the summit of Everest with Sir Edmund Hillary in 1953, India, and the people of Darjeeling in particular, celebrated.

After the successful climb of Everest, the Himalayan Mountaineering Institute (HMI) was established in Darjeeling in 1954, at Tensing's behest, to train Indian nationals in the sport of mountaineering. Over the years, several leading Sherpas have served as instructors, including Nawang Gombu, Sherpa Wangdi and Dorjee Lhatoo. Today, the Himalayan Mountaineering Institute is the leading organization for mountaineering training in India and runs a variety of courses for those aged between 12 and 50 years old. Students and HMI instructors have climbed several high peaks in the Indian Himalaya and have played a leading part in promoting mountaineering in India.

The Institute also houses a popular museum, one of whose attractions is the telescope presented by Adolf Hitler to Rana (Queen) Shamsherjung of Nepal.

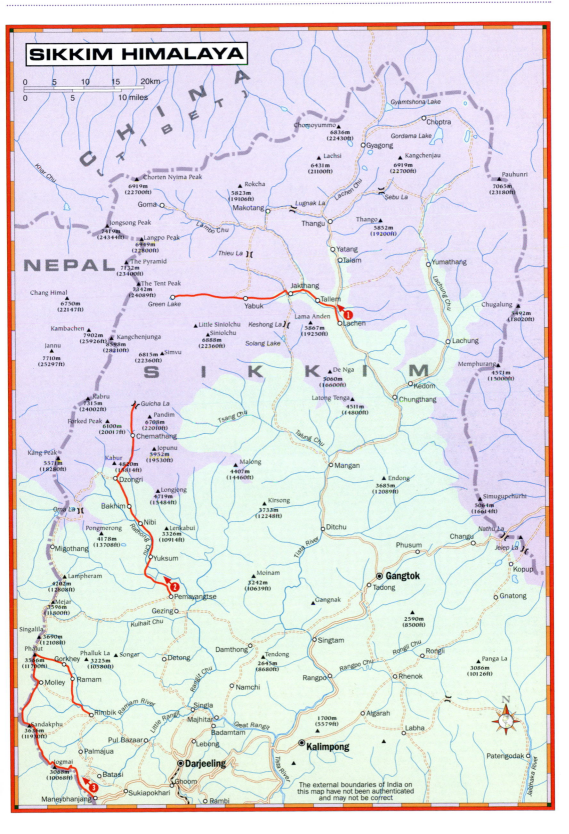

TREK 1: TO GREEN LAKE, NORTH SIKKIM

This is a very picturesque trail which combines natural beauty with spectacular views of high peaks. There are vast tracts of thick forest, with several varieties of rhododendrons, other colourful flowers, and birds and many waterfalls on both sides of the trail. Kangchenjunga was one of the first peaks to be attempted by expeditions before World War II. As Nepal was closed, the approach from Sikkim, via the Zemu Glacier, was followed instead. Pre-war Everest expeditions also passed through North Sikkim and this trail was part of their route. Today, it is still largely unexplored country as not many parties have been allowed access to Green Lake.

TREK ESSENTIALS

LENGTH 3 weeks; 92km (57 miles). Walking from Lachen: 3 days to Yabuk, 3 days to Green Lake; same route back and time to acclimatise.
ACCESS From Delhi or Calcutta, fly to Bagdogra or train to New Jalpaiguri. Good roads to Gangtok and Lachen.
HIGHEST POINT Green Lake (4935m/16190ft).
GRADE Medium.
SEASONS March–April and September–early November.
RESTRICTIONS Special permit required and some areas restricted to foreigners. Fees for entry into the National Park. Check requirements with a travel agent in advance (see page 31). Indian nationals can obtain permits in Gangtok.
FURTHER OPTIONS Scrambles and walks around Green Lake.

Kangchenjunga massif as seen from Green Lake.

From Gangtok, a 96-km (57-mile) drive passes through Rongo, Mangan, Singhik to Toong Bridge. Here, the Lachen (from the west) and Lachung (from the east) nalas converge to form the Tista river. After crossing the bridge, the road follows the left side (western) to Lachen, via Rongpu. On the way there is a magnificent Bolshoi Bridge – of Russian design – built almost 492m (1500ft) above the riverbed.

Lachen (2730m/8950ft) is a sleepy traditional village with a monastery. Arrangements for porters and food for the trail will have to be made in advance. It is best to spend a day acclimatising here before setting off to Green Lake.

Lachen to Yabuk

Walk to Zema, where the Zemu Chu merges with the Thangu Chu River. After crossing the bridge, the trail turns west to follow the left bank of the Zemu Chu to Green Lake. The trail for the first 6km (3¾ miles) is fairly straight and broad, but several landslides hamper the route after this. After a further 6km (3¾ miles) you will reach Tallem (Jadong) (3240m/10620ft) at the junction of Lhonak Chu with Zemu Chu. Make the first day's camp here in the wide open ground.

From here on, the trail enters some of the most magnificent forest areas for which Sikkim is famous. Cross a bridge to climb steadily through forest to Shobuk. The trail then descends steeply for 12km (7½ miles) to Jakthang, (3430m/11250ft), a small clearing in the forest and the second day's camp.

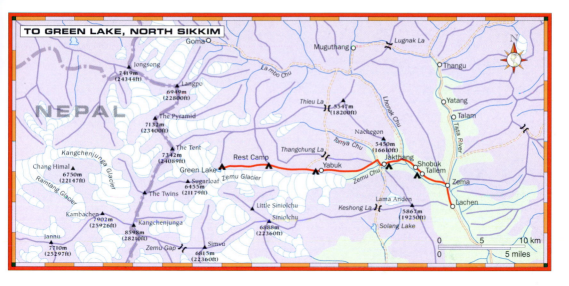

The valley in the south leads to the historic pass of Keshong La and descends to Talung Monastery, Sikkim's most sacred monastery. The monastery can be seen in the distance, but there is no bridge to cross the valley to reach it.

The trail continues through forest on the third day. After a short climb it crosses a bridge over Thombak Chu. This river, draining from the north, leads to the Thieu La pass and Muguthang towards the Lhonak Valley. There are several ascents and descents on the route, and the trail is frequently wiped out by floods. Find a place to descend towards the bank of the Zemu Chu and follow the trail beside the river. After a tiring 8-km (5-mile) day you will reach the camping ground of Yabuk, (4040m/13250ft). This is a fairly small area and increasingly cold and windy near the glacier.

Yabuk to Green Lake

The trail now enters the moraine field of the Zemu Glacier, crossing boulders and pebbles much of the way. This is a tiring route with increasing altitude and it is almost like walking in a high-altitude desert. However, one of the benefits is that the first good views of the mountains are visible. Siniolchu and Simvu can be glimpsed briefly across the glacier and at many turnings you will see Kangchenjunga rising in the distance.

Continue past some old campsites, dating back to the Survey of India, until you reach Rest Camp, 8km (5 miles) further on (4725m/15500ft). This camp is at the mouth of the wide Lhonak Valley descending from the Thangchung La to the north. Because of the boulder fields on the present trail, large expeditions using yaks have travelled via Thangchung La to reach their base camp at Green Lake. Unfortunately for the average trekker, this beautiful trail is not open as yet.

Rest Camp got its name from the early German expeditions in the 1930s. As the name implies, it was used by tired climbers to rest and recover while attempting Kangchenjunga and other peaks. This is the last camp where firewood is available.

On the last day the trail continues in similar terrain along a moraine ridge. But now the views

Lama Angden peak from the rest house in Lachen.

as many days as you possibly can. You will have to be properly acclimatised as the lake is at an altitude of almost 5000m (16405ft). Furthermore you will need to bring adequate fuel supplies with you.

Scramble up the moraine ridge and look down to the vast Zemu Glacier, which has several small lakes and pools, and is joined by several other glaciers. Across the Zemu Glacier rises Siniolchu (6877m/22563ft), with fluted ice ridges. Douglas Freshfield, who saw many mountains in his time, called this the most beautiful mountain in the world. Next to it rises Simvu (6812m/22350ft), which actually has four summits. The ridge of Simvu falls to Zemu Gap, a prominent depression in this vast ridge. This gap was last crossed by HW Tilman in 1938. To the west rises the giant Kangchenjunga massif. The south, central and main peaks are clearly visible, rising thousands of feet from the flat Zemu Glacier, creating one of the most magnificent and fearsome ice and rock walls ever seen. The northeast spur, which prevented early attempts to climb the main peak, is visible near the summit on the right.

Further to the right, almost in the northwest, a large glacier leads to Sugarloaf Peak (6455m/21179ft). Because of the vastness of the Zemu Glacier the distant peaks of Bhutan can also be seen. Prominent amongst them is Chhomolahri (7315m/24001ft), which rises to the east like a broad pyramid. The scenery is magnificent here and the mountains seem near enough to touch.

Walk-out via Lachen
The return trek follows the same route to Lachen and then a drive to Gangtok.

of the surrounding peaks are very clear and the walk is in high mountain country. It can get very windy by afternoon and, as the valley widens, the cold and the wind increase.

The final destination, Green Lake Camp, 6km (3¾ miles) further on (4935m/16190ft), is in a vast open ground with a wonderful view. The lake itself has dried out. This is a place to enjoy for

ALEXANDER CSOMA DE KOROS

The valleys of Kinnaur and Zanskar and the hill station of Darjeeling will always be associated with the Hungarian scholar Alexander Csoma de Koros. Born in 1784, he started his travels at the age of 34 and lived in Subathu, from where all treks began at the time, in the Shimla Hills.

Koros travelled the Hindustan-Tibet road to Kinnaur and lived at the Kanam Monastery from 1827 to 1830. Here he learned the Tibetan language and compared it with European dialects. Much of his work is still housed in the Kanam Monastery, which has a large library of books on Tibetan scriptures.

Later, he visited various parts of the Himalaya and lived in the Phuktal Monastery in Zanskar and the Ringdom Monastery near

Kargil. Visitors to these monasteries today can see stone tablets which have been carved in his memory. In all, Koros spent 22 years travelling, longer than any European since Marco Polo.

In March 1842 Koros reached Darjeeling, where he met Dr Campbell, leader of the early Everest expeditions. Koros contracted a fever a few days later and died on 11 April, at the age of 58. He was buried in Darjeeling cemetery, where his grave can still be seen.

See also *The Great Tibetologist Alexander Csoma de Koros* by Hirendra Nath Mukherjee

TREK 2: DZONGRI TO GUICHA LA

There are only a few trekking routes around the Kangchenjunga National Park that are open to visitors. One trail, to Guicha La, starts from Pemayangtse. The trail climbs steadily to cross a ridge at Dzongri, then proceeds north to the Onglathang Valley to reach Guicha La at its head. The return is by the same route. It is a traditional trek which follows a picturesque route past lush vegetation and wonderful mountain views until it reaches a high pass. The training courses of the Himalayan Mountaineering Institute are conducted in these valleys and trekkers have passed through here for decades.

Pemayangtse (2082m/6830ft) is 76km (47½ miles) by road from Darjeeling. Situated on a ridge, this well-known place is home to the second oldest monastery in Sikkim. Camp here for acclimatisation and views of the Kangchenjunga range before starting the trek. Note that it is essential to become acclimatised; many trekkers have suffered altitude sickness on this walk.

Pemayangtse to Dzongri

The trail heads up through terraced fields of rice, barley and corn, and is dotted with Nepalese, Sherpa and Lepcha huts. Crossing first the Rimbi Chu and then the Rathong Chu, the trail passes several other mountain streams. The trail then heads 16km (10 miles) up to the holy grounds of Yuksom (1780m/5840ft). The monastery, cloaked in perpetual silence, looms above. The first King of Sikkim, His Highness Funchook Namgyal, was crowned here by His Holiness Gyalwa Latchan Chembo, the same man who brought Buddhism to Sikkim in 1641. There is a stone throne on which the King sat for his coronation and the footprints of Gyalwa Latchan Chembo have also been preserved. About 3km (2 miles) away is the residence of Gyalwa Latchan, which was later converted into a monastery, the first of sixty-seven to be built in Sikkim.

A land of barley and apples, Yuksom provides beautiful vistas of mini-lakes with the Himalaya in the background. You can spend the night here in tourist huts or in a hotel.

TREK ESSENTIALS

LENGTH 2½–3 weeks; 112km (70 miles). Walking from Pemayangtse: 3 days to Dzongri, 4 days to Guicha La; same route back and time to acclimatise.

ACCESS From Delhi or Calcutta, fly to Bagdogra or take the train to New Jalpaiguri then drive 90km (56 miles) to Darjeeling. Pemayangtse is 76km (47½ miles) from Darjeeling and 170km (106¼ miles) from Gangtok.

HIGHEST POINT Highest trekking point: 4940m/16210ft Guicha La. Passes: Dzongri, 4030m (13220ft); Guicha La.

GRADE Strenuous.

SEASONS March– April and September–early November.

RESTRICTIONS Foreigners require state permits. All trekkers pay charges to Forest Department and Kangchenjunga National Park authorities.

FURTHER OPTIONS Combine with a trek to Sandakphu (see Trek 3, page 50).

The trail now runs through rice fields and wooded hills abounding in flora and fauna then passes through moss-laden forests of oak, spruce, chestnut, fir, pines, giant magnolias and rhododendron; a botanist's paradise. There are many varieties of exotic birds, butterflies and orchids. Among the animals here are Himalayan brown bears, black bears, and the barking deer. Sambar, marble cats, Blue sheep, Tibetan antelopes, wild asses, Himalayan wild goats, red pandas and musk deer are also found at various

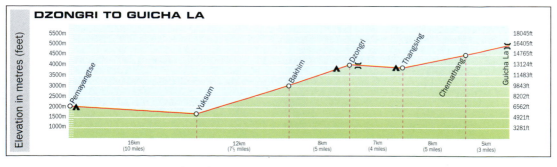

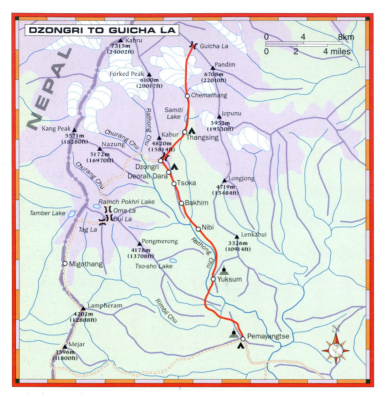

DZONGRI TO GUICHA LA

altitudes. It takes six hours' climbing to cover 12km (7½ miles) before reaching the Bakhim Forest Bungalow (3005m/9860ft).

Each step to Dzongri (4030m/13220ft), 8km (5 miles) and 6 hours away, leads on to the world of the Kangchenjunga massif. The steady and demanding climb continues through gullies with grazing yaks and mountain sheep, and past Tsoka, a Tibetan resettlement centre, which is the last village on the way. From here you should see the first sight of Sikkim snow.

After Phithang, a small clearing, the trail leads up into a rhododendron forest to Deorali Dara ('the meeting place of men and mountains'). There are spectacular views of the massive ranges of the Sikkim mountains and its peaks from here. Straight ahead is the third highest peak in the world, the legendary Kangchenjunga, in all its glory, surrounded by many other peaks. The mountains are particularly beautiful at dawn and dusk, when tinted in the softest of hues. Pygmy bushes of *cryptomaria Japonica* grow here, the dry leaves of which the locals gather to offer as incense to their family gods. You can stay overnight in tents or at the Dzongri Tourist Bungalow.

Dzongri to Guicha La

Seven kilometres (4½ miles) from Dzongri, a four-hour trek leads through meadows and valleys down into a lovely valley at the base of Jopunu Peak. Surrounded on all sides by massive mountains is a forest with a mountain stream slicing through it.

To reach the camping ground of Thangsing (3930m/12900ft), 7km (4½ miles) down the valley, you have to cross a wooden bridge over the stream. From Thangsing there is a clear view of the majestic peak of Pandim, which is considered sacred by the Sikkimese and mountaineers are not allowed to attempt it.

Situated at the base of Pandim Peak is Lake Samiti, sacred to the locals and to pilgrims from the plains. The trek up to Lake Samiti from the

Mist lingers over dense Sikkim forest.

camp at Thangsing is flat and surrounded by mountains. After pitching tents you can walk on the ridges surrounding the lake; and the higher you go the more breathtaking is the view of the lake.

Although some trekkers rush to Guicha La from Thangsing in a day, it is better to camp overnight on the way so that you can make the most of the breathtaking scenery. Set off early in the morning, and walk uphill in the direction of Guicha La. Chemathang is 8km (5 miles) from Thangsing and will take you 6 hours of walking towards Kangchenjunga through the giant

Prayer flags visible through the mist on the breathtaking vantage point of Guicha La.

Onglathang Valley. The trail to Chemathang is surrounded by many peaks and passes glacial lakes. There are also views of numerous glaciers on the way. After traversing loose boulders, rocks and sharp ridges, the trail reaches the old camp of Chemathang (4500m/14760ft), a very calm and serene place.

Guicha La (4940m/16210ft) is only 5km (3 miles) further on, but due to the altitude this excursion takes almost four hours. This is the northernmost and highest point of the trek. The climb starts through and over lichen-covered moraine and the approach to the pass is steep and over rugged terrain. The trail is faint.

It is best to make as early a start as possible, in good weather, for optimum visibility because the landscape visible from Guicha La is lovely. Kangchenjunga towers across the Talung Valley, north of the pass. There is a vast panorama sweeping towards the south.

If you wish to observe local customs you could add a piece of cloth, or a traditional *kata*, to the prayer flags on the pass, to seek the blessings of the mountain gods.

After a short rest, it is best to descend while the light is still good and proceed straight to Thangsing (bypassing Chemathang) near Samiti Lake, and camp there.

Walk-out via Pemayangtse

The return journey takes 4 days walking out by the same route: via Thangsing (bypassing Chemathang), then climb to Dzongri, descend to Bakhim, Yuksom and Pemayangtse. If you wish to vary the return journey, you could drive to Tashiding Monastery from Yuksom and then proceed to Gangtok.

SHERPA ANG TSERING

Ang Tsering, who lives in Darjeeling, is probably the oldest climbing Sherpa today, a legend in his own lifetime. Born in 1903, he is the only surviving member of the 1924 Mallory–Irvine expedition.

Ang Tsering was on Nanga Parbat with several pre-World War II German teams. He and Sherpa Gay Lay were with Will Merkle when all three were caught on top of the ice-wall during a storm in 1934. Ang Tsering came down as ordered and survived. The other two perished. It was an epic descent in difficult conditions: he subsequently lost several toes and was in ill health for many months.

To honour him and other Sherpas for achievements in the German expedition to Nanga Parbat in 1936, the German order of the Red Cross was issued to the Sherpas in the name of Adolf Hitler by the German Alpine Club. Three such certificates arrived in Darjeeling. As the Sherpas could not read, they decided to distribute one each, irrespective of the name on the certificate. Thus a certificate awarded to Kitar Sherpa is now with Ang Tsering. This is the only one which can be seen in Darjeeling as the other recipients, Sherpas Kitar and Kokuli, both died soon after on expeditions.

TREK 3: SINGALILA RIDGE TO SANDAKPHU

This trek follows the famous Singalila Ridge, a prominent spur of high ground that lies at the southern end of a long crest, which runs down from the Kangchenjunga massif and forms the border between Sikkim and Nepal. One of the unavoidable necessities of trekking in the Himalaya is that the best views are had from high up but the trek along this ridge, passing through small settlements, is perhaps the most scenically rewarding in the Himalaya. There are spectacular panoramic views of Kangchenjunga, Makalu, Everest, Lhotse and a host of other peaks all seen in one stretch.

TREK ESSENTIALS

LENGTH 2 weeks; 89km (55½ miles). Walking from Maneybhanjang: 3 days to Sandakphu, 4 days to Rimbik.
ACCESS From Delhi or Calcutta, fly to Bagdogra or take the train to New Jalpaiguri, then make a 90-km (56-mile) drive to Darjeeling. Trail starts at Maneybhanjang, 31km (19 miles) from Darjeeling (via Ghoom) and ends at Rimbik.
HIGHEST POINT Sandakphu (3636m/11930ft).
SEASONS March–April and October–December are best. Low altitude makes trekking possible in winter.
GRADE Easy.
RESTRICTIONS None.
FURTHER OPTIONS Trek to Guicha La (see Trek 2, page 47) can be combined with this trail.

From the hill station of Darjeeling a short drive of 31km (19 miles) brings you to the small settlement of Maneybhanjang (1981m/6500ft) in the southeast. This is at one end of the Singalila Ridge and on this trek you will be traversing the ridge from its southernmost point to the northern end, where it enters Sikkim State. There are plenty of houses and lodges on this trek for food and overnight accommodation.

Maneybhanjang to Sandakphu

The first part of this walk, 12km (7½ miles) to Tonglu, (3078m/10100ft), a small ridge-top settlement, climbs steeply to reach the main ridge. On

the way you will catch tantalising glimpses of the Kangchenjunga massif ahead, as the trail zig-zags up through the rhododendrons. There are many Nepalese tea-houses beside the trail, and you can either stay overnight in a comfortable trekkers' hut (booking needs to be made in advance of your trip) or camp.

On the second day, the treks starts off downhill through the picturesque Nepalese village of Khanyakuta where you can stop for lunch. You will see several Nepalese villages along the Singalila Ridge, which reflect the gradual migration over the border that has been taking place for the last few hundred years. The route then continues back to the ridge after a short climb to an overnight camp at Kalapokhari (3100m/10170ft), 13km (8 miles) further on. This is a relatively easy and short walk that is designed to aid proper acclimatisation before you progress to Sandakphu.

The next day, start the long climb up to the Singalila Ridge proper. After a pleasant hour's walk with good bird-spotting potential, it takes a further two hours and a steady haul up to Sandakphu, (3636m/11930ft), 8km (5 miles) further on. The reward is a remarkable panoramic view. The whole snowy ranges of Bhutan, Sikkim and Nepal, about 320km (200 miles) long, a wonderful mass of mountains looking like a wall of snow, is visible. The gigantic and towering Kangchenjunga, with its other peaks, Kabru, Kumbhakarna (Janu) and Pandim, dominates the scene. To the left of these peaks (to the west) Everest (8848m/

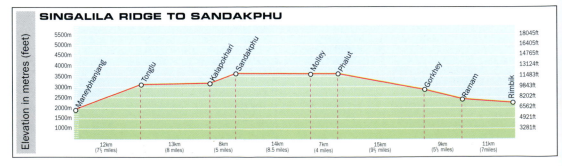

SINGALILA RIDGE TO SANDAKPHU

29030ft), graceful and majestic, can be seen in the distance, along with Lhotse.

You can stay overnight in a trekkers' hut at Sandakphu, or camp. Make sure you get up very early the next day because at sunrise there are glorious panoramic views of Everest, Makalu, Chamlang and Kangchenjunga from here.

Sandakphu to Rimbik

This is only a short walk but it pays to make an early start and find a prominent viewpoint so that you can see the magnificent sunrise from Sandakphu. Later the trail passes through one of the most spectacular sections of the Singalila Ridge, up and down, but never too demanding. There are ever-changing views of the snow-

Crossing a stream near Ramam.

The once-a-month family ritual of washing in freezing cold mountain stream water!

capped Himalaya to the north and northwest. This will be one of the finest day's walking you will ever have. You can make a slight detour from the main trail and camp at Molley (3535m/11600ft), 14km (9 miles) further on.

Climb up to the ridge once again and rejoin the main trail. This is a lovely, easy walk and continues to Phalut (3566m/11700ft), 7km (4½ miles) further on, where you can camp. The vegetation here is alpine, an undulating ripple of dwarf rhododendron bushes and shrubs of poisonous aconite. Phalut forms the junction between Nepal, Sikkim and West Bengal and is a very

beautiful area to visit. The hills are all barren and from here it is only 48km (30 miles), as the crow flies, to Kangchenjunga.

Next day, on leaving Phalut the trail descends steeply for 15km (9 miles) through a rich forest of rhododendrons and magnolias, teeming with bird life, to Gorkhey village. The lower hills are covered with moss-laden trees, many different varieties of rhododendron, silver firs, pines, spruce, chestnuts, oaks, giant magnolias and hemlocks. Gorkhey village (2390m/7840ft) is a small settlement on the border with the northern part of western Sikkim (though foreigners are not allowed to cross into Sikkim via this point). Next day, continue the descent for 9km (5½ miles) to make an overnight stop at Ramam (2490m/8500ft).

Continue the descent through forest the following day to reach the picturesque market town of Rimbik (2331m/7650ft). For the first hour, descend to the Siri Khola River, after which it is an easy 11-km (6¾-mile) walk to Rimbik.

Rimbik is a mainly Sherpa town, very different from other villages on the trail and quite busy on market day (Tuesday), with locals from surrounding villages coming to buy and sell their products. Rimbik, a Lepcha word, means *ling-gip*, 'the place where the swing is'.

You can either stay in Rimbik overnight in a lodge or drive to Kalimpong or Darjeeling, which takes four hours.

Drive-out via Maneybhanjang and Ghoom

Drive to Kalimpong (93km/58 miles, via Maneybhanjang and Ghoom), which was once an important trade centre between Bhutan and Tibet. This lovely, laid-back town with a pleasant climate is now famous for its orchid nurseries and handicrafts. Until 1959 Kalimpong was a major centre for the wool trade. Large caravans would start their journey to Tibet via Nathu La and Jelep La passes from here, and there are signs that these passes are to be reopened for trade. Kalimpong is a good place to end your trip and relax before driving to Bagdogra (76km/47½ miles) for flights or to New Jalpaiguri (80km/50 miles) for trains.

SHERPA TENSING OF EVEREST

Darjeeling was the home of the legendary Sherpa Tensing, born in the village of Thami, Nepal in 1913, the eleventh of thirteen children. Tensing's ambition from childhood was to climb Mount Everest, and he accompanied several expeditions attempting to do so, both from the northern and southern routes.

Tensing almost reached the summit with Raymond Lambert's Swiss expedition in the autumn of 1952, but it was not until he joined Lord Hunt's British expedition as head Sherpa that he, along with Sir Edmund Hillary, became the first to stand on the summit of Everest – on 29 May 1953.

Tensing later served as the Director and advisor to the Himalayan Mountaineering Institute until his death in 1986, during which time he never climbed again. Sherpa Tensing was cremated on a hill above the Institute, where a memorial has been erected in his memory.

SIKKIM DIRECTORY

REGIONAL TRANSPORT
Take the train to New Jalpaiguri station from Delhi or Calcutta. Alternatively, fly to Bagdogra airport, which has connecting flights to Delhi and Calcutta. Take a bus or taxi to Darjeeling and Gangtok.

REST HOUSE/HOTEL LOCATIONS
Bakhim, Chhiya Bhanjang, Chungthang, Darjeeling, Dzongri, Gangtok, Kalimpong, Lachen, Lachung, Mangan, Pemayangtse, Phalut, Sandakphu, Thangu, Yumthang.

Bronze statue of Tensing Norgay at Darjeeling.

REGIONAL TOURIST OFFICES
Sikkim Tourist Information Centre, Mahatma Gandhi Marg, Gangtok, tel (91-3592) 22064, 23425, 25277, fax (91-3592) 25647
Darjeeling Tourist Office, 1 Nehru Road, Darjeeling (WB) 734101, tel (91-354) 54050, 54102
Sikkim Tourist Information Centre, New Sikkim House, 14, Panchsheel Marg, Chanakyapuri, New Delhi 110021, tel (91-11) 3015346
Sikkim Tourist Information Centre, 4c Poonam Building, 5/2 Russell Street, Calcutta 700017, tel (91-33) 297516, 298983, fax (91-33) 2458479

RESTRICTIONS
Rules for foreigners entering restricted areas have recently been relaxed to promote tourism. Foreigners can visit Gangtok, Rumtek, Phodong, Pemayangtse and the Yuksom–Dzongri trekking route on the basis of restricted area permits, available through regional tourist offices or Indian embassies abroad. These allows foreigners to visit Gangtok, Rumtek, Phodong and Pemayangtse for a period of fifteen days.

For Dzongri, Changu and Yumthang Valley the rules are tighter. Organized foreign tourist groups consisting of not less than four persons, sponsored by recognized Indian travel agencies, can be issued permits up to fifteen days for trekking in the Dzongri area of west Sikkim. Note that permits for visiting Dzongri are issued only by the representatives of the Sikkim government in New Delhi. Groups in this area have to be accompanied by a liaison officer provided by the government of Sikkim. Similarly for visiting Changu Lake and the Yumthang Valley, foreigners are required to be in a group of four or more.

Areas other than those mentioned above can be visited, but require a special permit which is more difficult to get. These permits are obtained from the Ministry of Home Affairs, New Delhi.

LOCAL PLACES OF INTEREST
Darjeeling: Trek to Tiger Hill, Chaurasta Mall, Tensing Memorial, Zoo, Himalayan Mountaineering Institute, Tea gardens, Rope Ways, War Memorial at Batasia Loop.
Around Darjeeling: Sandakphu, Singla Bazaar, Phalut, Chhiya Bhanjang.
Darjeeling Hill Railway: Now declared a 'World Heritage Railway'. Leads from New Jalpaiguri to Darjeeling.
Gangtok: Tibetology Centre, Phurba Chorten with 113 prayer wheels, Tsuklakhang Monastery in King's Palace, Deer Park, Enchey Monastery.
Places around Gangtok: Rumtek Monastery, Phodong Monastery, Martam village resort.
Kalimpong: Once a trading town, now a quiet British-style hill station with old buildings.
North Sikkim: Kabi Lungtsok Memorial Pillar, Singhiek for views of snow peaks, Yumathang Hot Springs, Singba Rhododendron Sanctuary near Lachung.
West Sikkim: Yuksom, Peling, Pemayangtse.

5
KUMAUN AND GARHWAL

In the northern direction there is a noble-souled mountain called the Himalaya. He is Nagadhiraj, the Lord of All Mountains, with his extending arms fathoming the eastern and western oceans. He stands unsurpassed as the measuring rod of the earth.

(Kalidas, *Kumarsambhava*)

Kumaun and Garhwal are in many ways the centrepiece of the Indian Himalaya, dominated by the awe-inspiring mountain wilderness of the Nanda Devi Sanctuary. Closed at present for environmental reasons, trekkers can still enjoy the majesty of the Nanda Devi ('she who gives bliss') from the lower hills or by trekking around them. The Garhwal region is of considerable significance in Hindu mythology, and Badrinath on the Alaknanda is one of the four holy places of pilgrimage – the others being Kedarnath, Jamnotri and Gangotri.

The view of the Bandarpunch Range from the Kush Kalyan Plateau.

The bazaar in Joshimath is an important trading centre.

part of Kumaun, known as the Byans Valley, comprises the River Kali, running from Lipu Lekh to form the boundary between India and Nepal. The Kuthi, Darma and Lassar rivers merge into the Kali at various points. Vyas rishi, a sage who wrote the *Mahabharat*, is believed to have lived here, giving the area its name. The old pilgrim route to Manasarovar passed along the Kali and continues to be frequented by many today.

The main Gori Valley from Munsiary to Milam is known as Johar. Residents

Originally there was only Kumaun, but the British created Garhwal out of the western areas of Kumaun for administrative convenience and to pacify local kings. Ethnically, both areas resemble each other, but the demarcation in people's minds eventually became complete. Later, there was a movement to once again merge both the areas, and, in answer to this demand, in November 2000 the state of Uttaranchal was created.

Kumaun

The three major divisions of Kumaun had links with each other and with Tibet. The easternmost

of the upper villages traded with Tibet in the summer months and during the off-season reaped a harvest of *jowar* (maize). This harvesting gave them and the area the name of *jowari bhotia* (now Johar). Here a solid stone track leads over the Unta Dhura Pass into Tibet. With the closing of trade, the area has lost its trading importance and wealth but has become a popular route for trekkers.

Danpur, the westernmost part of Kumaun, gets its name from the generosity of its people, who gave free food to travellers (*dan*: donate, *pur*: place). In the old days when the passes to Tibet closed early due to early winter snow, the Tibetans who were left on the Indian side of the border were looked after by the people of this area, who supplied them with food and shelter until the passes opened again. Danpurians are regarded as the best porters and the most faithful – they accompanied the Shipton–Tilman party during the 1934 exploration of the Nanda Devi Sanctuary.

The Danpur area consists of two major valleys: the Pindari and the Sunderdhunga. The Pindari Glacier has Traill's Pass at its head and the peaks of Nanda Khat to its north and Nanda Kot to its south. The pass can be dangerous, and was the scene of fatal accidents for Indian (1970) and Japanese (1972) parties crossing it during attempts on Nanda Khat. Sunderdhunga ('beautiful stones') is a lovely valley into which the legendary British explorers Shipton and Tilman descended from Sunderdhunga Khal in 1934. This was the exit route which they strongly warned against using and has not

HOLY GANGA

To a pilgrim, a river is like a mother goddess, evoking love, devotion and reverence, so it is understandable that in ancient India people worshipped the Ganges (Ganga). In Indian mythology, the Ganges was brought to earth from heaven by a *rishi* (sage) named Bhagirath. The *rishi* endured a long penance so that India could have a perennial water source. However, the force of the Ganges was so strong that Shiva had to break her fall on his head so that she would gently descend to earth. His presence is symbolised by the Shivling Peak, towering above the source of the Ganges. Thus the River Ganges is supposed to flow on the earth to wash away the sins of mankind, and its source is a centre of meditation for sages.

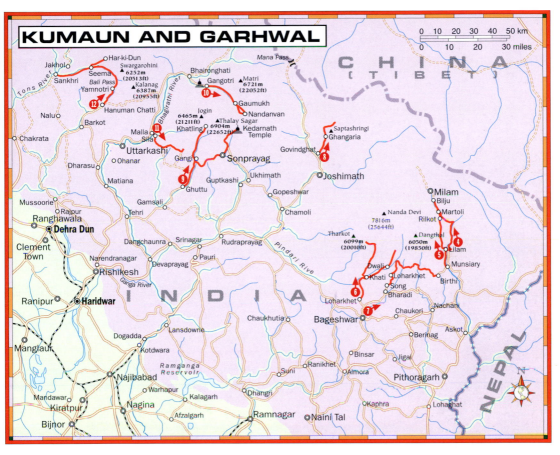

KUMAUN AND GARHWAL

been repeated. The area was visited again in 1944 by Wilfrid Noyce during his expedition to climb Tharkot. Maiktoli (6803m/22321ft), first climbed by Eric Shipton in 1934, has a formidable south face, an imposing 1800m (5906ft) wall seen from the Sunderdhunga Valley which was climbed by a Japanese party in 1977.

The jewel of the Kumaun–Garhwal region is, without doubt, the Nanda Devi Sanctuary. Until 1934, the gorge of the Rishi Ganga and the immediate area around Nanda Devi was among the least known and most inaccessible parts of the Himalaya. The mountain stands in a vast amphitheatre, and there is no point in the ring of mountains round the sanctuary lower than 5200m (17061ft), except in the west where the Rishi Ganga has carved out a formidable gorge.

Garhwal

Central Garhwal comprises the mountainous area around the Saraswati–Alaknanda river system and the Dhauli Valley. Hindus call Garhwal *devbhoomi*, which means the sacred valley of the gods. Adi

A Kumauni lady in traditional dress.

Shankracharya (c.800 AD), the guru who led the revival of Hinduism, established four temples at the four corners of India. The northern temple is at Badrinath (*badri*: wild berries, which grew here in plenty, *nath*: lord). He was said to have trekked across the Mana Pass and the statue at the temple bears a resemblance to Buddha (Bodhisatva) and the symbols of Vishnu. This is the earliest record of travel in the Himalaya.

Religion was at the heart of travel in this region. In 1624 the Jesuit priests Antonio de Andrade and Manuel Marques crossed the Mana Pass to Guge in Tsaparang province, Tibet. Later the mountaineer and botanist Frank Smythe visited the area in 1937, and, with his flair for writing, documented the region for posterity. WH Murray's 1950 expedition is perhaps the best

Archway at the entrance to the Nanda Devi Temple, Martoli.

known, and covered the area exhaustively.

West of Badrinath is the mighty Gangotri massif. The major glaciers here are the Gangotri, Chaturangi and Raktavarna, which lie adjacent to each other. The main valley is that of the Bhagirathi River – the Gangotri Temple is the last settlement, and the roadhead. At Gaumukh ('cow's mouth'), you can see the source of the Ganges emerging from the depths of the glacier, and the shape of the ice formation is indeed like a cow's mouth. Opposite it is Shivling (6543m/ 21468ft), a towering pinnacle of rare beauty – and of equally severe technical difficulty. It was only after the development of artificial climbing techniques that serious attempts were made on this mountain.

West of the Bhagirathi Valley, but more easily reached from Har-ki-Dun and the Tons River, is a most attractive trekking and climbing arena comprising the four peaks of Swargarohini and the Bandarpunch Range. The area first came into prominence when the Doon school masters – RL Holdsworth, JTM Gibson, JAK Martyn and Gurdial Singh – used this area to offer a Himalayan experience to their wards during their summer holidays. The tradition was continued, and this is where generations of Indian trekkers still go to climb and ski.

This completes the brief sketch of the major areas in the 'land of the gods'. Fittingly, as it began with the Christian fathers, the southernmost part of Kumaun ends with E Stanley Jones and his Christian ashram at Sat Tal, near Nainital. This is a Methodist Church, but the style and name is that of a Hindu organization. Earl Denman, who attempted Everest alone and secretly with Tensing Norgay in 1947, lived here for many years until he died in the late 1970s. In some way, Denman symbolises the attraction of Kumaun and Garhwal for trekkers.

THE LEGEND OF MADHOSINH RAWAT

Madhosinh Rawat is just one of the many legendary figures of the Milam Valley. A simple Milamwal who served the trading caravans to and from Tibet, Madhosinh ran a tea shop between the Unta Dhura and Jainti Dhura passes on the famous Indo-Tibet trade route.

This valley is deserted, barren and has strong Tibetan winds lashing along it which could prove lethal to anyone trapped between the passes during storms. Carrying wood to this barren terrain from far-away Girthi, Madhosinh served food and tea to the caravans, saving many from certain death. The caravans to Tibet sang praises of Madhosinh Rawat and his legend is kept alive in traditional songs of Milam, as in the following couplets:

If we stop, we stand rooted like great mountains.
If we walk, we sail through life.
We remember you at each step
and in doing so make you immortal.

TREK 4: BIRJEGANJ DHURA AND THE RALAM VALLEY

Munsiary is situated at a vantage point between two prominent valleys that stretch towards the north. The valley on the left (due north) is that of the Gori Ganga River, known as the Milam Valley. The adjoining valley to its right, leading northeastwards, is the Ralam Gad, the Ralam Valley. This contains the Kalabaland Glacier, with peaks such as Chiring We and Suitilla at its head. The main village deep inside the valley, from which it takes its name, is Ralam. Above the village on the Ralam–Milam watershed is the easy pass, the Birjeganj Dhura, used by villagers to go to the Milam Valley. This pass offers some unparalleled views.

Located on the slopes of the Gori Ganga Valley, Munsiary is accessible by road from Almora via Bageshwar. The trail north begins here.

Munsiary to Ralam

To start the trek you have to descend to the river and cross it by bridge. From here, the lowest point of the trail, climb steadily towards Lilam, 12km (7½ miles) further (1810m/5940ft). There are a few huts, a school compound and open places to stay or camp in. But it can be very hot and Lilam is also renowned for flies. There is a police post where you have to register.

After Lilam, leave Trek 5 and go east across the river to Paton village (2100m/6890ft) en route to the Ralam Valley where the trek will be followed the next day. Cross the Gori Ganga by bridge and start climbing to Paton village. The trail is wide and the village is about 10km (6 miles) away. Go on to Pilthi Gad, a small river flowing from the east and merging with the Ralam Gad. There are open grounds to camp near the confluence.

On the third day the trail gets wilder as you proceed deep inside the Ralam valley. There are constant ups and downs but no major climbs. Meadow after meadow is crossed on this shepherd's trail. After 10km (6 miles) you will reach a huge cave, Sapo Udiar (3015m/9890ft), with several large

TREK ESSENTIALS

LENGTH 2 weeks; 110km (68 miles). Walking from Munsiary: 4 days to Ralam, 2 days to Martoli, 4 days to Munsiary. 2 days back to Delhi via Kathgodam.

ACCESS Train to Kathgodam from Delhi then drive to Almora (88km/55 miles), then 72km (45 miles) to Bageshwar, then Munsiary. Trailhead extends to Darkot.

HIGHEST POINT 4666m/15310ft (Birjeganj Dhura). Passes: Birjeganj Dhura.

GRADE Medium.

SEASONS Mid-May to mid-November (not July–August).

RESTRICTIONS Foreign trekkers require permits to visit the Ralam Valley.

FURTHER OPTIONS Treks to Milam or to Bhadeli Gwar from Martoli (see Trek 5, page 62).

boulders nearby, good for rock climbing. Gurkha soldiers are said to have stayed in this cave during the invasion of Kumaun and now locals use it for shelter while travelling.

The last stage to Ralam village is a long one covering 16km (10 miles). But it is generally a flat trail and as the valley widens, so does the vista. To the east, peaks such as Shivu (lord Shiva), Rajrambha ('celestial fairy') and Chaudhara ('four cornered')

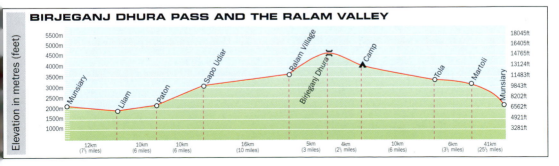

BIRJEGANJ DHURA PASS AND THE RALAM VALLEY

Elevation in metres (feet)

5500m 18045ft
5000m 16405ft
4500m 14765ft
4000m 13124ft
3500m 11483ft
3000m 9843ft
2500m 8202ft
2000m 6562ft
1500m 4921ft
1000m 3281ft

Munsiary — Lilam — Paton — Sapo Udiar — Ralam Village — Birjeganj Dhura — Camp — Tola — Martoli — Munsiary

12km (7½ miles) · 10km (6 miles) · 10km (6 miles) · 16km (10 miles) · 5km (3 miles) · 4km (2½ miles) · 10km (6 miles) · 6km (3½ miles) · 41km (25½ miles)

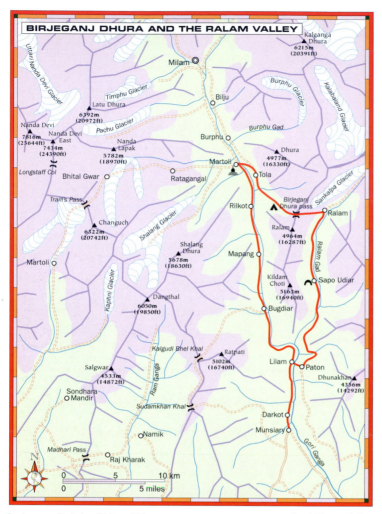

BIRJEGANJ DHURA AND THE RALAM VALLEY

Kalganga
Dhura
6215m
(20391ft)

Milam

Burphu Glacier

Kalabaland Glacier

Uttari Nanda Devi Glacier

Timphu Glacier

Bilju

Latu Dhura

6392m
(20972ft)

Pachu Glacier

Burphu Gad

Nanda Devi
7816m
(25644ft)

Nanda Devi
East
7434m
(24390ft)

Nanda
Lapak
5782m
(18970ft)

Burphu

Dhura
4977m
(16330ft)

Longstaff Col

Bhital Gwar

Martoli

Tola

Traill's Pass

Ratagangal

Rilkot

Birjeganj
Dhura pass

Sankalpa Glacier

Changuch
6322m
(20742ft)

Shalang Glacier

Ralam

Ralam
4964m
(16287ft)

Martoli

Shalang
Dhura
5678m
(18630ft)

Mapang

Kaphni Glacier

Dangthal
6050m
(19850ft)

Kildam
Choti
5163m
(16940ft)

Sapo Udiar

Ralam Gad

Bugdiar

Kalgudi Bhel Khal

Ratpati
5102m
(16740ft)

Lilam

Paton

Salgwar
4533m
(14872ft)

Ram Ganga

Dhunakhan
4356m
(14292ft)

Sondhara
Mandir

Sudamkhan Khal

Darkot

Namik

Munsiary

Gori Ganga

Madhari Pass

Raj Kharak

N

0   5   10 km

0   5 miles

Rocky campsite below Birjeganj Dhura.

can be seen. In summer you will see several groups of shepherds. Finally the trail reaches Ralam village (3650m/11975ft), which consists of about a dozen houses with large stony compounds. There is also a school and a lovely view. From the village, a trail to the north leads to a unique meeting of three glaciers. The Kalabaland, from the northwest, descends to merge with the Yankchar from the southeast. They join to form another glacier called the Sankalpa, which descends southwards to the Ralam Valley. The glaciology of this area and its unique formations are well documented. To the east of Ralam village, a deep notch in the ridge can be seen. This is the Yankchar Dhura Pass, which was traditionally used to cross over to the Ralam Pass and to the Lassar Yankti Valley. The 1950 Scottish Himalayan Expedition (see page 61) crossed this and the Ralam Pass during their fascinating journey.

Ralam to Martoli

Birjeganj Dhura Pass is situated directly above the Ralam village in the west on the watershed of the Milam Valley. A broad trail, starting near the village, leads to the top. It climbs gradually and zigzags up the slope, opening into a grand view towards the east and the north. The pass (4666m/15310ft) is reached after a 5km (3 miles) climb. Once on the pass a wide panorama opens up in front, which has to be seen to be believed. From the direction the trail has climbed, Rajrambha, Chaudhara, the sharp peak of Suitilla and several others are visible. But the best view is towards the west. The entire northern wall of the Nanda Devi Sanctuary is clearly visible, with the twin peaks dominating the heights on the left. You could spend hours counting the peaks and looking at this view with a sense of wonder.

There is no place to camp near the pass so descend towards the west. After about 200m (656ft) the trail is not too steep and descends to grassy meadows above the village of Tola (3432m/11260ft). By the stream at about 300m

(986ft) above the village there is an ideal place to pitch tents. It is almost mandatory to camp here as the Nanda Devi peak's east face (7816m/25644ft) is seen in a unique profile. Due to its position, the sun disappears directly beyond these peaks, giving it a wonderful silhouette. Be sure to get up very early in the morning the next day as the pre-dawn play of light on these peaks is worth a thousand sunrises. The first rays touch the peaks when everything else is in darkness and the gradual awakening of all the peaks and valleys is a breathtaking sight.

As the trail descends to Tola, the magnificent peaks of Hardeol and Tirsuli are seen in all their splendour. Finally you reach the valley and the small village of Tola where people go about their work blissfully in the shadow of the great panorama above them. Spend a night at this village or cross the bridge over the Gori Ganga to climb 6km (3½ miles) further on to Martoli (3374m/11070ft), which is on the Milam trail.

Milam to Munsiary

The return trek follows the Milam Glacier trail (see Trek 5, page 62), and takes four days; Milam to Rilkot, Bugdiar, Lilam and Munsiary. But with a long descent upon good trail, and weather permitting, a day can be saved on the return walk. It is preferable to arrange transport or take a local bus or taxi from Darkot to Munsiary to avoid the last 5km (3 miles) walk up to Munsiary.

Drive-out via Munsiary to Kathgodam

It is a long two-day drive to Delhi and civilization. Drive past Kalamuni Pass and Birthi to Tejam (57km/35 miles), which is a major junction. The road is always open (except the Kalamuni Pass section, which is sometimes blocked in the rainy season or during winter). Chakori lies 47km (29 miles) ahead on the main road and is a good place to enjoy some of the best close-up views of the Nanda Devi Sanctuary peaks. Owing to the location of Chakori, the peaks appear as if they are almost within touching distance. It has vast open places with old tea gardens and a newly built rest house.

If you start early the next day you can drive via Bageshwar (47km/29 miles) and Almora (72km/45

Walking along a rocky river bed in the Ralam Valley.

miles) to arrive in Kathgodam (88km/55 miles) by late evening. A convenient overnight train reaches Delhi the next morning.

THE SCOTTISH HIMALAYAN EXPEDITION

In 1950 an expedition led by the well-known Scottish mountaineer WH Murray explored the valleys of the Garhwal and Kumaun. They visited Milam and spent a few days there. Murray wrote about the Dancing Girls of Milam, traditional dancers who still perform today, but now only on festive occasions. The historic village of Milam once had about 500 homes; now with trade closed in this area the inhabitants have gone to the plains and only the ruins are left. A handful of families live in the ruined houses for a few months of the year.

TREK 5: MILAM GLACIER

The people of Johar, as the Milam Valley is locally known, were traders whose caravans crossed from India into Tibet by the high passes of Unta Dhura and Kungribingri La. Once the trading season was over, the entire population of Milam and the surrounding areas moved down to Munsiary or lower during winter. To help the trade and yearly migration, the British built a wide trail lined with stones with well-marked resting points, exactly 12km (7 miles) apart, which was considered a comfortable distance a laden porter should travel in a day. Trade stopped with the Indo–China conflict of 1962 and these once-prosperous villages are now deserted. However the trail still exists, linking the villages and beckoning trekkers.

TREK ESSENTIALS

LENGTH Two weeks; 82km (51 miles). Walking from Munsiary: 3 days to Rilkot, 3 days to Milam, 4 days to Munsiary; 2 days back to Delhi via Kathgodam.

ACCESS Train to Kathgodam from Delhi and drive to Almora (88km/55 miles), then Bageshwar (72km/45 miles) and on to Munsiary. Trailhead extends to Darkot.

HIGHEST POINT 3424m/11234ft (Milam).

GRADE Medium.

SEASONS Mid-May to mid-November (not July-August).

RESTRICTIONS None.

FURTHER OPTIONS Treks in side valleys to base camp of Nanda Devi East at Naspanpatti and to Bhadeli Gwar at Danu Dhura Pass. Or link up with Trek 4 (see page 59) to Birjeganj Dhura.

Munsiary is the starting point of this trek – as for Trek 4. Situated on the slopes of the Gori Ganga Valley, it is accessed by road from Almora via Bageshwar.

Munsiary to Rilkot

To start the trek you have to descend almost to the river and proceed on the right bank just short of Milam village. The trail is an ancient trade route which is well built and maintained, and has traditional halts. The Milam Glacier is further up at the head of the valley, while a trail towards the

northeast leads to Unta Dhura Pass, which is a restricted area.

The Milam valley extends north from Darkot or Shailapani (1800m/5900ft), which is 5km (3 miles) from Munsiary. The trail to Milam begins here. Continue descending steadily until you reach the river at Jimighat, another 5km (3 miles) away. From this, the lowest point of the trail, climb steadily towards Lilam, 2km (1¼ miles) further (1810m/5940ft). There are a few huts, a school compound and open places to stay or camp in, as well as a police post where you have to register. A trail leads eastwards across the river to Paton village en route to the Ralam valley (see Trek 4, page 59).

The trail during the trek borders the Gori Ganga River, which is seen in various guises as it passes through a narrow gorge and then opens up to a variety of mountain views. A little beyond Lilam, the original trail was washed away in floods in 1995 and a detour was built going higher on to the ridge above Lilam. This has added 4km (2½ miles) with a 1400m (4953ft) climb. The old trail is now restored except at one point which should be cleared soon (enquire when you reach Lilam). Follow the trail to Bugdiar, 12km (7½ miles) away, via Raurgari. The trail climbs steadily amid a forest contained in a narrow gorge. At Bugdiar (2450m/8040ft) there is a small rest house and a police post. You may camp a little further ahead along the trail.

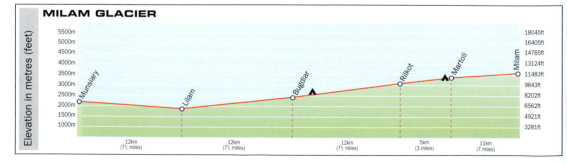

MILAM GLACIER

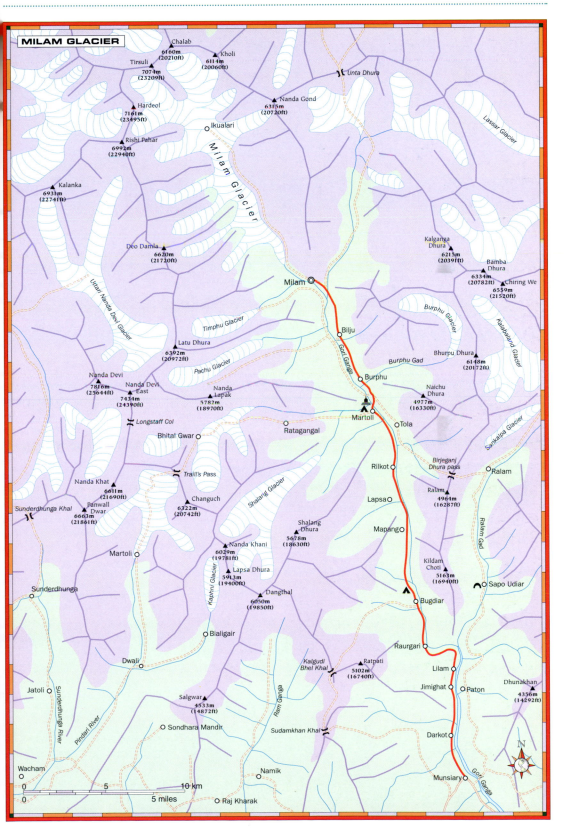

MILAM GLACIER

Chalab
6160m
(20210ft)

Kholi
6114m
(20060ft)

Unta Dhura

Tirsuli
7074m
(23209ft)

Nanda Gond
6315m
(20720ft)

Lassar Glacier

Hardeol
7161m
(23495ft)

Rishi Pahar
6992m
(22940ft)

Ikualari

Milam Glacier

Kalanka
6931m
(22741ft)

Kalganga
Dhura
6215m
(2039ft)

Bamba
Dhura
6334m
(20782ft)

Chiring We
6559m
(21520ft)

Deo Damla
6620m
(21720ft)

Milam

Uttari Nanda Devi Glacier

Timphu Glacier

Bilju

Gori Ganga

Burphu Glacier

Kalabaland Glacier

Latu Dhura
6392m
(20972ft)

Pachu Glacier

Burphu

Burphu Gad

Bhurpu Dhura
6148m
(20172ft)

Nanda Devi
7816m
(25644ft)

Nanda Devi
East
7434m
(24390ft)

Nanda
Lapak
5782m
(18970ft)

Martoli

Tola

Naichu
Dhura
4977m
(16330ft)

Sankalpa Glacier

Longstaff Col

Bhital Gwar

Ratagangal

Rilkot

Birjeganj
Dhura pass

Ralam

Nanda Khat
6611m
(21690ft)

Panwall
Dwar
6663m
(21861ft)

Traill's Pass

Changuch
6322m
(20742ft)

Shalang Glacier

Lapsa

Ralam
4964m
(16287ft)

Ralam Gad

Sunderdhunga Khal

Martoli

Kaphni Glacier

Nanda Khani
6029m
(19781ft)

Lapsa Dhura
5913m
(19400ft)

Shalang
Dhura
5678m
(18630ft)

Mapang

Kildam
Choti
5163m
(16940ft)

Sapo Udiar

Sunderdhunga

Bialigair

Dangthal
6050m
(19850ft)

Bugdiar

Raurgari

Dwali

Kalgudi
Bhel Khal

Ratpati
5102m
(16740ft)

Lilam

Jimighat

Paton

Dhunakhan
4356m
(14292ft)

Jatoli

Salgwar
4533m
(14872ft)

Ram Ganga

Sundardhunga River

Pindari River

Sondhara Mandir

Sudamkhan Khal

Darkot

Wacham

Namik

Gori Ganga

N

0   5   10 km

0   5 miles

Raj Kharak

Munsiary

THE LEGEND OF GURKHA KYUL

In the ruins of Milam village lie the legends of the past. Gurkha Kyul is a fortified building, built out of the heaviest stone, by a *rani* (queen) who used it as protection against a Gurkha invasion. She erected cairns that looked like humans on surrounding ridges, some of which can still be seen. The Gurkhas were kept away, scared for a while, and were unable to identify the Rani as she wore male attire. One morning at Ranikot (where the Gori Ganga and Goenkha Gad meet), a little outside Milam, she washed her face with both hands. According to custom, a man washes with only one hand while a woman uses both. She was thus identified and killed.

On the next day descend along the trail, by the side of the river and bypassing a small temple of Nahardevi under an overhanging rock. After about 8km (5 miles) and 4 hours the trail reaches the deserted village of Mapang where there

The trail follows the Goenkha Gad near Milam.

are some tea stalls. En route there are some excellent huge rock walls, which are a major attraction for rock climbers. The trail at this point may be covered with snow during early summer and road builders have erected wooden log bridges in places where care needs to be taken. Passing another deserted village (Laspa), you will reach Rilkot (3250m/10660ft), having covered the 12km (7½ miles) stage. Rilkot is at the northern end of the Gori Ganga Gorge and from here the valley widens to give good views of Hardeol (7151m/23462ft) and Tirsuli (7074m/23210ft), the peaks at the head of the Milam Valley.

Rilkot to Milam

Though the trail continues along the main valley towards Milam, it is advisable to make a short detour west of 5km (3 miles) to Martoli village (3400m/11150ft). About 2km (1¼ miles) ahead of Rilkot a wide trail leads to Martoli, situated at the edge of Lwan Gad Valley, a side valley of the Milam Valley. Martoli village has a temple dedicated to the goddess Nanda Devi and has a partial view of the famous twin peaks named after her. The stone temple is about 1km (⅔ mile) above the village and has a lovely arch from which many bells have been hung as offerings. There are several camping grounds near the temple, with good forest and a stream nearby. The valley further west leads to Bhadeli Gwar (two days' journey) and is one of the finest of the unspoilt green valleys in the area. Another branch of the Lwan Gad leads to Naspanpatti, the traditional base camp site for climbers attempting Nanda Devi East. It offers wonderful views of the peak and is a two day return trek.

Martoli itself is deserted and situated at the edge of a cliff. It has been well documented by Dr Tom Longstaff (during his first exploration in 1910) and HW Tilman and H Adams Carter, who passed through here (after exiting from the Nanda Devi Sanctuary) in 1936. To the east, across the Gori Ganga Valley, are wonderful views of the Birjeganj Dhura Pass and Chiring We (6559m/21520ft).

From Martoli, descend further northeast to reach a small bridge over the Lwan Gad. The trail now rejoins the trade route to Milam. After 3km (2 miles) the trail crosses the main bridge over the Gori Ganga and continues on the left bank. A short climb brings you to Burphu village (3350m/10990ft). The scenery is spectacular as the valley opens up. The north faces of the Nanda Devi peaks, several peaks on the Nanda Devi Sanctuary wall and Hardeol group are visible, particularly from Bilju village, which is about 4km (2½ miles) ahead. The trail continues horizontally to reach Milam in another 4km.

Mule herders lead their animals across a valley floor near Milam.

Milam ('place of meeting') (3424m/11235ft) is a large village with a police post where passports will be checked. It has a small shop and a rest house with many open grounds to camp in. The Goenkha Gad flows in from the northeast, draining the Tibetan watersheds whose passes are about three days' strenuous walking from here.

To proceed along the Goenkha Gad, cross the Unta Dhura Pass into the Girthi Ganga Valley in Garhwal and complete a circuitous route. At present, permits are reserved for Indian nationals.

The head of the Milam Valley leads to the glacier of the same name. After permission from the local police post, proceed into this valley for some distance to get a good view of Hardeol and other peaks. About 12km (7½ miles) ahead are the open grounds of Nital Thaur, which offer a magnificent view and are open for Indian trekkers to camp in and visit.

Milam to Munsiary

Allow four days for the return route: Milam to Rilkot, Bugdiar, Lilam and Munsiary.

Drive-out via Munsiary to Kathgodam

As for Trek 4, the drive-out from Munsiary involves a long two-day journey to Delhi. The road from Munsiary towards Tejam (57km/35 miles) is tarmacked and is always open – except the Kalamuni Pass section, which may sometimes be blocked in the rainy season or during winter. Some 47km (29 miles) ahead is Chakori, a good place to enjoy close-up views of the Nanda Devi Sanctuary peaks.

By starting early the next day you can drive via Bageshwar (47km/29 miles) and Almora (72km/45 miles) to arrive in Kathgodam (88km/55 miles) by late evening. A convenient overnight train reaches Delhi the next morning.

MILAMWAL

The people of this valley are known by the names of their villages. A person hailing from the Milam Valley would be called a Milamwal while a villager from Martoli is known as a Martolia. Many men from this area have played historic roles in the early explorations of the Himalayan ranges.

The famous Pundit Surveyors, Narain Singh and Kishen Singh Rawat - employed by the Survey of India to penetrate deep into then forbidden Tibet - hailed from Milam. Under disguise they gathered much information on Tibet, based on which maps were prepared.

In 1926 Ruttledge, who was then the District Commissioner, and Wilson crossed the difficult Traill's Pass from the Milam Valley to Pindari. Their guide was Diwansing Martolia who was almost considered a *lata*, someone of very low intelligence. After crossing the pass, when Ruttledge discharged him, he returned by a pioneering route directly over the high snow pass of Danu Dhura.

In appreciation, Ruttledge, who was a high official of the British Government, awarded him a *jagir* (grant of land) and a rifle. But Diwansing was swindled by local villagers and these awards were sold off.

In the last few decades many Milamwals have excelled in different fields, such as Hukam Singh of the Indo-Tibet Border Police. Travelling with *mawasas* (migrating families) he completed his education with great difficulty and in poverty. After joining the police force he rose to be Deputy Inspector General, a high-ranking officer in the Indo-Tibet Border Police Force, and was one of India's most famous mountaineers by the time of his death.

PANCH CHULI GROUP OF PEAKS

The most visible symbol in the Kumaun valleys are the peaks of Panch Chuli, named after the five Pandava brothers from the Indian epic *Mahabharata*. The peaks represent their cooking hearths (*chulis*) where they cooked their last meal before ascending to heaven. From the bungalow at Munsiary at sunrise, the sun's rays are reflected upwards into the sky from these peaks. The reflection is repeated in the evening, a little after sunset, best seen in the Darma Valley to the east.

The Panch Chuli peaks lie in the Eastern Kumaun and are seen to great advantage from the Kalamuni Pass and Munsiary. They form the watershed between the Gori and the Darma Ganga valleys. The eastern approaches are through Sona and Meola Glaciers. The Uttari and Dakshini Balati glaciers guard the western approaches. The peaks are numbered NW to SE, I (6355m/20851ft), II (6904m/22652ft), III (6312m/20710ft), IV (6334m/20782ft) and V (6437m/21120ft). Naming the peaks from west to east breaks with the tradition of giving the highest peak the lowest number, but the nomenclature has become too well established to be changed now.

Early Expeditions from the East

The mountaineering history of these peaks began with the British mountaineer Hugh Ruttledge (1929). He saw the group at close quarters from high up on the Sona Glacier. He examined the routes and thought that the north arête (sharp ridge) might be possible. After 21 years two teams examined the eastern approaches. WH Murray (1950) and his Scottish team followed the Ruttledge route. They intended to reach the north col and follow the northeast ridge; however, they found the terrain too difficult. Just 20 days later came Kenneth Snelson (British) and J de V Graaff (South African). They reached the upper Sona Glacier by early September and found that its head was a cradle of 182m (600ft) cliffs blocking the route to the northeast summit's ridge.

They considered the south ridge, but wrote: 'The ridge towards south col has a rather easier gradient but it is very broken, and heavily corniced.' They too abandoned their attempt on the southeast face after 122m (400ft).

After these attempts, the eastern approaches were left alone. Two more teams in 1970 and 1988 also tried them unsuccessfully.

Attempts from the West

The western approaches were tried one year after Murray. In 1951 Heinrich Harrer and Frank Thomas (Austrians) were joined by two Sherpas and a botanist. Though their account in the *Himalayan Journal* is not very explicit, their photographs in the archives clearly indicate that they pioneered the route through the Uttari Balati Glacier, bypassing three ice-falls. Together with the Sherpas, Harrer reached the Balati Plateau and examined the north and west ridges. They tried the west ridge but a Sherpa fell off on hard blue ice. Harrer gave up. They spent only 16 days on the mountains but during that time they pioneered the route which was followed by all subsequent expeditions from this side.

Wrong Claims

In 1952, the Indian climber PN Nikore followed the Harrer route and his attempt in June almost coincided with an attempt by another team led by DD Joshi which included Major John Dias. Both teams reached the Balati Plateau. Nikore returned in 1953 and claimed a solo ascent of the peak. Without any convincing proof, he was disbelieved and the claim ignored.

Group Captain AK Chowdhury led a team sponsored by the Indian Mountaineering Foundation to this group in 1964. Following the Uttari Balati Glacier, they reached the Balati Plateau. Their cursory attempt on peak II failed. They then claimed ascents of Peaks III, IV and V in two days (and two peaks on the same day).

These peaks stand above the southern valley of Pyunshani and are completely unapproachable from the Balati Plateau. To climb these peaks, as claimed, the party would have had to climb over very difficult terrain covering almost 10km (6 miles) in one day, above 6300m (20670ft) crossing low cols. The party had mistakenly climbed three distinct humps situated near their camps and running east–west from peak II instead of peaks III, IV and V, which broadly run north–south. At first, the so-called summitters either refused to reply to queries, or were adamant in their claim. The records were corrected after 28 years, when the mistake was pointed out by the 1992 Indian–British expedition, and the mistake was ultimately accepted by the sponsors.

A beautiful panoramic view of the peaks in the Panch Chuli group. From left to right: peaks I to V.

First Ascents

The history of the Panch Chuli group continued with two large expeditions from the Indo-Tibet Border Police. The first team in 1972 was led by Hukam Singh. They powered their way to the Balati Plateau via the Harrer route and made the first-ever ascent of peak I. Repeating their route, Mahendra Singh led another team in 1973. The entire route on the southwest ridge was fixed with almost 3000m (9843ft) of rope. On 26th May 1973, 18 people climbed the summit of Panch Chuli II, the highest peak of the group.

The mountain was then left alone for some 18 years. In 1991 two routes were climbed via the eastern approaches by teams from the Indian Army. The first team followed the Sona Glacier, climbed the northeast slopes to reach above the north col and established a camp on the north ridge. The ridge was followed to the top, and thus the route suggested by Ruttledge in 1929 was finally completed after 61 years. The second army team followed Murray's route to the upper Meola Glacier. They pitched a high camp following the southeast slopes to the east ridge. The summit team broke the cornice to reach the top, and thus the route suggested by Snelson–Graaff was also completed, after 41 years.

Last Climbs

The scene finally shifted back to the west. The Indian–British expedition 1992 (jointly led by Sir Chris Bonington and Harish Kapadia) followed the route along the Uttari Balati Glacier to the Balati Plateau. On the way the team divided into groups to climb Sahadev East (5757m/18889ft), Menaka (6000m/19686ft) and Rajrambha (6537m/21448ft). On peak II, a team of three climbed the southwest ridge. It was a hard climb on ice, keeping well away from the hanging cornices. Compared to the earlier ascent, only 60m (197ft) of rope was fixed on the ridge. This was only the second ascent of the southwest ridge, made after 19 years.

Another team of two pioneered a new route up the steep and icy west ridge, with bivouacs. They descended the southwest ridge completing the traverse. Thus the route tried by Harrer was completed after 41 years.

The 1992 expedition later made the first ascent of peak V. On this peak Stephen Venables, a leading English mountaineer, fell while returning from the peak. He survived despite serious injuries and was airlifted in a daring helicopter rescue from the high camp. Peak IV was climbed in 1995 by a team from New Zealand. Peak III still remains unscaled, though it was attempted by two expeditions from Bombay in 1996 and 1998, both of which resulted in accidents.

TREK 6: SUNDERDHUNGA AND PINDARI VALLEYS

This is one of the most popular trekking areas in Kumaun. As in Nepal, there are convenient rest houses (government-run lodges) at each stage. It offers the freedom to trek without any *bandobast*, or great preparations, but on the other hand you will be in the company of many other trekkers, especially in May and October which is India's holiday time. However, this does not diminish the area's beauty nor the fun of trekking in it. The trail from Loharkhet is broad and crosses the gentle Dhakuri Khal to enter the Pindari River Basin. Descending into the valley, the trail gradually rises towards the Pindari Glacier. The final viewpoint, called Zero Point, gives a wonderful view of the Pindari Glacier ice-fall.

TREK ESSENTIALS

LENGTH 2 weeks; 130km/81 miles (both valleys). Walking from Loharkhet: 2 days to Khati, 4 days to Sukhram, 4 days back, 3 days Khati to Zero Point.
ACCESS Train to Kathgodam from Delhi and drive to Almora (88km/55 miles) then Bageshwar (72km/45 miles further). A road leads from Bageshwar to Song, the trailhead.
HIGHEST POINT 3600m (11810ft). Passes: Dhakuri Khal (2902m/9520ft).
GRADE Medium.
SEASONS Early May to late November (not July–August, when there will be heavy rains).
RESTRICTIONS None.
FURTHER OPTIONS Visit the Kafni Glacier from Dwali.

A road leads from Bageshwar to Song via Bharadi (40km/25 miles). This is the trailhead though the road is being extended. Camp at Song or stay in a rest house at Loharkhet (2000m/6560ft), 3km (2 miles) above, which is connected by road.

Loharkhet to Khati

Loharkhet is in the Saryu Valley. From the bungalow, follow the broad trail climbing steadily up towards the Dhakuri Khal (2902m/9520ft). The climb is steep, rising almost 900m (2953ft) in 9km (5½ miles) and there is no water available en route. Unfortunately this trail is being converted into a jeep track and when that happens it will be the end of the lovely forest in this area. At present Dhakuri is a broad pass situated on a forested ridge offering a wonderful view of some of the peaks on the southern wall of the Nanda Devi Sanctuary. Dhakuri rest house, 2km (1¼ miles) lower down (2700m/8860ft), is about an hour away as you descend into the Pindari Valley. There is a lovely forest with summer strawberries surrounding the rest houses, which are themselves something of an eye-sore. There is a gorgeous view towards the Sunderdhunga Valley.

Next day the trail continues to zigzag down through the forest. Once it reaches the lowest point, the trail turns eastwards towards Khati (2050m/6725ft), the largest village in the area. The people of these villages have regular contacts with each other and, like the Dhakuri Khal, there are several smaller crossings towards the ridge in the east. For example, Khati Khal (3000m/9840ft), which villagers cross to reach the Saryu Valley, leads to Juni. These crossings are inviting and can be easily undertaken with a guide to link up with Trek 7 (see page 71) in the

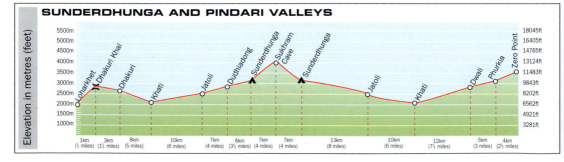

SUNDERDHUNGA AND PINDARI VALLEYS

Saryu Valley. Khati is a junction of two trails; one to the east going to the Pindari Glacier and the other going north to the Sunderdhunga Valley.

Khati to Sukhram (the Sunderdhunga Valley)

The Sunderdhunga Valley runs northwards from Khati and it takes four days to reach the high cave at Sukhram. The return to Khati village is by the same route.

From Khati, the trail descends near the point where the Pindari and Sunderdhunga rivers meet. Going over a bridge, the trail continues up and down north into the Sunderdhunga Valley on the right bank, passing village huts and several fields. After 10km (6 miles) the trail reaches the village of Jatoli (2500m/ 8200ft). This is a friendly village with a small rest house and food available, and is the place where Shipton and Tilman recuperated after their descent from the Nanda Devi Sanctuary in 1934. They left Nanda Devi by the Sunderdhunga Khal and descended into the valley in a hair-raising example of mountaineering, which has not yet been repeated.

The trail now enters a thick forest and climbs 7km (4¼ miles) to a small clearing called Dudhiadong (2847m/9340ft), 'the place of white stones'. Climbing and zigzagging further through the forest to the next stage can be strenuous as the trail is badly damaged in some places. But after 6km (3¾ miles) the trail reaches the junction of the valley at the Sunderdhunga central meadow (3206 m/10520ft). The hut is small, but the camping sites are breathtakingly lovely. You could make this your central camp and visit two different valleys from here.

The trail continues north to the Maiktoli Valley towards the Sunderdhunga Khal. There is an alternative camp at Sukhram (4000m/13125ft) 7km (4¼ miles) further on.

The route along the valley in the northeast is best avoided as there is a danger of falling stones.

The trail to Sunderdhunga Valley, near Jatoli.

TRAILL'S PASS

From Zero Point on the Pindari Glacier, the depression seen at the top of the Pindari ice-fall is Traill's Pass, leading to Martoli. The pass was first reached in 1830 by GW Traill, the first Deputy Commissioner of Kumaun, who, in the words of AL Mumm, 'exercised a benevolent and active despotism from 1817 to 1835'. He was searching for a shorter route from the Pindari Valley into the Milam Valley, which was a major trade route into Tibet, and there were talks of building a six-foot wide path across the pass. The present trail to Pindari is along parts of this trail and some traces can still be seen on the left bank of the Pindari River higher on.

The pass became popular with early explorers; after Traill, it was crossed by the Schlagintweits (1850), Ruttledge (1926), the Japanese Nanda Kot team (1936), Osmaston and the surveyors (1938), Arnold Heim (1937) and SS Khera (1941); and has been crossed twice in the last decade.

A better trail climbs 450m (1476ft) above the Sunderdhunga alp to reach open ground. From here there is a fabulous view of the Maiktoli Peak's south wall (6803m/22321ft). This is one of the highest walls in the Himalaya and is unclimbed, though the peak was scaled through an ice-fall on the right.

A narrow stone and wood bridge crossing the Sunderdhunga River.

Continue traversing the slopes further (take care when crossing some of the *nalas*) until you reach the Sukhram alp. The Tharkot (6099m/20011ft) Range is clearly visible from here, with several other subsidiary peaks lining the horizon. In 1944, the British mountaineer Wilfrid Noyce made the first ascent of Tharkot and Bauljuri peaks, and there have been further ascents since 1963.

From the camp at Sukhram, enterprising trekkers can visit Devi Kund (4500m/14760ft), 5km (3 miles) away, with a guide. This lake is visited by local villagers during the time of the annual pilgrimage.

Khati to Zero Point (the Pindari valley)

The head of the Pindari Valley is about two days' trek from Khati. However on your return from the Sunderdhunga Valley you can avoid staying at Khati and proceed to Dwali (2910m/9550ft), 12km (7½ miles) further ahead, where a tourist hut is located. Follow the broad trail for 5km (3 miles) to Phurkia (3203m/10510ft), which is the last tourist hut in the valley. For a view of the Pindari ice-fall, which is about 500m (⅓ mile) wide and about 4km (2¼ miles) long, go on to Zero Point (3580m/11745ft), a place marked on the lateral moraine ridge that gives a wonderful view of the ice-fall. Note the route to Traill's pass (see box), which is located on the top of the ice-fall and can be dangerous to approach. There are vast open grounds nearby and you can either camp here or return to Phurkia or Khati for the night.

Walk-out via Khati to Song

The return trek can be quick. Leave Khati early and, after crossing Dhakuri Khal, you will reach Loharkhet/Song by late afternoon. Spend the night in Loharkhet rest house if you wish. Starting early the next day, drive via Bageshwar (47km/29 miles) and Almora (72km/45 miles) to reach Kathgodam (88km/55 miles) by late evening. From here, a convenient overnight train will take you to Delhi by the next morning.

TREK 7: SARYU TO RAM GANGA VALLEY

This is an all-weather, low-altitude trek which offers an excellent walk in remote, unknown valleys. Large grazing grounds, called *kharaks*, are a joy to camp on. The greenery and the forest at many places are breathtaking. From the passes, the snow-capped peaks of the Nanda Devi Sanctuary are visible. A large number of snow-capped peaks with rugged rock gorges on the Pankhwa Dhar can be seen from the upper Ram Ganga valley. If you proceed further east across the Rur Khan Pass, there is an unforgettable view of the Panch Chuli Range. However, Rur Khan should only be crossed when it is not snow-bound.

Song is situated in the Saryu Valley. There is a camping ground below Song (1400m/4600ft) on the banks of the river, and porters and mules are readily available. The road extends to Loharkhet, 3km (1¾ miles) above Song and Munar and 3km (1¾ miles) further along the river.

Song to Namik

Make an early start as the weather in the valley can be very warm during the summer months. Proceed to Munar on a part-built road. The trail then climbs steeply to Supi (1810m/5940ft), a lovely little village situated on two levels. Energetic trekkers may go up to the upper village where there is a small temple. However, the usual trail from the lower village crosses the slopes for 10km (6 miles) until it descends to meet the Saryu River again at Bhadratunga camping ground (1600m/5250ft). There is a temple dedicated to the goddess Bhadratunga set in the thick forest.

Ahead, cross the bridge over the Saryu River to the left bank. The trail now climbs steeply along the Khalpata Valley leading to the village of the same name. There are several ups and downs and the trail is generally amidst thick forest. Four kilometres (2½ miles) above Khalpata village is Nigaliya Kharak (2240m/7350ft), an ideal camping site with a lovely stream flowing nearby. This is also surrounded by a forest and is the first of the several open *kharaks* you will come across.

The trail continues to climb 800m (2625ft) to reach Madhari Pass on the next day. This pass is the

dividing ridge between the Saryu and the Ram Ganga watershed. It is a long, forested ridge and can be crossed at several points. The final approach is through a wide open ground from where on a clear day the peaks of Nanda Devi can be observed.

A steep descent leads into the Ram Ganga Valley in the east, past several beautiful *kharaks*, one after the other, with the trail loosing height rapidly. Raj Kharak is a lovely grazing ground to camp on, but sometimes water is scarce here, in which case you will have to descend 8km (5 miles) to the Lower Raj Kharak (2520m/8270ft).

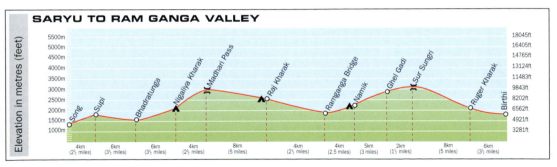

SARYU TO RAM GANGA VALLEY

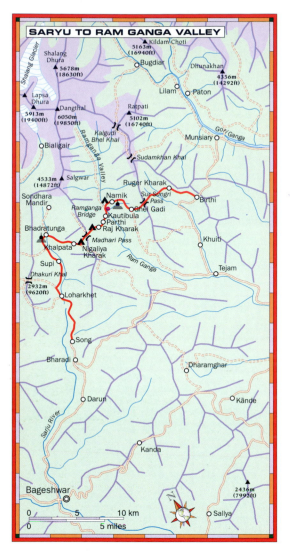

take the bus to reach either Bageshwar or Tejam. You could also visit the Namik Glacier, which is at the head of the valley, from here.

For this trek, a broad trail continues to climb from Namik village towards the Sur Sungri Pass. It leads through some interesting forest until it reaches a camp-site at Upper Ghel Gadi (2900m/9515ft), 5km (3 miles) further on. Next day, the climb to the pass takes about 2 hours. The pass is named Sur Sungri (3240m/ 10630ft) after a local legend (see box). From the pass, looking westwards across the Saryu Valley, the entire panorama of Pankhwa Dhar and the snowy peaks of the Nanda Devi Sanctuary are visible. The ridge to the north leads up and above to Sudam Khan. It is quite challenging, with some great views of the Nanda Kot Range.

There are two routes ahead from the Sur Sungri Pass. Descend about 200m (656ft) to an opening, where the route divides. Take the left-hand fork, traversing the upper Jakala valley, where the trail descends gently to cross the main river. Camp in the forest after a climb of about 500m (1640ft). Next day, cross Rur Khan pass and descend the slopes above Munsiary. This pass offers excellent views of the Panch Chuli group of peaks (see pages 66-7), but is generally snow-bound for long periods and, if porters are not well-equipped to walk on the snow, the route can be complicated.

The other, gentler, alternative is to turn right on the main trail down the Jakala Valley. Through a forest and across several side streams the trail emerges 8km (5 miles) later on *kharaks* which are used by shepherds from Birthi village. Camp on the Ruger Kharak (2240m/7350ft) after your descent.

Starting leisurely the next day, descend steeply again to the main road for 6km (3¾ miles) and walk up to Birthi, a small village with few facilities. Buses or transport (if arranged in advance) can be taken to proceed to Munsiary in the northerly

The trail continues the steep descent into the Ram Ganga Valley, passing Parthi village (4km/2½ miles) and ahead to Kautibula (2km/1¼ miles). The river has to be crossed 2km ahead, but the bridge (1870m/6135ft) over the rushing waters of the Ram Ganga is fit only for humans to cross. Mules will have to be unloaded and the luggage carried across. From the bridge a broad trail leads to the school in Namik village, 4km (2½ miles) away. This is a fairly large and prosperous village, full of activity. The best camping ground is above the village at Bhagwati temple (2270m/7450ft).

Namik to Munsiary

Namik is a meeting place of trails. From here you could walk down the valley to Gogina and Leti and

SUR SUNGRI PASS

In the local Kumauni language, a tiger is called *sur* and boar are known as *sungri*. According to one legend, a tiger was once accosted by a boar on this pass. As the boar did not yield the tiger became rather angry. To vent his anger he dug a large hole near the pass (which is prominently seen near the pass today). After a long chase the tiger leapt from the nearby slopes for the final kill, but he fell in his own pit and died.

Above: On Pankhwa Dhar with Nanda Khat and Panwali Dwar Peaks in the background. *Right:* Crossing a tricky bridge on the Saryu River.

direction. The road leads across Kalamuni Pass (2748m/9015ft) (for views of the Panch Chuli group) and to Munsiary (36km/22 miles). You may wish to spend a day in Munsiary (2200m/7220ft), a quiet one-street town with a rest house and hotels.

Drive-out via Munsiary to Kathgodam

As for Trek 4, the drive-out from Munsiary involves a long two-day journey to Delhi. There is a tarmac road from Munsiary towards Tejam (57km/35 miles) which is always open – except the Kalamuni Pass section, which may sometimes be blocked in the rainy season or during winter. Some 47km (29 miles) ahead is Chakori, a good place to enjoy close-up views of the Nanda Devi Sanctuary peaks.

By starting early the next day you can drive via Bageshwar (47km/29 miles) and Almora (72km/45 miles) to arrive in Kathgodam (88km/55 miles) by late evening. A convenient overnight train reaches Delhi the next morning.

TREK 8: VALLEY OF FLOWERS AND HEMKUND

The high *bugiyal* (grazing grounds) and the valleys of Garhwal are renowned for their flora. Nearly all the valleys in the Garhwal burst into bloom with a wide variety of flowers in July and August. But it was Frank Smythe who, on entering the Bhuidhar Valley (then known as Bhyundar Valley), named it the Valley of Flowers. The valley is situated near the well-known shrine of Hemkund (Lokpal) and is off the main road to Badrinath. Thousands of pilgrims visit every year and today this valley is one of the best-known and most popular places in the Himalaya.

TREK ESSENTIALS

LENGTH 1-2 weeks; 52km (32 miles). Walking from Govindghat: 2 days to Ghangaria, 1 day to Hemkund (Lokpal), 1 day to the Valley of Flowers, 1 day return to Govindghat.
ACCESS Good rail connections from Delhi to Haridwar or Dehra Dun. Taxis from Haridwar or buses from Rishikesh to Joshimath then Govindghat.
HIGHEST POINT Hemkund (Lokpal) shrines 4150m/13615ft. Passes: none.
GRADE Simple.
SEASONS Early May to early October.
RESTRICTIONS Permission required to camp or to do botanical research. Entry fees and camera charges payable upon entry.
FURTHER OPTIONS The Bhuidhar Pass (north) and the Khunt Khal (south) lead out from the Valley of Flowers. Permits for access to Bhuidhar and camping required.

A well-maintained road links Haridwar–Rishikesh with Joshimath, (1890m/6200ft) which is the administrative centre of the area. The road runs the length of the Alaknanda River, which forms the Ganges by merging with the Bhagirathi at Devprayag (see box, page 89). A variety of hotels line the route and in the pilgrim season (June and September are peak times) it may be diffi-

cult to find good accommodation. Joshimath itself is a lovely little place perched on a slope high above the meeting point of the Alaknanda which drains water from Badrinath, and the Dhauli Ganga which drains the Nanda Devi Sanctuary. It has many restaurants and is a vibrant place during the season.

Govindghat to Ghangaria

You need to start early from Joshimath to reach Govindghat, which is 18km (11 miles) ahead en route to Badrinath. There is a gate system which restricts traffic to one way only at certain times. Govindghat is a busy little place full of porters and mules ready to carry luggage. There is a Sikh *gurudwara* (temple) here and ample facilities to stay and eat.

Govindghat (1860m/6100ft) is situated on the river bank of the deep Alaknanda Valley. A 2m wide (6ft) trail starts from here, crossing the river over a bridge and going all the way to Ghangaria. There are several food and tea stalls lining the route of the trek, and it is essential to be careful about water and food hygiene. You are likely to meet several pilgrims on the 1280m (4200ft) climb. The first point is Pulna village, 4km (2¼ miles) away. Ahead you will notice a side valley going to the east, towards the peaks of Hathi (6727m/22070ft) and Ghori Parvat

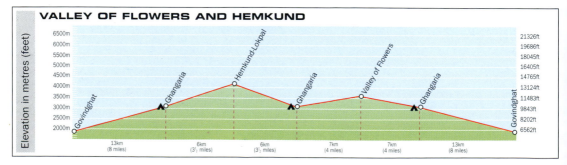

VALLEY OF FLOWERS AND HEMKUND

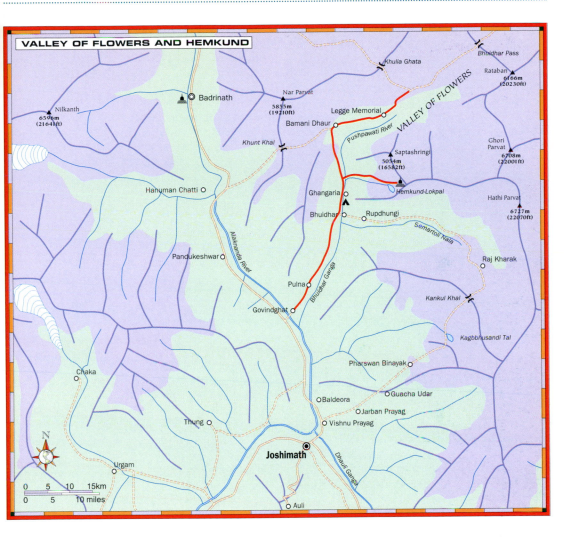

(6708m/22007ft). These high and lovely peaks can be seen from this trek. There is a memorial alongside the road to several mountaineers who have died on Hathi Parvat.

Bhuidhar village is another 5km (3 miles) further. The village and valley are named after a vast cave a short distance below the village (*bhui*: cave, *dhar*: balanced on). It is a friendly place with few houses and people here migrate to lower areas in winter. A side trail branches to the east to follow the Semartoli nala (if the bridge is intact) towards the glacier of the same name. After crossing a small ridge over a pass, the side trail goes on to Kagbhusandi Tal, a lovely glen, about three days away.

The main trail continues its steep climb for the next 4km (2½ miles). It enters a forested area and the route is lined with rhododendrons. Just before Ghangaria there is a wide open space

good for camping but there is little water. Ghangaria (3080m/10100ft) can be crowded in season and the rest house and the few small hotels are always packed. The place is rapidly expanding, and everything is much more expensive than elsewhere in the Garhwal.

Hemkund (Lokpal)

Ghangaria is the base from which to visit Hemkund (Lokpal) shrines and the Valley of Flowers. A steep, wide trail climbs some 1070m (3510ft) to the Hemkund (Lokpal) shrines (4150m/13615ft), which remain snow-bound until mid-June. During the months of July and August the lake is surrounded by brahma-kamal flowers (lotus, *Saussurea gossypiphora*). The lake, the ancient temple of Laxman and the Sikh temple are legendary sacred places (see box, page 77).

Trekkers on a rooftop in Bhuidhar village.

Visitors to the shrines are offered *prasad* (blessings) and hot tea, whatever the time of their visit. The lake reflects these shrines and the lovely panorama of the Saptashringi peaks which surround the lake. Though the Saptashringi peaks are only 5054m (16581ft) high they are are steep and challenging to would-be rock climbers. Enterprising trekkers can camp near the lake or stay in the *gurudwara*. Alternatively, return to Ghangaria completing the 12km (7½ miles) round trip.

Valley of Flowers

The Valley of Flowers is 7km (4 miles) from Ghangaria. The Pushpawati River flows from the Bhuidhar valley and meets the Hemkund Ganga at Ghangaria. A wide trail follows the Pushpawati river, first on the left and then on the right bank. A little ahead of Ghangaria lies the boundary of the Valley of Flowers National Park. An entry fee of Rs 100 for foreigners and Rs 20 for Indians is charged, plus Rs 50 for cameras. No camping is allowed inside the valley beyond this point except by prior permission obtained from the Chief

Conservator of Forests and the National Park Warden in Joshimath. After entering a gorge, the valley widens and can be seen in its entirety from the east. This place is locally called *bamani dhaur* ('cave of the Brahmin'). According to legend a Brahmin once lived here, telling visitors their fortunes and drawing their horoscopes (*kundali*). This he did by observing shadows on the long meadow across the river. At what time and on which day the shadow was to be observed depended on the person's date of birth. This meadow was therefore called Sri Kundalinisen ('meadow of horoscopes'), which is seen as a long meadow on the opposite bank of the Pushpawati River.

The Valley of Flowers has magnificent vistas. Straight ahead in the east stands Rataban Peak (6166m/20230ft), with the Nilgiri Parvat (6474m/21249ft) on the left. A deep depression between them is the Bhuidhar Pass (5090m/16700ft). In 1931, after their ascent of Kamet, Eric Shipton and Frank Smythe descended this pass to make the historic discovery of the Valley of Flowers (see page 78). Tragedy struck a member of the Himalayan Club here in 1991. Firdaus Talyarkhan, a lawyer from Bombay, was standing on the pass, alone and unroped, when a crevasse gave way beneath his feet. He fell into it and became wedged in the ice between the walls of the crevasse. His companions, after trying for hours to rescue him, went down towards Gamsali for help, but when they returned he was dead. His body was recovered nearly two years later when the crevasse widened naturally. Locals remember the incident and attribute it to supernatural forces in this valley.

A little ahead of Bamani Dhaur is a small meadow where stands the grave of Joan Margaret Legge. Inspired by Frank Smythe's work here, Edinburgh's Royal Botanic Garden deputed her to spend a few months in the Valley of Flowers with tragic results (see page 78).

To the north stands Nar Parvat (5855m/ 19210ft), which completes the wall surrounding the valley. Sir Edmund Hillary's Ocean to Sky expedition in 1978 completed its journey by the ascent of this peak. Immediately to the east is the easy pass of Khulia Ghata (5000m/16405ft), which leads to Badrinath. In the west lies the challenging Khunt Khal Pass (4425m/14518ft). In his book *The Valley of Flowers*, Frank Smythe gives a full record of flowers found here with their botanical names. Many visitors, based at Ghangaria, return to the valley for more detailed botanical studies.

A view from Bamani Dhaur of glorious spring blooms along the Valley of Flowers with the Kundalinisen Plateau to the right.

Govindghat

The return from Ghangaria to Govindghat (13km) is quick, descending on the wide trail, with tea stalls along the way. Local transport or taxis are available to proceed to other destinations.

Drive-out via Govindghat to Joshimath, Rishikesh and Haridwar

If you have a day to spare, visit the Badrinath shrine, 26km (16 miles) north of Govindghat. This is an ancient holy temple that has an excellent view of the Nilkanth Peak (6596m/ 21640ft). Alternatively pay a visit to Auli which is around 3km (2 miles) away as the crow flies and is easily reached by ropeway or along the 16km (10 miles) winding road that leads from Joshimath. This is a vast open meadow with a good view of many of Garhwal's peaks, particularly those of Nanda Devi. There are excellent rest houses here and from late December to April, Auli is a popular ski-resort visited by skiers from all over the world.

If you leave early from Joshimath, you can cover the 287km (178 miles) to Haridwar in a day to drive ahead or catch a train to Delhi. Alternatively, you can stay in one of the several rest houses en route or, from September to March, you can take a rafting trip on the Ganges starting near Rishikesh.

HEMKUND (LOKPAL)

Situated above Ghangaria village is a lovely lake called Lokpal at 4150m (13615ft), which Hindu pilgrims on the way to Badrinath have been visiting for centuries. It was believed to be the place where Laxman (the younger brother of Ram, in the epic *Ramayana*) meditated. Laxman's other name was Lokpal, the 'protector of the masses'. Lokpal was originally called Homkund (literally, 'lake of snow') and after Laxman's meditations the river issuing from it became Laxman Ganga, later Hemkund Ganga.

There is another legend associated with Lokpal. In the holy scripture of the Sikhs, *Dasham Granth*, Guru Govind Singh mentioned a lake with seven peaks surrounding it as a place where he had meditated in his past life. Scholar Bhai Bir Singh of Amritsar decided to search for such a place. In 1932, he visited Badrinath, where he observed many Hindu pilgrims climbing up the Bhuidhar Valley to Lokpal. Returning in 1936 he made further inquiries and reached this lake, which did lie at the foot of seven peaks. It was marked on the map as Saptashringi. Bhai Bir Singh declared this to be the lake where Guru Govind Singh had obtained *nirvana* in his past life and decided to build a *gurudwara* (temple) there. Havildar Sohan Singh was deputed to this task in 1939 and built a small shrine next to the ancient Laxman temple. This was expanded in 1974 with a wide footpath leading to it, was named Hemkund, which means 'lake of solace', and has since become an important Sikh place of worship.

FRANK SMYTHE'S VALLEY OF FLOWERS

In his book *Kamet Conquered*, Frank Smythe nicknamed the Bhuidhar Valley (then known as Bhyundar) in the central Garhwal as the Valley of Flowers in 1931. To mountaineers the Bhyundar Valley will always be known as the Valley of Flowers. It is a place of escape for those who have wearied of modern civilization. You would have to descend in winter to warmer and less snowy levels, but for half a year those in search of beauty and solitude can find peace in the Valley of Flowers.

To the southeast of the shrine of Badrinath, in the Garhwal, is the small village of Bhuidhar. Frank Smythe and his team, including Eric Shipton and RL Holdsworth, climbed Kamet (7756m/25447ft) in 1931. Like true explorers they decided to return by a high pass instead of the usual trade route. They crossed Bhuidhar Pass (5150m/16897ft) and descended into the north Bhuidhar Valley. Like many valleys in Garhwal, this one was in full bloom. With its wide meadows and seemingly endless loveliness it must have seemed like paradise after the hostile and barren slopes of Kamet.

The valley was visited in 1862 by Colonel Edmund Smith, and by TG Longstaff together with Arnold Mumm and Charles G Bruce in 1907. But it took Frank Smythe's scientific eye and philosopher's heart to recognise it as the Valley of Flowers. Since then many have traversed the valley's high passes and thousands visit it every year. Today it is one of the best-known valleys in the Indian Himalaya.

After his first brief visit in 1931, Smythe returned to the valley in 1937 and stayed for four months. Each week botanical specimens were sent to Joshimath and then on to Edinburgh where they were housed in a specially built hot-house in the Royal Botanic Garden. Nanda Singh Chauhan (aged 85 in 1999) who worked with Frank Smythe, vividly remembered 'Dr Smythe' as a 'pukka British sahib' and talked fondly of him.

'The sahibs had a very comfortable and huge camp for months together. Supplies used to arrive from Ranikhet regularly and everything was well organised.' This was hardly surprising, for Smythe was well known for his appreciation of the finer things in life.

Inspired by Frank Smythe's work, Edinburgh's Royal Botanic Garden sent Joan Legge to spend a few months in the Valley of Flowers. With porters she trekked across the lower foothills, reached Joshimath and finally Govindghat on 25 June 1939. She walked up slowly, collecting samples along the way. On 4 July she went up the slopes towards Khulia Garva, slipped and fell to her death. Legge's sister requested that her body be buried in the valley. All the items she carried and collected were listed and sent to England and a small grave was built where she lay. Her sister visited the site in 1940 and erected a small memorial, which still stands there, with the following inscription from the Bible:

I will lift up mine eyes unto the hills
From whence cometh my help

Since this grave is the only point of reference in the valley most visitors who reach here believe, rather erroneously, that it was Joan Legge rather than Frank Smythe who discovered the Valley of Flowers.

Today the Valley of Flowers is a national park and is well-preserved. This valley owes much to Frank Smythe. The name he gave it caught on and he made the place famous. As a result trekkers, non-mountaineers and even weekend visitors find their way to this easily accessible place of glorious beauty. Outsiders now know that there is much more to the Himalaya than shrines and snow.

The golden blooms of the Valley of Flowers in autumn.

TREK 9: BHILANGANA VALLEY TO KEDARNATH

This is a beautiful valley in central Garhwal, situated between the two historic temples of Gangotri and Kedarnath. The ancient pilgrims' route passes through the lower half of the valley and this can still be followed. The forest, wildlife, alpine flowers and the friendly villagers are other attractions. There are excellent views of the snowline at the head of the valley. A visit to the Khatling Glacier and its ice-fall is possible. This valley is at its best during early autumn, when the forest changes its moods and the snowline is more visible.

The starting point of this trek, Ghuttu, is reached by road from Dehra Dun via Tehri and Gamsali.

Ghuttu, Khatling Glacier to Gangi

The first part of the trek is all along the right bank of the Bhilangana River. There are two villages en route (slightly above the trail) with rest houses, and excellent places to camp. Even if you do not reach Ghuttu until afternoon you will still be able to proceed 10km (6½ miles) on the trail to Reeh (2132m/6700ft). The trail climbs steeply at first but then becomes gentle and it is a beautiful walk.

The next day begins with a steep climb of about 500m (1640ft) on a broad trail. There are lovely views from its highest point and from then on the trail descends and flattens to reach Gangi village, 10km (6½ miles) (2584m/8480ft). This is a rather strange place with a tradition of intermarriage, resulting in genetic defects and a rapidly reducing population. Gangi commands a fabulous view over the neighbouring fields and of the Panwali Ridge seen to the east.

The trail leads along the valley to Kalyani, 5km (3 miles) ahead. It takes about 3 hours to walk this short distance as the climb is steep in places. But the camping ground at Kalyani is in a clearing in the forest and it is worth spending a night there.

A similar trail continues the next day. You will need to cross several streams and should take

care at every crossing. Several higher peaks can be seen at the head of the valley. The most prominent amongst them is Thalay Sagar (6904m/22652ft) which rises like a colossal monolith. Its shining walls contrast with the other peaks on the same ridge, such as the Jogin and the Gangotri groups. In the centre of the valley are two large glaciers, Khatling being the more prominent of the two.

TREK ESSENTIALS

LENGTH 2 weeks; 131km (81 miles) (including Kedarnath). Walking from Ghuttu: 5 days to Khatling Glacier, 2 days to Triyugi Narayan, 2 days to Kedarnath. Return via Gaurikund to Rishikesh.

ACCESS Train from Delhi to Dehra Dun then taxi or bus to Tehri (125km/78 miles) then Ghuttu, the trailhead, 64km (40 miles) ahead via Gamsali.

HIGHEST POINT Khatling Glacier (3600m/11810ft). Passes: Khimkhola (3545m/11630ft).

GRADE Medium.

SEASONS Late May to November (avoid in monsoons).

RESTRICTIONS Kedarnath Valley open late April to early November only.

FURTHER OPTIONS Combine with Trek 11 to Shastru Tal (lake), or visit Vasuki Tal above Kedarnath and Madhyamaheshwar.

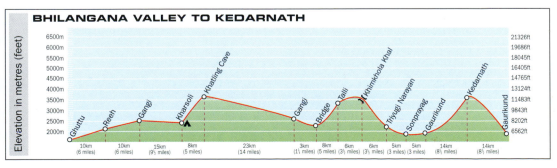

BHILANGANA VALLEY TO KEDARNATH

Elevation in metres (feet)

6500m (21326ft), 6000m (19686ft), 5500m (18045ft), 5000m (16405ft), 4500m (14765ft), 4000m (13124ft), 3500m (11483ft), 3000m (9843ft), 2500m (8202ft), 2000m (6562ft)

Ghuttu · Reeh · Gangi · Kharsoli · Khatling Cave · Gangi · Bridge · Talli · Khimkhola Khal · Triyugi Narayan · Sonprayag · Gaurikund · Kedarnath · Gaurikund

10km (6 miles) · 10km (6 miles) · 15km (9½ miles) · 8km (5 miles) · 23km (14 miles) · 3km (1½ miles) · 8km (5 miles) · 6km (3½ miles) · 6km (3½ miles) · 5km (3 miles) · 5km (3 miles) · 14km (8½ miles) · 14km (8½ miles)

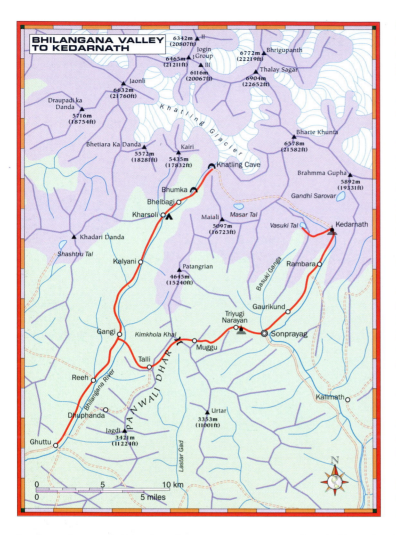

BHILANGANA VALLEY
TO KEDARNATH

Camp at Kharsoli (2900m/ 9515ft), 15km (9 miles), or go on slightly further to Bhelbagi (3110m/10200ft) for the night. There are several camping places and shepherds' huts along this route.

Bhumka Cave (3200m/ 10500ft) is only about 2km (1¼ miles) beyond Bhelbagi. Tamakund, 3km (2 miles), and Khatling Cave, 3km (3600m/ 11810ft), are a little disappointing to stay in after the lovely camps down in the valley. To see the glacier at close quarters you have to camp near it, but as you near the mountains the view disappears. You may instead prefer to stop at Bhumka and make a long day trek to the Khatling Glacier and back. This depends on clear weather and an early start.

About 2km (1¼ miles) beyond Bhumka lies a bridge across the main river. If you cross this to the left bank, you can trek to Kedarnath Temple by a high-level route via Vasuki Tal. This is a difficult and complicated trail and should be undertaken only with a qualified guide and proper gear.

Return by the same route to Gangi village for the next part of the trek. It is a 20-km (12½-mile) walk but mostly downhill and not too tiring. Alternatively, stop at one of the many shepherds' camps on the way back.

Gangi to Triyugi Narayan

Traditionally, pilgrims trekked from temple to temple. One such trail, linking the Budha Kedar Temple (near Gamsali) with Kedarnath, passes through the Bhilangana Valley. It offers some of the best views in Garhwal.

From Gangi, the trail descends steeply for 3km (2 miles) to the Bhilangana River in the centre of the valley (2365m/7760ft). The trail climbs steeply up the opposite slopes through forest and then wild grass meadows. There are a few *bugiyals* on the way and in the season you will meet shepherds. The climb ends at Talli after 8km (5 miles) (3472m/11390ft) where it meets the traditional

Camping on the exposed ridge at Panwali Kanta.

broad pilgrim trail. Check the availability of water on the ridge before the climb to Talli, because in autumn the water supply dries out.

The trail follows the Panwali Kanta, or Panwali Dhar ('ridge of winds'), the next day. It runs northwards and is almost flat, with no vegetation on either side, but the views it offers are fabulous. In the north stands the majestic Thalay Sagar (6904m/22652ft) with Jogin I (6465m/21211ft), Rudugaira (5818m/19089ft) and Jaonli (6632m/21759ft) completing the arc of mountains on the left (northwest). Immediately above the Khatling glacier and next to Jogin I in the west a prominent snow depression, Auden's Col, is visible. This was crossed by JB Auden, the well-known geologist and brother of the British poet. On the right (northeast) of Thalay Sagar stands Bhartekhunta (6578m/21582ft) and Kedarnath Peak (6940m/22770ft), and the view stretches to Chaukhamba (7138m/23420ft).

Follow the ridge until the trail descends from Khimkhola Khal (3545m/11630ft) to Muggu Chatti. *Chattis* (pilgrim rest houses) were built to provide shelter for pilgrims. The trail now descends steeply from 3650m (12000ft) to almost 2250m (7300ft). Follow the broad trail until you reach the small village and temple of Triyugi Narayan (2250m/7380ft) after a total walk of 12km (7½ miles). Triyugi Narayan is one of the many exquisite temples of the Garhwal, dedicated to Lord Shiva (Triyugi; 'lord of three worlds'), and is associated with the Bhilangana Valley (see box, above right).

Triyugi Narayan to Kedarnath

From Triyugi Narayan, Sonprayag is a 5-km (3-mile) walk away on the main road to Kedarnath, from where you can get transport to Gaurikund, 5km further on. From Gaurikund follow the Mandakini River valley for 14km (9 miles) to Kedarnath. This is a popular pilgrim's route and the trail is lined with food stalls. As you reach the wide, open valley of Kedarnath (3584m/ 11760ft), the temple is visible in the centre with a huge mountain chain as a backdrop. Alternatively, if pressed for time, take transport to Rishikesh from Sonprayag.

There are many one-day walks possible from the Kedarnath bazaar, such as Gandhi Sarovar (a small glacial lake to the north) or a climb to Vasuki Tal, where literally hundreds of brahma-kamal flowers are found and carried as an offering to the temple. Best of all is the view of the peaks that line the northern horizon.

BHILANGANA AND TRIYUGI NARAYAN

The ancient temple of Triyugi Narayan, where the trek from the Bhilangana Valley ends, has a legend linking it to the valley. Shiva, while meditating in the Himalaya, forgot the promise he had made to Parvati that he would marry her. To remind him, Parvati disguised herself as a *bhil-kanya* (daughter of a forester, or *bhilangana*) and created the beautiful valley with a river. With such beauty and the dance of the river, the light of love kindled once again in Shiva's heart. He realised his mistake, so they married without delay at the nearest temple, Triyugi Narayan.

Walk-out via Kedarnath to Gaurikund and Rishikesh

The return trek is via Gaurikund (14km/9 miles) from where you can take a bus or a taxi to Rishikesh during the pilgrim season (the road closes when the first snows fall). The road goes via Rudraprayag (67km/42 miles), an ideal place for an overnight stop, to Rishikesh (172km/107 miles). Continue to Haridwar (25km/15½ miles) or Dehra Dun (42km/26 miles) for onward trains.

The Kedarnath Temple beneath Kedarnath Peak.

TREK 10: GANGOTRI GLACIER

The Gangotri Glacier is one of the longest and, for Hindus, most sacred glaciers in the Himalaya. Because of the road, it is very accessible, but visitors who wish to proceed beyond Gangotri Temple must make sure they are properly acclimatised after the rapid ascent in altitude. Spend at least two nights in Gangotri before going on. The Gangotri Temple (3048m/10000ft), where devotees have worshipped for centuries, lies on the right bank of the river. The head of the Gangotri Glacier was once located here and the slopes nearby mark the glacier bed. In the background rises the majestic peak of Sudarshan Parvat.

TREK ESSENTIALS

LENGTH 2 weeks; 50km (31 miles). Walking from Gangotri: 4 days to Gaumukh, 3 days to Nandanvan.

ACCESS 192km (119 miles) by road from Dehra Dun or Haridwar/Rishikesh to Uttarkashi then via Harsil and Bhaironghati to Gangotri Temple, 88km (55 miles).

HIGHEST POINT Tapovan (4463m/14640ft). Passes: none.

GRADE Medium.

SEASONS Early May to early October.

RESTRICTIONS None.

FURTHER OPTIONS Trek to Kedar Tal from Gangotri or extend the trek to Badrinath across Kalindi Khal (with permits).

The first two days are best spent in exploring the Gangotri Temple area (3048m/10000ft) and in acclimatisation. The present temple was built in the eighteenth century by the Gurkha general Amar Singh Thapa, and visitors can witness the evening ritual of *aarti* (worshipping the river Ganges). The priest walks out of the temple precinct and makes circular movements with his hands, in which he carries a plate with flowers, lighted lamps and glowing incense. As the lights make geometric patterns in the still air, he chants ancient hymns. The scene is awesome, and witnesses feel a sense of spiritual involvement. In the gathering darkness of the evening it is a mystical sight, and even if you are not a Hindu it is an uplifting experience.

The tiny village on the opposite bank is lined with ashrams (religious retreats) and giant deodars and conifers. There are several walks down the river to the marble slopes where the river in one spectacular sweep falls about 100m (328ft). To the south a trail leads to the Kedar Tal valley, which can be followed for a few kilometres through a lovely forest.

Gangotri to Gaumukh

The trail to Gaumukh, the present-day source of the Ganges, starts off steeply from the temple. As you walk further down the valley, different snow-capped peaks come into view. There are a few tea shops and *dhabas* on the way. The trail crosses several small bridges over the side streams and is fairly easy. Camp at Chirbasa (3606m/11830ft) after 7km (4½ miles) in fairly open ground a little below the trail, which has a small rest house. Though many rush ahead to Bhojbasa, if you can it is better to stay here to become properly acclimatised.

After a couple of kilometres the Bhagirathi peaks are visible on the horizon to the left. Soon the terrain is devoid of any vegetation except a few birch trees which gave the name to the place of the next stop, Bhojbasa (*bhoj*: birch), 7km (4½ miles) ahead. Once there was a birch forest here but now only a few trees remain, the rest having been cut for the pilgrims and food stalls. All the ancient Hindu scriptures were written on *bhoj* leaves which last for a long time. Bhojbasa (3792m/1440ft) is

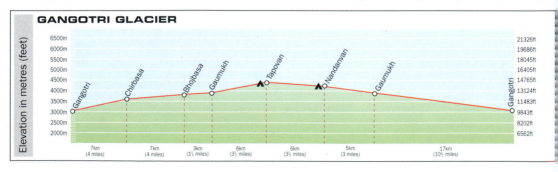

GANGOTRI GLACIER

a vast open ground and the ashram of Lal Baba will accommodate visitors. There is a rest house built by the Garhwal Mandal Vikas Nigam which provides very basic amenities.

If you are not trekking to Tapovan you should visit Gaumukh (3892m/12770ft) and return to Bhojbasa or Chirbasa the same day. Gaumukh, (literally 'cow's mouth') is 3km (2 miles) beyond Bhojbasa and there are some tea shops located here. Water rushes out from a vast ice-cave at the edge of the Gangotri Glacier and many peaks can be seen. Prominent amongst them is Shivling (6543m/21468ft) which dominates the valley.

Gaumukh to Tapovan to Nandanvan

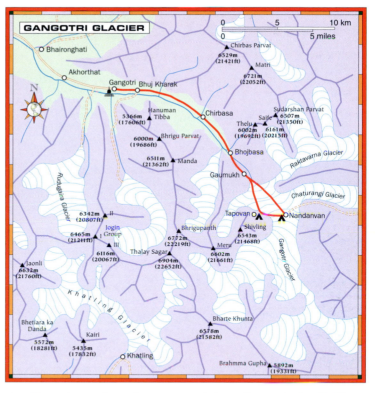

Tapovan is a vast meadow on the left bank of the Gangotri Glacier. There is a proper trail leading here from Bhojbasa, 6km (4 miles) away. From Gaumukh the trail climbs the moraine steeply and then divides in two. Turn right, across the moraine. Do beware of loose scree and stones, particularly those that have been dislodged by returning parties. After crossing the moraine, Tapovan (4463m/14640ft) appears like a green oasis, with Shivling for a backdrop. There is a marked similarity between Shivling and the Matterhorn. Marco Pallis, who visited the Gangotri Glacier in 1933, wrote of Shivling as, '... a horrid-looking mountain with a striking resemblance to the Matterhorn... beautifully alluring, hideously inaccessible.' Since the first ascent in 1974 many routes have been climbed.

There are several places to camp on the Tapovan Plateau from where you can observe the vast Garhwal panorama. Several Hindu sages have stayed and meditated at this plateau and their thoughts

have been passed down the centuries in literature. The peaks surrounding the Gangotri Glacier are named according to Hindu mythology. To the east rise the Chaukhamba peaks ('four pillars of earth'), signifying Brahma, the creator of the world. Towards the north the peaks are named after Vishnu, the preserver.

The gleaming roof of the Gangotri Temple.

PEAK: SAIFE

Ascend the snow-covered slopes in the southwest to reach the conical summit. The trail is broad and is maintained by workers during the pilgrim season until you reach Gaumukh. Follow the right hand side of the Gangotri Glacier towards Nandanvan and turn east into the Raktavarna Glacier. This is a large glacier with red stones (from which it gets its name, *raktavarna*: 'blood-complexioned'). Two feeder glaciers join it from the north: the Thelu Glacier and the Swetvarna ('white-complexioned') Glacier, which has many white stones.

Base Camp

After a long day's walk on the right bank of the Raktavarna Glacier you will reach the junction with the Swetvarna Glacier. This is a good place to establish a base camp at 4800m (15750ft).

High Camp

Turn into the Swetvarna Glacier and climb to the centre of the glacier. The initial sections of the trail cross scree and large stony areas. The going is tiring but never dangerous, although some open crevasses need to be crossed. After a walk of about 4km (2½ miles) and 5 hours you will reach the flat central moraine where there are several suitable places to establish a high camp (5400m/17710ft). This camp commands a wonderful view. To the head of the valley rises the majestic peak of Sudarshan Parvat (6507m/21349ft) which dominates the entire valley. On the ridge falling south of this pinna-

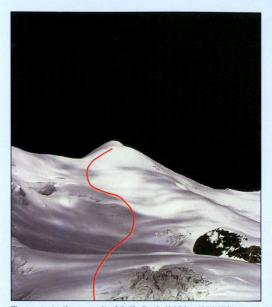

The route to the summit of Saife Peak (6161m/20215ft).

cle is the peak of Saife (6161m/20215ft) (see map on page 83). This a lovely conical snow pyramid with several approaches.

Saife

A prominent southeast ridge falls from the summit to the glacier. This peak can be easily climbed in a long day by going up this ridge and following the slopes on the left. It is basically a snow-plod and except for a few crevasses there are no other technical difficulties to be encountered. From the summit a grand view of all the peaks of the Gangotri Glacier are visible, particularly those of Shivling and Sudarshan Parvat.

This peak was first climbed in 1981 by an Indo–French expedition. The summitter skied down from the summit to the camp on the glacier within minutes. The slopes of this peak are ideal for a ski-descent, but you must take care to avoid the crevasses. In early June the entire Swetvarna Glacier is covered with snow and it is perfect both for cross-country skiing and mountaineering. The Swetvarna Valley offers other easy climbs such as Koteshwar I (6080m/19950ft) and Koteshwar II (5690m/18670ft).

CLIMB ESSENTIALS

SUMMIT Saife (6161m/20215ft)
PRINCIPAL CAMPS Base camp: Swetvarna glacier, 4800m (15750ft). High camp: 5 hours higher, 5400m (17710ft).
GRADE A long but easy snow slope leads to the summit. This is also an excellent peak for a ski descent.
MAP REFERENCE See sketch-map Trek 10, Gangotri Valley.

Towering opposite Tapovan and seen from the Gangotri Temple is the peak Sudarshan Parvat, named after a round weapon, or *chakra*, Lord Krishna or Vishnu holds in his hands. And to the south of course stands Shivling, the peak on which Shiva, the destroyer of the world resides, completing the holy trinity.

Cross the Gangotri Glacier to the right bank in a traverse up and down the moraine. Though a faint track exists, hire an experienced guide for this section. It will take about three hours to cross the glacier and another hour to climb the steep moraine walls at the other end. Nandanvan (4337m/14230ft) is at the junction of the meeting of the Chaturangi ('colourful stones') and Gangotri glaciers. The Chaturangi glacier leads to Kalindi Khal and across to Badrinath, linking the two holy shrines. From the Nandanvan meadow you get a very different view of the Meru and Manda peaks which are in line with Shivling.

Walk-out via Gangotri

From Nandanvan descend to Gaumukh on a well-defined trail over partly loose scree for 5km (3 miles) until you reach the main trail. The return journey is quick with a night's stay at Bhojbasa or Chirbasa, depending on weather and the time available.

From Gangotri there are several buses in the morning to Uttarkashi and beyond. Taxis are available for all destinations.

> ## SEVEN YEARS IN TIBET
>
> The road to Gangotri Temple crosses a high bridge over the Jadh Ganga River at Bhaironghati, 9km (5½ miles) before the temple. This is a historic valley leading to Tibet, which was the scene of an epic journey made by Heinrich Harrer, recounted in the film *Seven Years In Tibet*. Harrer, an Austrian (see Panch Chuli feature), was interned by the British during World War II at Dehra Dun. After an initial failure Harrer escaped with Hans Kopp and met up with another pair, Peter Aufschnaiter and Bruno Treipel. Crossing the Jamuna and Algar valleys and Nag Tibba, they managed to reach Nelang. Finally, on 17 May 1944, the two groups crossed into Tibet a little north of the Gangotri Valley via the Tsang Chok La (pass) (5240m/17192ft).

The Bhagirathi Peaks seen from the Tapovan Meadow. From left to right: peaks II, III and I.

TREK 11: KUSH KALYAN AND SHASTRU TAL

Called 'the Lake District of Garhwal', the area has several lakes situated on both sides of a beautiful high ridge, the Kush Kalyan. At its head is Shastru Tal, named after the brahma-kamal flower which grows profusely around here. The name 'Shastru' seems to have originated from the Sanskrit word *sahastra*. According to legend, a king performed ablutions on the shores of this lake by offering a thousand (*sahastra*) flowers to Lord Vishnu. As he finished offering the 999th flower, Vishnu made the last one disappear. Without hesitation, the king submitted his own head as the last offering to complete the *puja*, or ceremonies. Since then the lake has been visited by pilgrims, especially during the holy month of *shravan* (generally August) when the flowers bloom in their thousands.

TREK ESSENTIALS

LENGTH 2 weeks; 72km (45 miles). Walking from Malla: 4 days to Lamb Tal, 2 days to Shastru Tal and back.
ACCESS Trains to Dehra Dun from Delhi and other parts of India. 192km (119 miles) by road from Dehra Dun or Haridwar/Rishikesh to Uttarkashi. Malla, the road-head, is 24km (15 miles) further along the road to the Gangotri Temple.
HIGHEST POINT Shastru Tal (5000m/16400ft). Passes: Chuli La (3580m/11745ft), Kyarki Khal (4077m/13375ft).
GRADE Average.
SEASONS Mid-June to October.
RESTRICTIONS None.
FURTHER OPTIONS Approaches available from Pinswar and Bhilangana valleys.

Uttarkashi, the major halt on the way to the holy shrine of Gangotri, is the local district headquarters. Situated on the banks of the Ganges, it has many ashrams and temples. Recently Uttarkashi has expanded but like all Himalayan towns the growth is haphazard. There are several hotels in the bazaar but the Garhwal Mandal Vikas Nigam's rest house is the best (reservations advisable during the pilgrimage season). A little above the town is the Nehru Institute of Mountaineering, with its sprawling campus amidst pine trees. Its museum and library illustrates various facets of Indian mountaineering.

The road to the Gangotri Temple follows the right bank of the Bhagirathi Ganga until it reaches the small village of Malla after 24km (15 miles). Malla has a large school and is connected by several buses and taxis, particularly during the pilgrim season (May to October). Bhatwari, the local *tehsil* (district) headquarters, is nearby.

Malla to Lamb Tal

The road at Malla (1500m/4920ft) descends about 200m (656ft) to the Bhagirathi Ganga bridge, 1km (⅔ mile) away. Cross the river and pass a beautiful temple. Form here a broad track climbs steadily for 6km (3½ miles) to Silla, (2040m/ 6690ft), a large, rather uninviting village where the majority of the population works away in the cities or in Uttarkashi. If you get here before noon, keep walking. Otherwise, spend the night at the village school as the track ahead climbs steeply and, for quite a distance afterwards, there is no water available.

The climb continues on a broad track to the east. Many shepherds use this trail to go to Kush Kalyan and you are guaranteed to get some company on the way. At about 3000m (9840ft), (after 3km/2 miles) there is a clearing and water is available; this is the only camping site on this climb. On the second day, the climb continues to the Kush Kalyan Plateau. Though the track is broad and safe, the climb to the Chuli La (3580m/11740ft) is rather steep. The track winds up the slope through

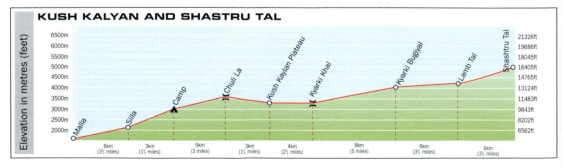

KUSH KALYAN AND SHASTRU TAL

thick forest and climbs continuously until it comes to a little opening below Chuli Peak. From here the trail zigzags below the peak and descends through meadows to a group of small huts, known locally as Bagi settlement. This is the Kush Kalyan Plateau ('plateau of blessing'). From here on the trail follows broad green pastures, one after the other. The best campsite (3300m/10825ft), 8km (5 miles) from Silla, is a little before Kush Kalyan.

On the third day, the trail continues to the *bugiyals* (meadows) of Kush Kalyan, where you will find several shepherds camping here with their flock. Milk and milk products can be easily obtained from them. The track then descends to a saddle, above the shepherd settlement at Mati. From this saddle the trail climbs, gradually at first, along a ridge to reach Bhowani Bugiyal. From here it climbs rather steeply for about 4km (2½ miles) to Kyarki Khal (4077m/13370ft). The trail proceeds along the Kukhli Dhar, after which it gradually descends about 300m (984ft), to the camping ground at Kyarki Bugiyal (3900m/12790ft), 12km (7½ miles) further on.

There are stunning views in the evening, particularly of the Bandarpunch Range (see box). In front is Jaonli (6632m/21753ft) and in the distance is the deep Bhagirathi Valley, which leads to the Gangotri Temple. With green meadows, snow-capped peaks and the company of shepherds, this is a great place to be.

On the fourth day the trail crosses the *bugiyals* to a grassy slope which has to be climbed to its top. The views are staggering as the trail climbs further onto a ridge from the Kyarki Plateau. The ridge, covered with flowers, has the Bandarpunch massif in the background. The Jaonli Peak can be seen rising to the north. It is a magnificent setting, this lush green *bugiyal* with the herds of goats and sheep grazing around.

Once on the Kukhli Dhar the trail reaches a well-made footpath, constructed by the British District Commissioner for the benefit of pilgrims going to Shastru Tal. Locally called *chhe phuti path* ('the six-foot-wide path') the path follows the route from Tehri to Budha Kedar and then to the villages of

The snow-capped peaks of the Bandarpunch Range seen from Lamb Tal.

THE BANDARPUNCH RANGE

The view from the Kush Kalyan Plateau is a sight for the gods. In the evening and early morning there is a beautiful panorama of the Bandarpunch massif. JTM Gibson, a renowned British educationalist who stayed in India after Independence attempted each of these peaks in the 1950s and climbed several of them. He introduced young Indian mountaineers to the sport of mountaineering, particularly in these ranges.

Viewed from Kush Kalyan, to the right stands Kalanag (6387m/20955ft), the highest of the lot. It rises like a black serpent, as its name implies. In the centre rises Bandarpunch (6316m/20722ft), the monkey's tail. Both these peaks were attempted several times by Gibson with different parties from the Doon School, where he was the headmaster. Bandarpunch was climbed by one of his teams in 1950 when Greenwood, Tensing Norgay (later of Everest fame) and Sherpa Tsering reached the summit. Kalanag defied two attempts by Gibson, in 1953 and 1955, and was finally climbed by another party from the Doon School in 1968. Today it is perhaps the most well-known (and most often climbed) peak in the Garhwal.

Further left is Bandarpunch West (6102m/20020ft), scene of a bold attempt by Gibson and Tensing Norgay who followed the sharp south ridge but only just failed to reach the summit. This peak remained unsurmounted until 1984 when the first ascent was made by an Indian team from Bombay following the northern route through the highly crevassed Bandarpunch Glacier.

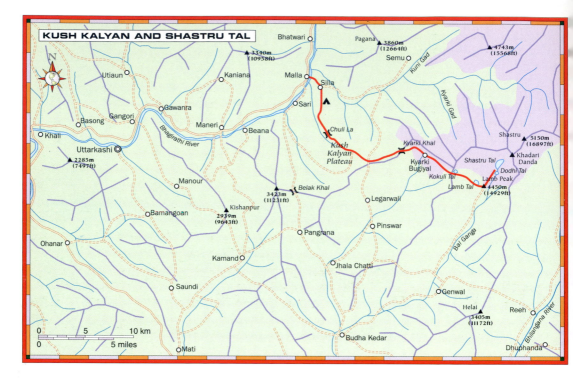

KUSH KALYAN AND SHASTRU TAL

Sheep graze on the rich summer grass at Kyarki Khal.

Jhala and Pinswar to reach Shastru Tal, joining it with Masar Tal, a lake above Pinswar village. It has beautiful views and a gentle gradient and can be followed to return via the Bal Ganga Valley.

After about a kilometre there is a dilapidated *dharamsala* (rest house). Such *dharamsalas*, the traditional Hindu rest houses for pilgrims, were built by the local administration during the British period (1910–45). Mostly paid for by charity or government funds they provided (and still do) a temporary shelter for a night or two. Normally there are no attendants nor is any food available at such places in remote areas.

After a climb of about 200m (656ft) the track passes Kokuli Tal and continues above Lamb Tal (4300m/14100ft). Shastru Tal is 6km (3½ miles) from here and an enterprising party can easily reach the lake. For a relaxed approach it is best to camp above Lamb Tal.

Shastru Tal and Back

The broad track climbs to a ridge above Lamb Tal, where there are fabulous views of the conical Shastru Peak (5154m/16910ft) above Shastru Tal, and other peaks.

The trail continues, descending at first then climbing gently to Dodhi Tal. From here it goes up steeply to Shastru Tal. The shores of Shastru Tal are about 2 hours' walk from Lamb Tal. As the lake is situated in a bowl it does not offer better views, but the surrounding cliffs make it an enchanting setting. Shastru Peak rises behind the lake like a sentinel. Several lakes can be seen on the way and are marked on the map on both sides of the ridge, amply justifying writer Bill Aitkin's soubriquet, 'the Lake District of the Garhwal'.

You can scramble up the small Lamb Peak (4550m/14929ft), rising above Lamb Tal. The view of Shastru Tal from here is magnificent. From June to September, brahma-kamal flowers grow in abundance. These are the most beautiful flowers seen at this altitude and there are many hundreds of them, if not thousands. Many local villagers trek up to the lake to collect these flowers which are used as offerings in various temples.

Shastru Peak (5154m/16910ft) is a conical landmark that rises behind the Shastru Tal in the north. From a camp at the Shastru Tal, at 5000m (16405ft) or just above, it is a good day's climb to the summit and back. It is not often climbed but there are some magnificent views of the Gangotri Range, with peaks such as Thalay Sagar (6904m/ 22650ft), Jaonli (6632m/21753ft) and Gangotri I (6672m/21890ft) also visible.

Walk-out via Shastru Tal to Bhagirathi Valley

You can return by the same route in about 3 days by descending steeply to the Kush Kalyan Plateau and further down to Silla and Malla to pick up transport back to Uttarkashi. But two interesting variations are also possible for a round trip.

The first is to detour to the south from the Kush Kalyan upper plateau towards Belak Khal. After crossing the plateau the path joins a trail from Budha Kedar to Belak Khal (3000m/9840ft). It then descends to the Bhagirathi Valley to meet the road at Lata, near Malla. This trail is about 10km (6 miles) longer than the route of ascent, but far less steep in descent.

The second route is completely different. It follows the broad trail from Lamb Tal to descend to the Bal Ganga Valley in the south. It descends to Pinswar and Jhala villages and thence leads to Bhudha Kedar, a Hindu shrine connected by road with Tehri town. From here you can reach Dehra Dun in a day.

THE GANGA DESCENDS

One of the most fascinating aspects of travel and trekking in the Garhwal is the forming of the River Ganges, the most sacred river in India. The majority of the water running off the Himalaya to the south flows into the Ganges which becomes a large body of water by the time it reaches the plains of India.

The Alaknanda River, the main tributary of the Ganges, rises north of Badrinath shrine at the confluence of the mythical Saraswati and Arwa rivers. It joins the Bhuidhar Ganga at the Valley of Flowers, from where it becomes a major river.

The main rivers of the Garhwal merge with the Alaknanda at five *prayags*: the 'holy meeting of rivers' (the purifying power of a river is strengthened at a confluence, just as its physical power is).

The Five *Prayags*

The first and highest is Vishnuprayag, where the Alaknanda, rushing down from Badrinath in a southeast direction is met by the Dhauli Ganga at Joshimath.

The second is Nandaprayag. Here the Nandakini River flows into the Alaknanda. The Nandakini runs off the western wall of the Nanda Devi Sanctuary. Between these two *prayags*, the relatively small Birehi Ganga joins the Alaknanda, a little to the south of Pipalkoti.

The third is Karnaprayag, where the Pindari River, flowing westwards from the Kumaun, merges with the Alaknanda. The Alaknanda now changes directions and flows westwards for a short distance.

The fourth is Rudraprayag ('ferocious meeting point'). Here the Mandakini River, running off the southern ranges of the Kedarnath valley and the Gangotri wall, rushes to merge with the Alaknanda.

The fifth and final *prayag* is Devprayag. The Alaknanda, a very large river by now, merges with the Bhagirathi, flowing southeast.

Many Hindus consider the Bhagirathi as the main source of the River Ganges. According to Hindu beliefs, the goddess Ganga descended to earth at Gaumukh on the Gangotri Glacier. The river then flows west till it meets Jadh Ganga or Jahanvi at Bhaironghati. Soon after Uttarkashi the river turns south, until at Tehri, the Bhilangana and Bal Ganga merge with it. Finally at Devprayag it meets the Alaknanda. Both the rivers lose their names and as the River Ganges it flows south to Rishikesh and Haridwar to emerge in the plains of Uttar Pradesh.

Finally, this large body of water, the Ganges and the Yamuna (from farther west) flow through the plains of Uttar Pradesh to merge with each other at Allahabad. It is believed that the mythological Saraswati, which disappeared near Badrinath, re-emerges at Allahabad, completing a trinity of rivers.

The Ganges takes in all the major rivers flowing south from the Indian Himalaya, draining large areas of snows, to flow into the Bay of Bengal. The Ganges is considered to be extremely sacred. Along with the Brahmaputra in the east and the Indus in the west, it forms the major source of water in India.

THE NANDA DEVI SANCTUARY

The centrepiece of the Garhwal–Kumaun region is, without doubt, the Nanda Devi Sanctuary, remarkable for its unique wild grandeur.

Until 1934 the gorge of the Rishi Ganga and the immediate area around Nanda Devi was the least known and most inaccessible part of the Himalaya. The mountain stands in a vast amphitheatre, enclosed by a ring of mountains, 110km (70 miles) in circumference, and about 6000m (19686ft) high. There is no point in the ring lower than 5200m (17601ft), except in the west where the Rishi Ganga, draining some 380km² (240 sq. miles) of ice and snow, carves out for itself one of the world's most formidable gorges.

The twin peaks of Nanda Devi (7816m/25792ft) and Nanda East (7434m/24391ft) stand majestically in the centre. The Nanda Devi peaks are beautiful from any angle, particularly when the first and the last rays of the sun are reflected on the summits.

Surrounding Peaks

There are several famous peaks on the rim of the Nanda Devi Sanctuary. From the east wall of the north sanctuary are Latu Dhura (6392m/20972ft), Deo Damla (6620m/21720ft), Mangraon (6568m/21550ft) and Rishi Pahar (6992m/22941ft) peaks. The sanctuary wall turns west from this junction and leads to Kalanka (6991m/22937ft) and Changabang (6864m/22521ft). It ends at Dunagiri (7066m/23184ft).

Towards the south stand the small but difficult twin peaks of Bethartoli Himal (6352m/20841ft) and Bethartoli South (6318m/20729ft). Further south is Trisul (7120m/23361ft). The wall then turns east and leads to Mrigthuni (6855m/22491ft), Devtoli (6788m/22271ft) and Maiktoli (6803m/22321ft). Across the depression of Sunderdhunga Khal stands Panwali Dwar (6663m/21861ft) and Nanda Khat (6611m/21690ft) to complete the circle. The sanctuary wall is divided into the inner and outer sanctuary. The Devistan peaks stand on the central dividing ridge.

Even more remarkable is the veneration that the Nanda Devi peaks hold in Hinduism, the folklore behind it and the tributes it has received from some of the finest writers of mountaineering literature. The sanctuary and the high peaks of Nanda Devi are the major barriers between the cold Tibetan winds and the plains of the River Ganges. Without the sanctuary to absorb the main thrust of the icy winds, the plains of the River Ganges, the granary of India, would be stripped barren. It is hardly surprising, then, that the peaks are worshipped as a goddess with some impressive folklore built around them. The name Nanda Devi itself means 'the bliss-giving goddess'.

Trek into the Sanctuary

It takes eight days to reach the base camp of Nanda Devi on the south side. The Rishi Ganga River forces its way through two gorges. The first one, near Lata village, cuts off any possibility of an easy approach, and therefore a route over two intervening ridges – the Dharanshi and Malathuni – was explored. Shipton and Tilman called this the Curtain Ridge. Near the second gorge of the Rishi Ganga a route was explored over precarious, rocky terrain.

The approach to the inner sanctuary will always be difficult. The route is: Lata, Lata Kharak, across Dharanshi Pass (4267m/14000ft) to Dharanshi Alp, across Malathuni Pass (4270m/14010ft) to Dibrugheta Alp, along the river to Deodi, Ramni at the foot of the gorge, Bhujgara half way through the gorge and Patalkhan across the main difficulties of the gorge. 'The Slabs' are the first of the challenges, where downward-sloping rocky slabs make for a precari-

Devtoli (left) and Maiktoli peaks on the southern wall of the Nanda Devi Sanctuary.

The Nanda Devi peaks rise up above the forest of Deodi, as seen from the approach to the historic Rishi Gorge.

ous crossing. A narrow staircase of stones ahead cuts across a huge wall. Just one slip and you would plummet thousands of feet down the gorge, aptly called the *vaikunth seedi* (the 'staircase to heaven') by locals. If you climb up this, you will reach the heaven of the Nanda Devi Sanctuary, whereas if you fall, you might reach heaven anyway.

Patalkhan is the first halt in the sanctuary. From Patalkhan, the route crosses the Rishi Ganga to enter the north side of the sanctuary.

Exploration of the Sanctuary

The first attempt to explore the routes to the sanctuary was made by WW Graham (1883), who could not possibly have made much headway and his claims to have climbed several peaks, such as Changabang, have been called into question. Dr Longstaff (1905 and 1907) was the next explorer. At first, with AL Mumm and CG Bruce he tried unsuccessfully to forge a route through the Rishi Gorge. He then approached from the east and reached a col – becoming the first person to see into the inner sanctuary. This col, on the shoulder of the east peak, is named after him. Hugh Ruttledge was next, and of the several routes tried by him, the most innovative went via the Sunderdhunga Col in the south, which Shipton and Tilman used to descend from the sanctuary in 1934.

The main peak of Nanda Devi was climbed in 1936 and over the years several ascents by many routes followed. The ridge between the twin peaks, nowhere less than 6700m (21983ft) and almost 2km (1¼ miles) long, was crossed by an Indo-Japanese expedition in 1976. Many peaks on the sanctuary wall have been climbed by expeditions of different nationalities since the sanctuary was opened to foreign mountaineers in 1974.

Unfortunately, too many expeditions in a short span put pressure on the sanctuary's fragile ecology. Logs were cut to make bridges, junipers burnt to keep porters warm and there was talk of building a footpath to the inner sanctuary for tourists. Local shepherds forged an alternative route into the inner sanctuary which allowed their herds to be taken into the main sanctuary for the first time. This was a fine piece of exploration but it led to much destruction of flora and the sanctuary had to be closed to mountaineers and locals alike. At the time of writing, the sanctuary remains closed, depriving a generation of mountaineers from enjoying the bliss of the goddess Nanda.

There is a lot to look forward to when the sanctuary reopens to mountaineers, such as the awe-inspiring west face of Nanda Devi. Many other peaks and routes are yet to be climbed. For whatever reason, the abode of the *rishis* (sages) will always be regarded as one of the world's natural wonders, the most prized mountain wilderness in the world.

TREK 12: RUINSARA TO HAR-KI-DUN VALLEY AND BALI PASS

The valleys of the western Garhwal have long been popular with trekkers and climbers. The glaciers and peaks in these valleys first became attractions when JTM Gibson and other teachers from the Doon School, Dehra Dun, came here in the 1950s to teach their young students the pleasures of appreciating nature. It is a lovely walk to the Har-ki-Dun Valley, a national park with superb views of the Jaundar Glacier and surrounding peaks. The trail to Ruinsara Valley from here leads through a forest and finally climbs over the Bali Pass to magnificent views.

TREK ESSENTIALS

LENGTH 2 weeks; 80km (50 miles). Walking from Sankhri: 3 days to Har-ki-Dun, 3 days to Ruinsara Valley, 3 days to Yamnotri.
ACCESS Trains from Delhi to Dehra Dun. Connecting taxis or buses for the journey to Sankhri, 200km (124 miles), crossing the hill station of Mussoorie on the way.
HIGHEST POINT Bali Pass (4880m/16010ft). Passes: Bali.
GRADE Medium with a difficult pass.
SEASONS Mid-June to October.
RESTRICTIONS None.
FURTHER OPTIONS Treks in the Har-ki-Dun Valley and to the head of the Ruinsara Valley.

The drive to Sankhri (1800m/5900ft) alone is beautiful, via the hill station of Mussoorie, then along the Yamuna River into the Tons Valley. The dense forest around Naitwar is inviting, with a rest house located at a vantage point. The entire Ruinsara–Har-ki-Dun area is a national park. Entry fees and camera fees are payable, and no shooting or hunting is permitted. Sankhri is a small village at the end of the road where the Supin River, draining the snow from the Kinnaur border, merges with the Tons. (See Trek 15, page 113).

Sankhri to Har-ki-Dun

Though there is a road suitable for jeeps to Taluka you should walk this stretch for better acclimatisation. The road is blocked in several places and dangerous at some turns. Taluka (1980m/6500ft), 12km (7½ miles) on, is a rather bleak place but full of *dhabas* and rest houses. On day two take the regular trail going east, which is lined with tea-houses in many places. You will need to cross several bridges as the path is generally on the left bank. After 2km (1¼ miles) a short climb brings you to the village of Dhatmir and the trail proceeds east for 10km (6 miles) to Seema (2500m/8200ft), where there are plenty of rest houses and tea shops. The next village, Osla, is on the opposite bank and about 60m (197ft) higher. The people of these valleys worship Duryodhan, the villain in the epic *Mahabharata*. The main deity is Mahasu and you will find several temples dedicated to him.

Har-ki-Dun is 9km (5 miles) further on, which takes about 5 hours. It is a beautiful walk, but may be crowded during the holiday time in India. The trail climbs the Kalkatti Dhar (named after the goddess Kali) and the view of Kalanag towards the Ruinsara Valley is excellent. There are rest house and *dhabas* (tea stalls) in the valley (average 3500m/11500ft). But the valley

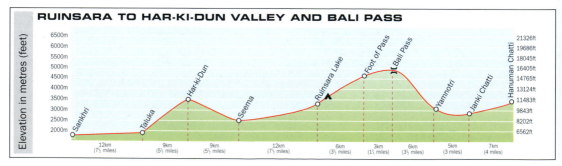

RUINSARA TO HAR-KI-DUN VALLEY AND BALI PASS

itself is always beautiful with views of the Jaundar Glacier and surrounding peaks. You could easily spend a couple of days in Har-ki-Dun and visit the Borasu Pass (4725m/15502ft), 5km (3 miles) northeast, which is on the watershed alongside Kinnaur. It is advisable to hire a local guide to trek in the area and to go in the right season when there is not too much snow around.

Har-ki-Dun to Osla (Seema) to Ruinsara Valley

Returning to Osla is easy and quick. It will take only about 4 hours to reach the bridge near the confluence of the Ruinsara Gad and the Tons. Seema is about an hour's walk downhill from here. But to reach the Ruinsara Valley you can turn southeast, along the Ruinsara Gad. Keeping to the right bank, the trail passes some wonderful forests interspersed with grazing grounds. After 12km (7½ miles) you will reach Ruinsara Lake (3350m/10990ft). The views from the lake are fantastic. At the head of the valley, Kalanag (6387m/20956ft) and Bandarpunch (6316m/20723ft) are visible. Camp here and spend a day acclimatising and enjoying the view. Make a day trip towards the head of the valley. It is basically a moraine walk of about 6km (3½ miles) and there are much wider vistas from here. The trail ahead leads to Dhumdhar Kandi Pass (5490m/18013ft) across to Harsil, but these are high passes and better left to well-equipped mountaineering parties. Jack Gibson, who visited these valleys several times, named the side valleys Toothache Valley, Ski Valley I and Ski Valley II from east to west. As the names imply, these valleys offer good skiing slopes when snow cover is firm until June (see JTM Gibson's book, *As I Saw It*).

Ruinsara Valley to Yamnotri

From the camp at the Ruinsara Lake a wide valley extends to the south, Gibson's Ski Valley II. Proceed along the slopes in the centre. There will be plenty of snow until late June, but after the rains the entire valley will be almost devoid of snow, except in the higher parts. It is 6km (3½

Arriving in Sankhri with its spectacular views of the national park in the Har-ki-Dun Valley.

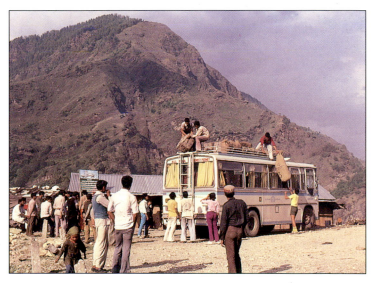

SWARGAROHINI PEAKS

These peaks are named after the five *pandavas*, heroes from the epic *Mahabharata*. They are believed to have ascended to heaven from these peaks. These are a group of beautiful peaks on the dividing ridge between the Har-ki-Dun and Ruinsara valleys. Peak I is the most difficult of the group and after being tried by several parties it was finally climbed by an Indian party from the Nehru Institute of Mountaineering.

miles) to the foot of the pass (4600m/15090ft), where you can camp. Next day, starting early, cross the upper slopes to reach the Bali Pass in about 2 hours (3km/1½ miles). Take care when crossing the final slopes, particularly when the route is snow-bound. The view from the pass is worth any difficulty encountered on the way. There is a magnificent panoramic view of the Swargarohini Peaks (see box above), the Ruinsara Valley and the peaks to the east above the Gangotri Valleys.

The descent on the other side is along a prominent ridge, steep to begin with, but soon

it becomes a well-defined track amid virgin forest. The views of thickly wooded valleys compensate for the lack of any high peaks visible on the Yamnotri side. Set up camp at a clearing in the forest, named Damni, as water is available here, or continue the descent to the pilgrim route near Yamnotri. Yamnotri Temple, 6km (3½ miles) from the pass (3185m/10450ft), may be something of a disappointment as it is a small temple located deep inside the valley without any view at all. There are hot springs near the temple but, for anyone wanting to bathe, the quality of hygiene is poor. You would be better off walking down the trail and staying at one of the *chattis* (pilgrims lodges), such as Janaki Chatti (2560m/8400ft) some 5km (3 miles) lower down.

Walk-out via Hanuman Chatti

Walk down the pilgrim trail to Hanuman Chatti (2400m/7875ft), 7km (4 miles) further on, which is a roadhead. Buses and taxis are available during the pilgrim season to drive to Dehra Dun (190km) via Dharasu and Chamba or via Mussoorie. There are rail and road connections from Dehra Dun to Delhi.

A camp at Ruinsara Tal with its spectacular views of Kalanag Peak in the Ruinsara Valley.

PEAK: KALANAG

Kalanag, meaning 'black serpent', is a prominent peak of the Bandarpunch Range. Of the three peaks of this range, this is the highest and easiest to climb. It is popular with many Indian climbers, especially students – a 15 year old student has ascended the peak. Nevertheless, with its height and location it offers a most wonderful and rewarding view from its slopes and from the summit.

View from Base Camp showing the route across the glacier to the summit of Kalanag Peak.

Follow the valley up towards its head. Turn south from the point where the glacier descends to meet the moraine ridge and climb the broad slopes of the peak.

Base Camp

The peak is at the head of the Ruinsara Valley and rises near the Bandarpunch Glacier with magnificent mountain views all around. From the base camp on the moraine ridge of the Bandarpunch Glacier – one day's walk ahead from Ruinsara Lake – continue walking on the moraine ridge until it flattens out. You will need to cross several side streams and ridges. The point where the ridge and the lower slopes of the glacier meet is the traditional site for an advance base camp, at 4880m (16010ft).

Chhotanag Camp

Climb the glacier in a wide arc, the route turning southwards towards a prominent col seen on the way to the summit. The main peak is seen rising like a serpent in one sweep. The steep black rock slabs on the southwestern slopes give the mountain its name. Climb on the upper slopes, steeper, and crevassed.

Camp just above a small peak of 5220m (17127ft) called Chhotanag (smaller serpent).

On the day of your ascent to the summit start early as the entire climb will be on snow. Late in the season there will be plenty of crevasses and the slopes will be icy. Continue up the steep slopes on the left to reach the col. Once above these you will reach the final summit slope. This slope is exposed and extends for a long distance but is not particularly difficult, rather it is a test of stamina. Finally, you will reach the summit. It is described as the fang of the serpent, as the summit is flat but narrow.

The view includes the Bandarpunch Range and the wonderful Swargarohini Peaks. Distant peaks include those of the Gangotri group to the southwest and the Rangrik group of Kinnaur to the east.

CLIMB ESSENTIALS

SUMMIT Kalanag (6387m/20490ft).
PRINCIPAL CAMPS Base Camp: one day beyond Ruinsara Lake, at 4025m (13200ft). Chhotanag: 5220m (17127ft).
GRADE An easy climb with one last steep slope near to the summit. Beware though of numerous crevasses.
MAP REFERENCE See sketch-map Trek 12, Ruinsara Valley (page 92).

PEAK: SWARGAROHINI II AND III

The Swargarohini Peaks. From left to right: peaks III, II and I.

to climb and several ascents have been made, the first in 1974 by a Canadian/British team led by DS Virk. Peak III (6209m/20370ft) was first climbed in 1984 by a team from Bombay led by Anil Kumar.

Route to summit: Follow a steep *nala* to reach a sharp ridge between Swargarohini peaks II and III. Follow this ridge to flatter ground for an uncomfortable camp. Form this camp peak II is attempted.

According to legend, the Pandava brothers of the epic *Mahabharata* climbed to heaven from the summit of these peaks, one for each of the five brothers. The peaks rise in a group dividing the Har-ki-Dun and the Ruinsara valleys.

Peaks of this group have attracted mountaineers for a long time. Peak I (6252m/20511ft), the main peak, defied climbers for several years but was finally climbed by the instructors of the Nehru Institute of Mountaineering, Uttarkashi in 1990. Peak II is only five metres (16ft) lower but is relatively easy

Base Camp

From the base camp near the Ruinsara Lake, proceed in a narrow valley to the north. This leads towards the narrow gorge between Swargarohini peaks II and III. After going for some distance, climb up the ridge on the left and proceed along it. The flat ground reached after a long climb on the ridge is the only place where a camp can be made.

From this camp proceed slowly and carefully to the col between peaks III and II. This col is the culmination of the long ridge and the nearer you get, the steeper the ridge. From the col turn right, towards the north, to climb an exposed ridge. Take great care when crossing but apart from this there are not many difficult sections. The peak is between the Har-ki-Dun and the Ruinsara valleys and there is a strong wind on the final ridge. The summit is a narrow point and the view of the ridge linking this peak with peak I is amazing. To the southeast rise Kalanag and other peaks of the Bandarpunch Range. Distant valleys in the south lead to the Yamnotri Valley across Bali Pass. Linked to these peaks from the col is Peak III of Swargarohini, which is also easy to climb. The northern slopes of the Swargarohini group can be approached from the Jaundar Glacier, but the climbing routes on these faces are challenging and no one has yet succeeded in climbing them.

CLIMB ESSENTIALS

SUMMITS Swargarohini II (6247m/20495ft); Swargarohini III (6209m/20370ft)

PRINCIPAL CAMPS Base Camp: near Ruinsara Lake, at 4100m (13450ft). Camp 1: 4720m (14500ft). Camp 2: 5340m (17520ft).

GRADE Long snow slopes with many crevasses. This is a difficult peak and care must be taken to carry enough equipment.

MAP REFERENCE See sketch-map Trek 12, Ruinsara Valley (page 92).

KUMAUN AND GARHWAL DIRECTORY

UTTARANCHAL STATE
This new Indian state, comprising the hill areas of Kumaun and Garhwal and separating them from the state of Uttar Pradesh, was formed in late 2000. Uttaranchal will be an important authority for trekkers, mountaineers and pilgrims visiting the mountain areas, and, in time, it is likely to introduce new regulations and fees and establish new offices. Its capital is now Dehra Dun.

REGIONAL TRANSPORT
Kumaun
Take a night train from Delhi to reach Kathgodam early in the morning. Road transport is available to reach Munsiary, Bageshwar and all other destinations.
Garhwal
For most areas of Garhwal take a night train to Haridwar (or slightly further on to Dehra Dun). Taxis and buses (from Rishikesh) are available to reach Joshimath, Kedarnath, Gangotri, Sankhri and other starting points for treks.

REGIONAL TOURIST OFFICES
Contact the offices below for transport and accommodation information.
Kumaun Mandal Vikas Nigam Ltd (KMVN)
Oak Park House, Nainital 263 001 (UP-India); tel (91-522) 36356; fax (91-522) 36897; e-mail kumaon@seeindia.com; www.seeindia.com
Garhwal Mandal Vikas Nigam Ltd (GMVN)
74/1 Rajpur Road, Dehra Dun 248 001 (UP-India); tel (91-135) 746817, 749808; fax (91-135) 744408; e-mail gmvn@nda.vsnl.net.in

NEW DELHI OFFICES
GMVN
102 Indraprakash Building, 21 Barakhamba Road, New Delhi 110001; tel (91-11)

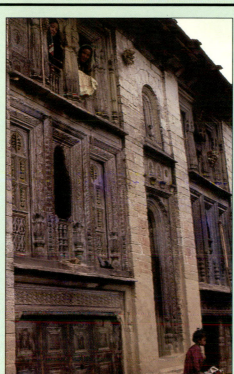
A Kumauni house with carvings.

3350481; fax (91-11) 3327713
KMVN
103 Indraprakash Building, 21 Barakhamba Road, New Delhi 110001; tel (91-11) 3712296

RESTRICTIONS
Kumaun
Eastern Kumaun: (Darma valley) This is still closed to foreigners but Indian mountaineers are now allowed entry.
Central Kumaun: The areas are open up to the Milam Glacier and Milam village. This gives mountaineers access to the Kalabaland glacier, lower Milam Glacier and Nanda Devi East. There are several high and unclimbed peaks here.
The Nanda Devi Sanctuary is closed for environmental reasons.
Western Kumaun: There are no restrictions in Pindari and the Sunderdhunga Valley area.
Garhwal
Northern valleys: The areas north of Badrinath and around Kamet are still closed to visitors and are within the Inner Line (see page 35). Some joint expeditions have been allowed here.
Major parts of central Garhwal such as Dunagiri, Uja Tirche and Panpatia Bank are open.
The western Garhwal area is completely open and is home to the Gangotri group and the the Bandarpunch Valley peaks.

LOCAL PLACES OF INTEREST
Bageshwar: Baijnath temples
Chaukori: Nanda Devi view and old tea gardens
Gulabrai, nr Rudraprayag: Jim Corbett Memorial
Kausani: Gandhi Ashram
Uttarkashi: Nehru Institute of Mountaineering
Joshimath: Ashram of Shankracharya
Okimath: ancient temple with carvings

6
HIMACHAL PRADESH

In a hundred ages of the gods, I could not tell thee of the glories of Himachal. As the dew is dried up by the morning sun, so are the sins of mankind by the sight of Himachal.

(The *Skanda Purana*)

The Indian Himalaya, particularly the areas of the western Himalaya, has been looked upon as a spiritual abode by Hindus and Buddhists since time immemorial. In 1971, the three major areas of the Himalaya were merged into one political entity to create the state of Himachal Pradesh, which contains the areas of Kinnaur, Spiti-Lahaul and Kullu-Kangra. Together they form some of the most inviting trekking areas in India with their vastly different culture, geography and history. Many of the trade and grazing routes have been followed for generations.

The Bhimkali Temple at Sarahan with Gushu Pishu (left) and Zangshu peaks in the background.

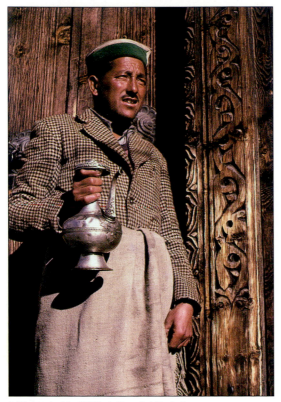

A Hindu priest in Chhitkul, Himachal Pradesh.

Although Himachal Pradesh (HP) is one of the youngest states in India, the hill kingdoms that comprise it can trace their history back hundreds of years. These hill kingdoms managed on the whole to maintain a state of independence until annexed by the British as part of the Punjab in the mid-19th century.

Kinnaur

The very name Kinnaur conjures up a picture of inaccessible valleys, of the Hindustan–Tibet road, of the mighty gorge of the Satluj River and of unfamiliar customs. It was in Kinnaur that the famous character Kim, created in the 19th century by British author Rudyard Kipling, travelled on his mission in the novel of the same name. But things have changed drastically since Kim's time, and many possibilities for trekkers and mountaineers have opened up.

While it used to take about two weeks' trekking to reach Kinnaur, national highway No. 22 now runs along the side of the River Satluj and is kept open almost throughout the year, connecting Kalpa with Rekong Peo, the headquarters of Kinnaur. The Satluj River literally cuts through the Himalayan chain near Shipki La and then runs through the centre of Kinnaur.

The earliest Western explorers of Kinnaur were the Gerard brothers in 1818, followed by Marco Pallis in 1933, who brought these valleys to the notice of trekkers and mountaineers. In 1952, the South African mountaineer Dr J de V Graaf reached Manirang Pass and climbed Manirang Peak (6593m/21632ft) to its northeast.

In Kinnaur there is a fusion of Hinduism and Buddhism. Every village has a temple and a *gompa* (monastery) and everyone worships at both. Like Kinnauri culture, the architecture is wonderful to behold. Kamru Fort, perched strategically on a hillock, and some exquisite gompas and temples are literally breath-taking.

Kalpa, situated in the centre of Kinnaur, is the district headquarters, with one of the finest views you are ever likely to see from the confines of a comfortable bungalow. The following is a description of that view, taken from the *Himalayan Journal*, Vol XXVII:

'From the forest bungalow at Kalpa, 9400 feet above sea-level and 145 miles from Shimla along the Hindustan–Tibet road, the Kailash massif is seen to advantage. The snowfields are so close that in spring the reflected light from the snows is painful to the eyes, while during the monsoon the sound of falling avalanches can be heard all day long.'

It is hardly surprising then, given the above description, that Lord Dalhousie, Governor-General of India at the time, made Kalpa a hideout and planned the blueprint of the Indian Railways here.

Spiti

Spiti literally means 'middle country' and it lies across the main Himalayan chain, between Tibet and India. The Spiti River flows in a rough northwest/southeast direction, cutting the valley into its eastern and western halves. At Khab it flows into the mighty Satluj, which carves out a formidable gorge for itself as it enters India near the Shipki La, about 10km (6 miles) from Puh. All these natural features can be seen from the road that runs alongside the rivers.

The western section of Spiti adjoins Kullu and Kinnaur. Proceeding upstream from the confluence of the Satluj, the first large tributary is the Pin which joins the Spiti a short distance from the Lingti confluence (on the opposite bank). Several passes – the Manirang, Ghunsarang, Tari Khango and Shakraode – lead into Kinnaur, while the famous Pin Parvati Pass allows access into the beautiful valley of Parvati in the Kullu.

Spiti first came to the notice of the outside

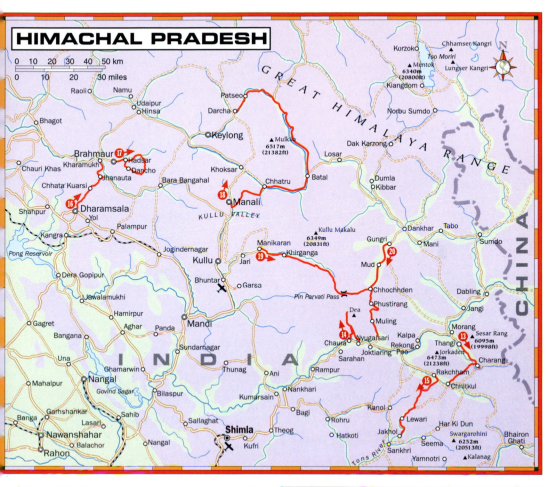

HIMACHAL PRADESH

world in 1945, in a rather infamous manner. Two Germans, Paidar and Schmaderer, escaped British wartime internment and, following in the footsteps of Heinrich Harrer and Peter Aufschnaiter (see page 85), escaped into Tibetan territory. However, they decided to turn back and it was on their return, at Tabo in Spiti, that Schmaderer was robbed and murdered.

The Spiti and Kinnaur valleys have been free of travel restrictions since 1993 and parties can now roam freely. This fabulous trekking country has a lot to offer visitors.

Kullu-Kangra

The Kullu Valley has long been a happy hunting ground for *shikaris* (hunters), trekkers and climbers alike. The British general CG Bruce (in 1912) and another Briton, JOM Roberts (in 1939), were two of the earliest explorers, and before a decent road was constructed, the most popular trekking routes in the Kullu Valley were over the passes in the Dhauladhar Range.

ABODE OF SHIVA

In Hindu mythology, Kailash is the legendary home of the god Shiva, and perhaps because of this many mountain ranges have peaks named Kailash. The Kailash Peak (6714m/22028ft) above Manasarovar in Tibet is the holiest, believed to be the centre of the universe.

For those who cannot make the arduous pilgrimage to Tibet there is Baba Kailash (6322m/20741ft) near the Tibetan border between the Darma and Kuthi valleys. In Garhwal (Gangotri) is Sri Kailash (6932m/22742ft), the easiest of Shiva's peaks to climb but the most difficult to view. Sri Kailash was first climbed by an Austrian team in 1938. Further west is Kinnaur Kailash (Jorkanden) (6473m/21239ft) above Kalpa, a very difficult peak. The trail that circumambulates this peak, known as Charang Ghati, is now a popular trek (see page 103).

The last peak is the Kailash of the Chamba district of Himachal Pradesh, also known as Mani Mahesh Kailash after the sacred lake to its west (see page 121). This is perhaps the most difficult of Shiva's abodes to gain entrance to.

The Kullu Valley is dominated by the River Beas, which rises at the Rohtang Pass. Across the Rohtang Pass lies Lahaul, a district that is almost completely bordered by the rivers Chandra and Bhaga, which eventually merge in the southwest corner to become the Chenab. Today, ease of access to this area is one of the main reasons for Kullu–Kangra's popularity.

Manali, which lies to the north of the Kullu Valley, is the most popular base for trekking in Himachal Pradesh, being both a starting point for many treks and a convenient stop en route to the Zanskar Valley or Ladakh.

Dhauladhar, a mountain wall, separates the Kangra and the Kullu valleys. The passes over this moderate range were the preferred bridle routes in

Kinnauri girls celebrating the *Phulej* festival at Rangrik monastery.

THE LINGTI PLAINS

The Lingti Plains lie above the River Lingti, and though it has a fine level expanse of grass, with abundant fuel (dema or Tibetan furze), it has no surface water and cannot be irrigated, so cultivation is impossible. Crossing the plains takes almost two days and its vast expanse is lined with peaks. The Manali-Leh highway crosses the plains at its eastern end.

Northeast of the Baralacha La, just above Lingti (Sarchu) Camp is a high, isolated square stone known as Phalang Danda or Lingti that traditionally marks the boundary between Lahaul (Himachal Pradesh) and Zanskar (Ladakh).

The River Lingti flows from the foot of Phirtse La, west of the Lingti Plains and northwest, passing the foot of the Phuktal Monastery. It merges with the Doda River to become the Zanskar River, flowing north.

the days before tarmacked roads were constructed. From the comforts o Dharamsala, the old district headquarters of the British administration, the upper grazing grounds and the mountains can be reached in two to three marches. The area was a weekend climber's paradise during the days o British rule and many of the modest summits have been climbed and the passes are crossed with regularity by trekkers and shepherds.

The major areas of interest fo climbers and trekkers today are the valleys surrounding Kullu and Manali Many of the treks follow old trade and grazing routes that have been used by the locals for centuries. The Solang nala, north of Manali, is dominated by peaks that offer both difficult and easy climbs. The Parvati Valley is a trekker's dream, with excellent prospects and some great route variations. The Pin Parvati Pass, which leads to Spiti offers a super vista.

The Manali–Leh highway, built in the 1960s after the war with China, runs for 473km (294 miles) and has brough road access to many of the trekking areas. Despite greater access and communication, there has not been an excess of trekking activity. To a mountain lover this is still an unknown and inviting area with several trekking routes and hundreds of unclimbed peaks.

TREK 13: ACROSS CHARANG GHATI

Amongst Buddhists and Hindus there is a tradition of circumambulation (walking around in a circle). This form of worship, called *parikrama*, is always done from left to right in a clockwise direction so that the deity, statue or icon is always on the right. There are several places in the Himalaya where pilgrims complete such circuits. The *parikrama* around the Kinnaur Kailash, considered to be the home of Shiva, is an age-old tradition. Lamas (priests) and pilgrims cross the Charang Ghati to complete the circuit around this range, whose highest peak is Jorkanden (6373m/20408ft). Since 1994, when the area was opened to tourists, this has become a popular trek. A great variety of scenery, local temples and the culture of the Kinnauris can be seen along the route. There may be a lot of snow on the pass until mid-July. August and September are the best months for crossing and for observing several local festivals on the way.

Thangi

Reaching Thangi (2650m/8700ft) is a pleasure in itself. Once inaccessible, it is now linked by a road with highway No. 22, which runs along the side of the Satluj River. Starting from the railhead at Kalka or Shimla, it is a long journey to Kinnaur, and sometimes vehicles are held up due to road-blocks. There is a direct bus that travels to Thangi from Shimla.

Thangi is situated at the entrance of the Tirung Gad River, which drains into the Satluj from the east. The district headquarters, Rekong Peo, is 41km (25½ miles) before Thangi. From here, the road follows the Satluj to Morang, where a dilapidated fort can be seen from the road. From here the 9-km (5½-mile) drive to Thangi is an exciting experience as you pass under huge cliffs and look down to the Tirung nala.

There are a few campsites where the road ends and there is a small (tolerable) hotel. The main village is about 100m (328ft) higher up. It has a small monastery and many houses, but no worthwhile place to camp as all the flat land has been used for farming.

Southwards, the valley across the Tirung nala leads to the Jorkanden Base Camp. This is the highest peak in the Kinnaur-Kailash Range and poses a stiff challenge to climbers.

TREK ESSENTIALS

LENGTH 2 weeks; 44km (27 miles). Walking from Thangi: 4 days to Charang, 3 days to Charang Ghati pass (includes ascent). Drive-out via Chhitkul.

ACCESS Train from Delhi to Kalka (near Chandigarh) and Shimla. Drive 226km (140 miles) to Rekong Peo then Morang, 32km (20 miles) and Thangi, 9km (5½ miles).

HIGHEST POINT Charang Ghati, 5200m (17600ft). Passes: Charang Ghati.

GRADE Medium; pass difficult.

SEASONS Mid-June to late October.

RESTRICTIONS Foreign trekkers must travel in groups of at least 4. Permits from District Magistrate at Rekong Peo. Charge to be paid.

FURTHER OPTIONS Combine with trek to Shaone Gad (see Trek 15, page 113).

Thangi to Charang

The trek proceeds along the Tirung nala. The road is being extended, rather slowly, from Thangi ahead into the valley and the first section of the trail is on this partly constructed road. After about 2km (1¼ miles) the trail descends towards the riverbed and then continues along the same axis. As there are huge walls rising on both sides the

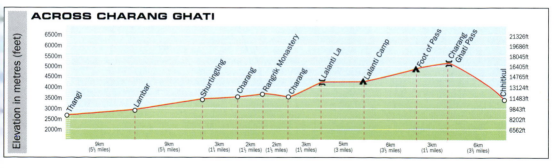

ACROSS CHARANG GHATI

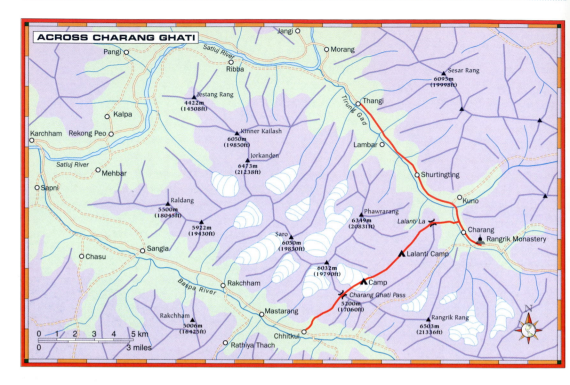

ACROSS CHARANG GHATI

Jangi
Pangi
Satluj River
Ribba
Morang
Sesar Rang
6095m
(19998ft)
Jestang Rang
4422m
(14508ft)
Thangi
Kalpa
Karchham Rekong Peo
Kinner Kailash
6050m
(19850ft)
Lambar
Satluj River
Mehbar
Jorkanden
6473m
(21238ft)
Shurtingting
Sapni
Kuno
Raldang
5500m
(18045ft)
Phawrarang
6349m
(20831ft)
Lalanti La
Charang
5922m
(19430ft)
Saro
6050m
(19850ft)
Rangrik Monastery
Sangla
Chasu
Lalanti Camp
6032m
(19790ft)
Baspa River
Rakchham
Camp
Charang Ghati Pass
5200m
(17060ft)
Rakchham
5006m
(16425ft)
Mastarang
Rangrik Rang
6503m
(21336ft)
Chhitkul
Rathiya Thach

0 1 2 3 4 5 km
0 3 miles

N

Charang Ghati Pass is a popular site for trekkers and pilgrims.

view is limited, but it is amply compensated for by a dense forest. Near Lambar (6km/3½ miles), the first halt, there are huge, smooth, granite walls on the right bank that rise almost 600m (19687ft) and are an attractive proposition for rock climbing. At Lambar (2875m/9430ft) there is an excellent camping ground on the left bank of the river. Visit the small village, about 50m (164ft) above the campsite; consisting of only a few huts, it is a peaceful place, with a giant tree at the entrance. Many of these villagers had not met any foreigners until as recently as 1995. The Lambar nala drains from a southern valley and merges with the Tirung nala here.

The second day's trek continues along the river and is even gentler than the previous one. There are no ups or downs to speak of. After about 5 hours and 9km (5½ miles), you will reach a bridge that crosses the Tirung nala. The open ground on the left bank is called Shurtingting (3410m/11190ft), and is the second day's halt. The valley in the north leads to Kuno village, but the area is prohibited to visitors without a special permit.

On the following day, it takes about 20 minutes to reach the camp of the Indo-Tibet Border Police, where permits and passports will be checked and entered in a register. From here, you can see the Tirung nala taking a prominent turn to the east. A new trail built above the nala leads directly to

Charang village (3km/1½ miles). However, the old trail, which is about 300m (984ft) higher, gives some excellent views of the Racho group of peaks. Amongst these is the highest peak in this part of Kinnaur, Rangrik Rang (6553m/21500ft), visible on the right along with the Mangla Khad Valley which leads to the Tibetan border. After an easy 3-hour walk you will come to Charang village (6km/3½ miles).

Charang is a large village extending along the ridge. It has a monastery with a courtyard where all the festivities are held, a small rest house in the village itself and a place for camping near it. The friendly villagers used to trade with the Chewrang Province of Tibet across the Khimokoul La, trade which is now being revived.

The route across the glacial moraine of the Charang Ghati Pass can be difficult.

The Rangrik Monastery (3680m/12075ft), 2km (1¼ miles) beyond the village, is the most sacred in Kinnaur. An excellent trail, used regularly by many villagers, leads to it. You can camp near this monastery as it has excellent open grounds. Nearby is another police post where you will have to register again and gain official permission before you may proceed along the main or the side valleys, due to the proximity of the Tibetan border. Before crossing the high Charang Pass you should stay on here for an extra day to acclimatise. Walk on the slopes near the village and visit the Tirung nala in the valley to aid this.

Charang to the foot of the Charang Ghati Pass

If you camped at the Rangrik Monastery, retrace your steps along the trail that leads to Charang village. From the rest house take the trail that forks towards the Charang Ghati Pass. There are several village trails that climb diagonally towards the ridgeline to the northeast.

The climb is gradual but longer than it at first appears. After about 4 hours you will come to a pass (Lalanti La), which is a small depression in the ridge. From here, the trail gets wilder and zigzags across slope after slope. At some places the trail is broken, particularly when it descends gullies. Once in the valley you will reach the Shurtingting nala which flows into the camping ground below. Follow this nala upwards along the

trail. A landslide has completely wiped out the trail to the Lalanti camping ground (4200m/13780ft, 4 hours' distant). You will have to climb up at least 250m (820ft) and then descend to get past, or you can try to follow the almost non-existent rocky route along the river.

The trail leads to a wide-open, beautiful valley which, in season, is covered with red plants. The plants are the reason why this valley is known as Lalanti ('the place of red plants'). There are many places to camp here. There is also a small dilapidated hut which is used on occasion by the police and by local shepherds.

Next day, the trail climbs along a broad valley. It is often windy but this is more than compensated for by the wide vistas of mountains, both in the nearby valleys and in the north, where several small peaks of the Sesar Rang Range are visible. After a couple of hours the terrain becomes rough and crosses several boulder-strewn fields. It is a tiring walk as the altitude is high. Finally, after 6 hours, almost at the foot of the pass, near a lake (4800m/15750ft) and away from the boulders, it is possible to pitch tents but the strong winds are likely to prove troublesome.

Charang Ghati Pass and Chhitkul

Begin the climb to the Charang Ghati Pass as early in the morning as possible, because a long day lies ahead. From the camp the pass is seen as a prominent depression in the ridge on the left. With a pair of binoculars (or sharp eyes) you will see prayer flags on the pass. The route is tricky and deceptive. Proceed along the remains of glacial moraines. Sometimes in summer these are covered with snow so have a guide break the trail for you to make the walking easier. Climb towards the pass for 4 hours until a final section, almost straight up about 80m (262ft), leads to the Charang Ghati Pass (5200m/17060ft).

The pass offers a vast and interesting panorama. In the Charang Valley several small peaks are visible, all beautiful and unexplored. The best view is towards the south, over the Baspa Valley. Across it you can see two more large valleys, which lead to the Borasu Pass and into the Garhwal region. Several snow-capped peaks in the distance are about 6000m (20000ft) high and mostly unclimbed. Though this is the traditional route of circumambulation of the Kailash massif, the main peak is not seen from anywhere on the trail, nor indeed from the pass.

The descent on the Chhitkul side is rather steep and there is a lot of scree at the beginning. Three plateaux have to be crossed. After a descent of about 200m (650ft) the first plateau is reached. Depending on the season, it will be full of stones or snow. The trail continues for 3 hours down the steep descent, zigzagging down the slopes,

Buddhist monastery in Chhitkul.

generally remaining in the centre of the valley. The second plateau is reached after a 600m (1969ft) descent. It is possible to put up one or two uncomfortable tents here in an emergency, though water is scarce.

The final descent is more gentle but takes 3 hours longer. The trail is now better defined and you will see signs of civilization in the form of small fences, animal tracks and sometimes human activity. The trail crosses to the right of the valley and becomes easier to descend.

The descent leads directly to Chhitkul village (3450m/11320ft). Once a remote village in the Baspa Valley, Chhitkul is now well connected by road and bus. It has, nevertheless, retained its Kinnauri charms. There is an ancient temple of a *devi* (goddess) here and several other traditional Kinnauri monuments. On reaching the village, you will almost immediately come across a monastery, the abode of the old Chhitkul Lama, a legend in himself.

The main valley extends towards Nagasti in the east (restricted at present) and is dominated by two lovely peaks, Thula and Chula, both still unclimbed. There are several treks possible from here, such as one to the Borasu Pass and another along the Shaone Gad (from Rakchham). (See Trek 15 for further information.)

Drive-out via Chhitkul to Sangla and Shimla

From Chhitkul you can travel by road (by pre-arranged transport, or by local buses) down the Baspa Valley. The drive to Sangla is beautiful and passes through a large forest near Mastarang and Rakchham. Sangla, reeling under the pressure of development, has some basic facilities available and there are a few places where you can get a square meal. There is also a beautifully located, large rest house.

From Sangla the narrow road joins the main road along the Satluj, at Karchham. From here you can return to Shimla or travel on to visit Kalpa.

KINNAURI NAMES

The naming of peaks and places in the Himalaya is a subject of serious study. The central part of Kinnaur was once called the Chini district after a village of the same name. However, *Chini* in Hindi also means China so the British changed the name in the 1940s to Kalpa, the name of an adjoining village.

Kinnaur has several dialects and each valley has its own, so much so that a Kinnauri from one valley may not even understand the language of another from a neighbouring valley. Some of the names in the area have different meanings in different places. Most of these names are appropriate to features on the ground; the locals may be illiterate but they are extremely knowledgeable about their areas and the early surveyors took this into consideration.

The Himalayan nomenclature combines many factors, such as language, location, local legends, beliefs and religion. Given below are the meanings of some of the names in Kinnaur.

Mani, or prayer stones, in Kinnaur are erected as offerings to the gods.

Villages/Others

Shurtingting	*Shurting*: a type of grass; *ting*: place of.
Lambar	*Lam*: on the way; *bar*: to stay – a place to stay on the way.
Thangi	*Thanen*: a place high up. The village is situated far above the river.
Kuno	In a corner. The village is in the corner of a nala.
Charang	Related to the Chewrang province of Tibet.
Kanam	Named after the legend of a lama who was given a stone shaped like a similar-sounding letter in the Hindi alphabet ('k' in English).

Rivers/Nalas/Valleys

Tirung	*Ti*: running water; *rung*: heap of stones – water running over a heap of stones. The river is rough and with a stony bed.
Tidong	*Ti*: running water, *dong*: where it falls.
Nisang	Hidden. This valley cannot be seen from the main road.
Mangla	*Marla*: a fertile valley.
Racho	A fork, like the two horns of an animal. A nala forking into two.

Peaks

Rang	Any mountain.
Rangrik	Made by a god, based on legend.
Phawra	*Phowar*: a place where big animals dwell. As several animals are found on this side valley of Tirung, the peak at its head is named Phawrarang.
Zangshu	*Zang*: gold; *shu*: place. A golden peak (in the Rupi valley).

Passes

Lamkhaga	*Lam*: many routes; *khaga*: pass. A pass with many routes.
Chhotkhaga	*Chhot*: smaller. A smaller pass.
Khimokoul	*Khim*: dog; *koul*: crossed in winter. The name of a pass to Tibet. A Tibetan dog, left behind by a caravan, crossed over this pass in winter.
Yamrang La	A regular pass.
Gunirang La	*Guni*: winter; *rang*: mountain. A winter mountain pass.
Mangshu La	*Mangshu*: hidden. A pass that is not easily seen.

TREK 14: THE SORANG VALLEY

Few valleys in Kinnaur are relatively unknown to visitors as the National Highway runs along the left bank of the Satluj River. However, to reach the valleys on the right bank you have to cross the river, which involves steep descents and ascents, and as a result some of these valleys have been more or less left alone. The Sorang Valley is one such valley where very few visitors have gone, despite the construction of the road and the fact that the traditional Hindustan–Tibet trail passes through Bara Kamba village.

There are several peaks, Kokshane, Zangshu and Gushu Pishu, which could keep climbers busy for years. Although low by Himalayan standards (rising to 5800m/19030ft), these peaks offer serious technical climbing challenges. With an easy approach, without any restrictions whatsoever, general availability of porters and supplies and lovely rest houses to stay in, this area is extremely enticing to trekkers and climbers, and could be regarded as the Himalayan equivalent to the European Alps.

TREK ESSENTIALS

LENGTH 2 weeks; 70km (43 miles). Walking from Chaura: 4 days to Rakpatang, 2 days to Palit, 3 days to Bara Kamba. Walk-out via Nyugalsari.

ACCESS Kalka (near Chandigarh) then Shimla by train from Delhi. Drive 172km (107 miles) to Sarahan. Chaura is 23km (14 miles) further on the Hindustan–Tibet road.

HIGHEST POINT Above Palit 4100m (13450ft). Passes: Dumti, 914m (3000ft).

GRADE Medium, with a trek on some unknown terrain.

SEASONS Mid-May to late October.

RESTRICTIONS None.

FURTHER OPTIONS Trek to Parvati Valley (Trek 19, page 127).

Chaura

As for other treks in the Kinnaur, you have to travel from Delhi to Kalka by rail and then to Shimla by the Hill Railway. Follow national highway No. 22 (the road along the Satluj River) until you reach Sarahan (2165m/7100ft). This is a lovely place to stay and a good place to acclimatise in the comfort of a rest house. The entire Kand Mahadev Range (including the Sorang Valley) is visible from here. From Sarahan, drive another 23km (14 miles) to Chaura (1460m/4790ft), the starting point for the trek. You will need to make arrangements in advance to hire mules or porters.

Chaura to Rakpatang

From Chaura, a broad trail descends rather steeply (500m over 2km/16405ft in 1¼ miles) to the Satluj River. Cross the bridge and start the 12-km (7½-mile) climb to Rupi village, which can be fairly strenuous, particularly during hot summer afternoons. It is safer to follow the longer trail leading to the village instead of the short cut that villagers follow when pressed for time. About a kilometre away from the village there is a well-maintained rest house (2350m/7710ft). Situated amidst a forest, it is a historic place where the entries in the log book date from 1915, and it has been described as the second best rest house in Kinnaur (the best being in Kalpa). Spend an extra day here if you can to walk in the forest, visit the village and climb to the ridgeline to the west. If you have even more time, you could ascend one of the smaller peaks, such as Jhandodya (4044m/13268ft), which is a hard day's walk from here.

Follow the trail that leads up to the ridge from the Rupi Rest House. It passes through lovely forest and reaches the ridge known as Dumti Dhar

THE SORANG VALLEY

(3100m/10170ft) in about three hours. The trail leads down the east side into the Sorang Valley, through an equally beautiful virgin forest. Camp near the Sorang Gad on the site of a dried-out lake in the valley floor.

The trail continues along the Sorang Gad on the right bank. About 2km (1¼ miles) upstream you will reach a prominent fork in the valley, the camping-ground of Dumti (2705m/8875ft). The Sorang Gad continues northwards while an unnamed nala turns northeast. This leads to the Kamba Khango Pass and, by a complicated route, into the Parvati Valley.

The Kand Mahadev Range from the Sorang Valley.

Travelling from Dumti along the Sorang Gad, the valley takes several turns and the forest gives way to shrubs. After 5km (3 miles), you will reach an enormous cave, Rakpatang ('the place of the cave'), which has a large camping ground at its entrance. This is an ideal site, especially for observing wildlife. There are black bears in the upper valley and you may also come across a rare musk deer. Amid a forest of apricot trees, pines and deodars on both banks, several birds such as the monal, vultures and the Himalayan eagle can be observed from this cave.

Rakpatang to Palit

Trek along the *shikari* (hunter's) trail (not well-defined but easy to find and follow) up the valley on the right bank, or if there is snow, on the central snow-tongues. After climbing about 600m (1968ft), the snow-capped mountains of Kinnaur in the south come into view, particularly the shapely peak of Hansbeshan (5240m/17191ft).

Ringvichina (3435/11270ft), another cave used by the *shikaris* is 6km (3½ miles) further on. It is a good place to camp near and observe the vista of peaks at the head of the valley, the highest being Kokshane (5625m/18455ft) and Zangshu (5695m/18684ft). The entire ridge is full of several challenging peaks. From the camp at Ringvichina you could climb to the ridge on the west and follow an ancient, difficult trail along the crest to descend directly to Rupi village.

Palit (3835m/12580ft) is 6km (3½ miles) further up the valley where three glaciers meet. The central glacier leads to the foot of Kokshane, and the one on the right leads to the Zangshu group.

THE SORANG VALLEY

- Parvati Glacier
- 5260m (17258ft)
- Zangshu
- Kokshane 5780m (18964ft)
- 4560m (14961ft)
- Zangsu Glacier
- Pishu 5672m (18610ft)
- Palit
- Kamba Khango
- Dea
- 5622m (18446ft)
- Kati 5185m (17012ft)
- Ringvichina
- Rakpatang
- Dumti
- Kut
- Dumti Dhar
- Sorang Dogri
- Rupi
- Sorang Gad
- Bara Kamba
- Chaura
- Satluj River
- Nyugalsari
- Taranda
- Jeori
- Solding
- Sarahan
- Termi 3978m (13052ft)

0 1 2 3 4 5 km
0 3 miles

PEAK: HANSBESHAN

As the road descends to the Satluj Valley from Narkanda, a steep pinnacle is visible in the distance. This is the peak of Hansbeshan, rising south of the Srikand Dhar. This shapely mountain stands on the ridge dividing the Satluj and Pabar valleys.

From the base of Hansbeshan Peak a col leads to the southern valleys. From here onwards, follow the steep ridge to the summit. The peak is steep and rocky. In June lots of firm snow may be encountered, while during the autumn season there will be plenty of scrambles and some steep rock sections to be climbed.

Base Camp

From the National Highway at Solding, a side road travels 17km (11 miles) to Nachar, a small village with a rest house. From here, a trail leads through beautiful forests to Nacharchot Dogri, 6km (3½ miles) from Nachar, a small village with several fields and summer houses. Set up Base Camp here (2840m/9320ft).

North Ridge

From Nacharchot Dogri, the trail climbs steeply to a ridge. As you ascend, the views all around open up. Camp on the flat ground above the ridge (3690m/12110ft). From here, the shapely peak of Hansbeshan is seen rising in the south.

North Face

On the next day, traverse the slopes to a prominent col seen to the south. Camp at the foot of the col (4400m/14440ft). From this camp you can soon reach the col, and then follow the ridge. The climb is steep and complicated. The ridge has pinnacles which will have to be negotiated carefully. At about halfway the ridge drops and reaches another mini-col. Climb the highly exposed final pinnacle to reach the summit.

Descend with care as the ground is a mixture of loose scree and steep rocks. Once back on the ridge, the col can be easily reached. Return by the same route.

CLIMB ESSENTIALS

SUMMIT Hansbeshan Peak (5240m/17191ft).
PRINCIPAL CAMPS Base Camp at Nacharchot Dogri, plus two high camps, one on the ridge, one at the foot of the summit.
GRADE Medium with steep rock climbs near the summit.
MAP REFERENCE See sketch-map Trek 14 (page 109), Sorang Valley, Kinnaur.

The north face of Hansbeshan (5240m/1719ft) with both the col and the mini-col clearly visible.

But the most exciting views are to the west, where a steep broken glacier leads to the Gushu Pishu peaks. These peaks are named after demons and to date there has been only one recorded ascent. At 5672m (18608ft), they are not particularly high but to climb them requires good technical skill. There are many climbs and walks possible from Ringvichina Camp and you could easily spend a week or more undertaking forays into side valleys, attempting peaks and traversing ridges. For a less physical challenge you could spend time observing the panoramas and the occasional wildlife.

Palit to Bara Kamba

Depending on the snow conditions it is possible to retrace your route the 14km (9 miles) back to Dumti camping ground. Alternatively you could follow the Sorang Gad down along the left bank across boulder-strewn ground. The trail continues along the left bank as the Sorang Gad becomes a torrent and it is not possible to cross it. The trail is winding, with ups and downs, but always through virgin forest. There are few camping grounds available en route and the best one is after 8km (5 miles) near Upper Sorang Dogri (2400m/7875ft). This is a wide open ground used by shepherds. The next day you will reach Sorang Dogri (2340m/7678ft) on a village trail. A trail leads across a bridge to Rupi in the adjoining valley. However it is easier to continue the valley descent to the village of Bara Kamba (2000m/6560ft), 6km (3½ miles) further on. This village has spectacular views of the Satluj Valley, a lovely temple with wooden architecture, many apricot farms, and a small forest rest house to stay in. Bara Kamba was once on the old trade route, traces of which can still been seen today on the way to Chhota Kamba village.

Drive-Out: Bara Kamba to Nyugalsari to Shimla

The walk does not finish at Bara Kamba. At first the village trail descends very steeply for 1000m (3280ft) to the banks of the Satluj. Cross the river by a traditional *jhula* (cradle) which is sent across on a cable with pulleys. There is an official attendant (usually) to pull a person across.

On the other bank, climb the steep 2km (1¼ miles) to the small town of Nyugalsari, which is 400m (1312ft) higher. Nyugalsari is on the National Highway and transport is available to return to Kalka (via Rampur-Bushahr, Narkanda, Shimla) for trains to Delhi. The road east leads to Rekong Peo (via Kharchham) for other destinations in Kinnaur.

On a vantage point near Hansbeshan Peak, Kinnaur.

THE HINDUSTAN-TIBET ROAD

Kinnauris have always travelled to Tibet for trade and several easy passes lead into Tibet from the valleys here. In days gone by, locals carried wool, cloth and wooden products in exchange for Tibetan salt, gold and other items. This trade developed over the centuries but was stopped by the Indo-China war of 1962. The route has been recently opened again to locals.

Journeys were made along the Hindustan (India) to Tibet Road, a six-foot wide track specially built for commerce, which started from the British headquarters at Shimla, and crossed many ridges to reach Narkanda. From here the trail dropped steeply into the Satluj Valley and followed the course of the river. With intervening ridges and cliffs, the trail climbed up steeply in places and then down again to the river. The most famous of such climbs was on the Rogi Cliffs near Kalpa. The path was so narrow and steep that some drowsy memsahibs were reported to have fallen off their mules.

Rest houses (dak bungalows) were built at convenient places along the road for rest at night. Most of these have wonderful views and are a delight to stay in. Lastly, the path crossed the Satluj River near Puh to climb across the Shipki La and enter Tibet. The present-day road follows a similar alignment with the same wonderful views.

PEAK: SRIKAND MAHADEV

The Srikand Mahadev Range, named after Shiva, is a long range starting from the north of Rampur town, and parallel to the Satluj river. It is the central range of southern Kinnaur and its highest point is Srikand Mahadev Peak. This straddles a high ridge and is seen as a high point on it with several equally higher points.

There are many approaches to this peak, but the best one, which is a good climb, is from the south. Follow a steep, faint trail to the northeast ridge then a long traverse to the summit. In June there may be lots of firm snow. In the autumn some steep sections of rock will have to be climbed.

CLIMB ESSENTIALS

SUMMIT Srikand Mahadev (5227m/17150 ft)
PRINCIPAL CAMPS Base Camp: Sogori (3200m/10500ft), High Camp 4500m (14760ft).
GRADE Easy, long ridge walk.
MAP REFERENCE See sketch-map for Trek 14 (page 109), Sorang Valley.

Base Camp

From Rampur-Bushahr go ahead to Jyura. Cross the Satluj and enter the valley in the north. A steep trail leads to Phancha, a large village. From here a shepherds' trail leads north to the head of the valley, Sogori. Set up Base Camp here (3200m/10500ft).

Northeast Ridge and North Face

From Base Camp the trail climbs steeply towards the ridgeline. The climb is a good scramble. There is hardly any path here and without a guide it will be hard to stick to the trail. Set up High Camp a little below the ridge on the flat, rocky ground (4500m/14760ft).

Next day the col on the ridge can be reached. Follow the ridge to the southwest and after a long, tiring climb you will reach the highest point, Srikand Mahadev (5227m/17150ft).

The view is in all directions and peaks of the Parvati Valley, Jorkanden and the Rangrik Rang group can be seen rising over the Satluj Valley. In the southeast is Hansbeshan and surrounding peaks.

Descend by the same route to Phancha village and to Jyura the day after.

The Srikand Mahadev Range with its highest peak in the centre.

TREK 15: ACROSS SHAONE GAD TO GARHWAL

This is an exploratory trek for those adventurous enough to discover their own trail over unknown terrain. Once there were several passes used by shepherds and traders that linked the Baspa Valley of Kinnaur with those of the Garhwal in the south. This was a far quicker route for trade and community contact than the (present) circuitous Hindustan–Tibet road. However, with the development of the road these passes fell into disuse, and few are crossed nowadays. For an adventurous trekker, this is an opportunity to follow a trail that might have been known in bygone times but is now unfamiliar, almost alien territory. Map-reading skills and/or a guide who knows the terrain are essential.

TREK ESSENTIALS

LENGTH Two weeks; 83km (52 miles). Walking from Rakchham: 3 days to Upper Shaone Thach, 2 days across Lamea Pass, 2 days to Lewari, 2 days to Dehra Dun.

ACCESS Kalka (near Chandigarh) then Shimla by train from Delhi. Drive 224km (139 miles) to Sangla, then 14km (9 miles) to Rakchham.

HIGHEST POINT 5100m (16730ft) above Lamea Pass. Passes: Lamea, 4920m (16140ft), Ratangdi Ghati, 4820m (15810ft).

GRADE Difficult.

SEASONS Mid-June to late October.

RESTRICTIONS None.

FURTHER OPTIONS Combine with trek to Charang Ghati (Trek 13, page 103) or ascents in and around the Shaone Gad Valley. High-altitude lakes in the Garhwal region.

Rakchham

Rakchham is 14km (9 miles) from Sangla on the road to Chhitkul. Sangla is the focal point of the Baspa Valley. There is a small rest house here but if you wish to camp in Rakchham, there are several sites near the river, or cross the bridge to the left bank. There are also some excellent sites about 4km (2 miles) ahead on the trail in a lovely forest. You should walk to Chhitkul to acclimatise before starting on the main trek – it has some fascinating temple architecture and the monastery of the Chhitkul Lama.

The lama, Sonam Gyatso, is nearly 100 years old. In his younger days he was a great traveller and explored areas in Zanskar, Ladakh and Tibet. While crossing the Charang Ghati Pass right above his village, he was trapped in a snowstorm and subsequently lost his toes due to frostbite. Today the lama spends time in *puja* (religious ceremonies) and meditation and is a respected figure in the Kinnaur valleys.

Rakchham to the Upper Shaone Thach

The trail starts from the Rakchham Rest House (3100m/10170ft). Follow the river towards the village and cross a bridge to reach the left bank. There is a wide track along the river, leading 4km (2 miles) upstream. There are some beautiful meadows on the way and a lovely forest at the end, almost opposite Mastarang village on the right bank. Turn into the valley towards the right, past a small house and a giant rock. The trail ascends the right slopes of a broad valley. It appears rather gradual and short but the climb is exhausting and stretches for six long kilometres (3½ miles). The valley flattens out at the head and it is possible to camp here, about 2km (1¼ miles) before a scree scramble (3850m/12630ft).

The valley then opens up to a beautiful grassy plain, known as the Rathiya Thach ('lower grazing ground'). You can still see the steel frame of an abandoned bunker, constructed by the Geological Survey of India, which has done a lot of work in

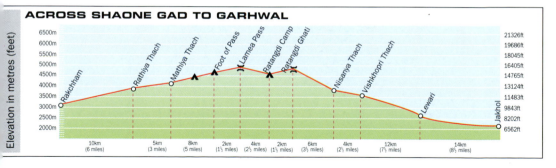

ACROSS SHAONE GAD TO GARHWAL

ACROSS SHAONE GAD TO GARHWAL

Charang Ghati Pass

Rakchham Mastarang Chhitkul

Sangla Baspa River

Rakchham
5006m
(16425ft) Rathiya Thach

Mathiya Thach

Camp Kimilay Pass

Camp

Nalgan Pass Lamea Pass

Ratangdi Camp Ratangdi Ghati

Nisanya Thatch
Vishkhopri Thatch

Rupin River

Supin River

Lewari

Jakhol

Doni

0   5   10 km

0   5 miles Sankhri

A trekker makes his way through fields near Rakchham.

this area studying the glacier and the terrain of the region in great detail. A large amount of geological data is now available on this valley.

Ahead, several streams have to be crossed and a small hill climbed. Above this is a wide open space, the last major camping area before the pass, known as the Mathiya Thach ('upper grazing ground') (4150m/13615ft). Many peaks are visible to the north and the Bilare Bange Glacier is to the east. Several peaks rise above this glacier, the highest touching 5555m (18226ft).

Spend a day here to acclimatise, because from here on the trail rises steeply to the pass. The small glacier in the southeast leads to the old pass, Singha Ghati, now in disuse. The approaches to this pass are broken and you would have to cross steep rock faces and ice-cliffs on both sides. But you can climb up on to a glacial moraine ridge towards it for a better view, becoming acclimatised in the process. Small hikes or scrambles are also possible up the many small surrounding hills which rise to 5200m (17061ft).

Across Lamea Pass

Singha Ghati was once the main pass used by the people of Kinnaur and Garhwal for inter-village travel. After its blockage the enterprising villagers opened a new pass from a side valley, called the Lamea Pass (literally, 'the longer pass').

From the Upper Shaone Camp at the Mathiya Thach, proceed southwards to the top of the ridge of the glacial moraine. Keep to the left of the main nala of the Shaone Glacier. There are huge cairns on the ridge and some on the trail. After the first cairn follow a faint path along the ridge. From a small col in the ridge a short distance ahead three valleys are visible. The one on the left goes nowhere, the central valley leads to the Singha Ghati (now in disuse), while the valley to the right (southwest) leads to the Lamea Pass, approached by a route that goes across the central valley.

Descend to the central valley and cross several tributaries of the main river. On the other side of the river is a huge moraine with large rocks. The trail is now almost non-existent and you have to cross these 'boulder-fields' by intuition into the side valley. On the left bank of the river there is a faint trail that gradually climbs towards a major depression in the ridge ahead. There are several more boulder-strewn fields to be crossed.

Before the final climb starts you will reach a small grassy camping ground near a stream. Either camp here or about a kilometre ahead on ground that is uncomfortable but is almost at the foot of the pass, enabling you to make an early start the following day.

The Baspa River passes through meadows near Rakchham, beneath the peaks of Shaone Gad.

The way to the pass is steep and uncharted. The moraine ridge ends abruptly at the foot of the pass and you then have to scramble 200m (656ft) up a near-vertical, unstable rocky surface to reach the cairns as there is no trail at all.

The view from Lamea Pass (4920m/16140ft) is beautiful in all directions, but most of all towards Kinnaur, where the smaller peaks of the Charang Ghati Ridge can be seen. Immediately below, the verdant Rupin Valley stretches invitingly to the southeast. If you decide to go this way, follow the Rupin River until just short of its meeting-point with the Tons River near Naitwar, a long 5 to 6 day trek. However by crossing the second pass, Ratangdi Ghati, you will arrive in the Supin Valley and can reach the road-head in 2 days.

To cross the Ratangdi Ghati, climb along the ridge on the east (left) from the Lamea Pass. It leads to a small open ground and a flat ridge. Descend the steep boulder-field ahead by moving diagonally to the left. The prominent depression seen on the ridge to the southeast (left) is the Ratangdi Ghati. Once you are about 1000m (3300ft) lower and have traversed about 2km (1¼ miles), you will come to two vast fields. One field has a lake and the other is a camping ground (4630m/15190ft), from where you can get a good view of the Rupin Valley as well as see some of the smaller peaks on the Ratangdi Ghati.

Across Ratangdi Ghati to Lewari

From the camp start early and find your way across the boulder-field on the left, towards the prominent notch (there is no defined trail). After a short scramble and then a descent (2km/1¼ miles) you will reach Ratangdi Ghati (4820m/15810ft). It is rocky but broader than the Lamea Pass, and is the divide between the Rupin (west) and the Supin (east) valleys. The former is in Kinnaur while the latter is in Garhwal.

From the pass, descend to the eastern valley.

VISHKHOPRI THACH

The *thaches* or *bugiyals* (grazing grounds) of the Garhwal valleys are the most beautiful places to camp on. They lie either beside river banks or on higher grounds, situated amid lovely, green, grassy slopes. During the grazing season, they are occupied by local shepherds, who unfailingly pay an annual visit to, and have traditional rights over, the grazing grounds. These friendly people generally come from different villages in the area and are not nomads in the strict sense of the word.

Vishkhopri Thach in the Supin Valley is very green, lush, and thickly covered with flowers. The name itself implies that the place is so full of fragrance you feel intoxicated. (*vish*: poison, *khopri*: brain). It lies at the junction of the Gogoyi Gad and the Supin River. On the western ridge lies the high-altitude Bhadrasar Lake, a two-day trek away. Continue along the ridge for another two days, and you will reach Lewari village.

In the east, a trail leads along the Gogoyi Gad to Devkira Pass (2 days). It then descends to Obra Gad and crosses another small pass to reach the well-known Har-ki-Dun Valley. The shepherds' trails that lead you there pass beautiful grazing thaches, one after the other. These are typical examples of what the *thaches* in Vishkhopri are like.

After a hard day's trekking you can set up camp at the foot of Ratangdi Ghati.

into a roaring river by the time it reaches Lewari (2700m/8860ft), 12km (7½ miles) further ahead. Along the trail there are beautiful grazing grounds which lead to a wonderful forest. The trail, though mainly descending, has many tiring ups and downs. Cross a bridge over the river about a kilometre before you come to the village of Lewari. It is best to stay in the school building or in its compound as everywhere else is crowded. Lewari is not often visited by outsiders and the friendly villagers will accommodate trekkers in their houses.

If there is still time, carry on for 2km (1¼ miles), to a steep descent which leads back to the Supin River. There is a lovely, isolated camping ground right next to the river.

Jakhol–Sankhri to Dehra Dun

From Lewari, take the *Chhe footi* path (a six-foot wide rough road; such inter-village roads were built as government community projects). This is a brilliant walk, gradually descending all the way. There is one tea shop along the road, at the junction of the Obra Gad and the Supin. The *Chhe footi* leads to the Obra Gad, another beautiful trekking area.

About 2km (1¼ miles) beyond the tea shop, cross a bridge over the Supin. The trail then climbs rather steeply to Jakhol village, which is situated about 1000m (3280ft) above the river. The valley is broad and you can stay either at the Forest Rest House in the village (100m/330ft higher up) or camp near the road where there is a water tank.

Jakhol is linked by an unsurfaced road to Sankhri (19km/12 miles) which is the starting point for several buses and the trek to Har-ki-Dun. There is a daily bus service to Jakhol in fair weather, and private jeeps are available, whose costs can be shared on a per seat basis. If transport is arranged in advance it may be possible to reach Dehra Dun the same night, as there is a tarmac road from Sankhri to Dehra Dun, generally in good condition.

There are rest houses at Sankhri, Naitwar, and Purola and the hill station of Mussoorie where you can stay on the way to Dehra Dun. From here there are several means available, by rail and road, to reach New Delhi or elsewhere.

The rocky terrain soon gives way to grass and a typical Garhwal landscape emerges, lush and green. Keep traversing towards the southeast (right) until the trail reaches the end of the moraine ridges. The broad valley of the Supin River can be seen at the bottom. Do not descend too quickly and keep traversing towards the right. The steep grassy slopes seen on the ridge are easy to cross as the grass-tufts are firm. Make sure you stay above a huge break (caused by a major landslide) in the nala. The trail then gradually descends and finally reaches the Nisanya Thach at the bottom, beside the main river.

After the rocky traverses over the two passes, this place is paradise. There are lovely, grassy meadows and pretty flowers to admire. This is truly shepherd country and you can follow a trail comfortably down the valley. There are places to camp almost everywhere and you could spend a couple of days exploring the head of the valley in the east, which leads to the Khimloga Pass, now disused.

Though it is tempting to camp at the Nisanya Thach, it is even better to continue about 4km (2 miles) down the valley to Vishkhopri Thach. On the way, notice the huge, strange-looking rocks called *Bhoti-ka-dera*. According to legend, a Tibetan king stayed here and these rocks are supposed to have been carved in his memory. Vishkhopri Thach (see box, page 115) is a beautiful place, at the junction of routes to nearby valleys.

On the last day of the actual trek the trail descends steeply, following the course of the Supin River, which starts as a small nala and turns

TREK 16: INDRAHAR PASS-DHAULADHAR

The Dhauladhar, which rises steeply from the plains of Punjab, is a great mountain getaway from Delhi and it takes only a few hours to reach the foothills. This range, though comparatively small by Himalayan standards, offers some exhilarating trekking and wonderful panoramic views of beautiful sunsets over the Punjab plains. For climbers these small peaks offer challenges that could keep them busy for years to come.

Mcleodganj (Dharamsala) to Indrahar Pass

Dharamsala was the district headquarters of the British administration of Kangra, Kullu and Lahaul until Indian independence in 1947. Today it is growing in importance due to the presence of the Dalai Lama, the exiled Tibetan spiritual leader, and many Tibetans have settled at Mcleodganj (1640m/5380ft), 10km (6 miles) to the north of Dharamsala. Several places in and around Dharamsala are named after the British generals who commanded troops here, such as General McLeod, by adding *ganj* (market) after their names.

The trail to the Dhauladhar Range begins northwards from the main bazaar in Mcleodganj. The Western Himalayan Mountaineering Institute (Manali) has an outpost here in a bungalow named Swargashram, which is worth a visit as the team who run it know the trails and passes of the Dhauladhar Range well. The well-defined trail leads to Triund (2975m/9760ft), 10km (6 miles) ahead. Though it is a wide trail purpose-built for visitors, it is steep and without any source of water, so you should make an early start.

Triund is on open ground on a ridge with a small rest house. If you wish to spend the night here you will need to make a reservation in advance with the Dharamsala Forest Department as this rest house is very popular with Indian trekkers, but there are also some good camping spots nearby.

Next day the trail climbs steeply to a ridge in the west and follows it to a small camping ground, Laka Got (3200m/10500ft), 5km (3 miles) away. Spend a night here to acclimatise because the trail then climbs very steeply towards the Indrahar Pass. The pass is seen as a deep notch in the centre of the southern ridge. Climb on the faint trail. On the way to the pass you will see an enormous wall on your right, the south face of Mon Peak. Try to cross the pass in a day as the camping place en route, a cave, is very uncomfortable and water is scarce. Lahesh Cave (3550m/11650ft) is 4km (2½ miles) nearer the pass, and can accommodate almost 40 people.

Indrahar Pass (4316m/14160ft) is 4km (2½ miles) further and offers wonderful views in all

TREK ESSENTIALS

LENGTH 10 days; 58km (36 miles). Walking from Dharamsala: 3 days to Indrahar Pass, 3 days to Kharamukh.

ACCESS Train to Pathankot from Delhi. Dharamsala is 90km (56 miles) by road from here. Mcleodganj is the upper part of Dharamsala. Occasional flights to airport at Gaggal, 13km (8 miles) away.

HIGHEST POINT Indrahar Pass (4316m/14160ft). Passes: Indrahar.

GRADE Medium.

SEASONS Late May to end June; October to end November.

RESTRICTIONS None.

FURTHER OPTIONS Trek across several other passes on the Dhauladhar Range. Joins Trek 17 (see page 121).

Crossing the bridge near Chanaota.

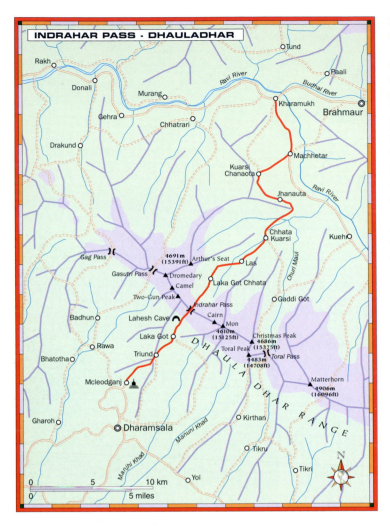

INDRAHAR PASS - DHAULADHAR

Chhata (3880m/12730ft), where you can camp.

From this camp on the north of the pass many climbs and scrambles are possible, and you can set up a base camp here. Towards the north is Camel Peak, with its distinct hump. Other prominent peaks include the twin peaks of Two-Gun (4469m/14663ft), Dromedary, Slab Peak and Arthur's Seat, all of similar heights. A serrated ridge called Arthur's Footstool is also inviting. All these peaks can be climbed in a day from the camp at the pass.

Towards the south, Cairn and Mon Peak (4610m/15125ft) are challenging summits, while across the valley Christmas Peak (4686m/15375ft), Toral Peak (4483m/14709ft) and some others are accessible. The 'Dhauladhar Matterhorn' has two of the highest summits of the Dhauladhar Range at 4971m (16310ft) and 4906m (16097ft) respectively. All these peaks are moderately difficult to ascend if they are approached from the base camp at the north of the pass, but from the south they provide a formidable challenge, particularly in the snow and ice which prevail until late June.

Indrahar Pass to Kharamukh

Camp near the pass then continue the descent for 6km (4 miles) to a small shelter called Las (3000m/9842ft), This is a natural shelter under an overhanging rock used by local shepherds, with an open ground nearby. You will see some excel-

directions. You could be standing on snow yet the Punjab plains simmering in the heat may be visible to the south. To the north several peaks of the Kishtwar area can be seen, including Brammah Peak (6416m/21051ft) and Sickle Moon Peak (6574m/21569ft).

A 3km (2 miles) descent, initially very steep, leads to flat ground, locally known as Laka Got

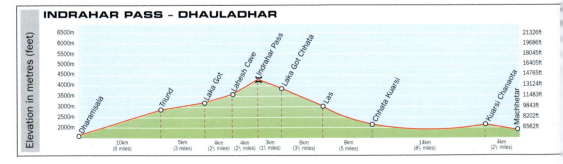

INDRAHAR PASS - DHAULADHAR

Brammah (left) and Sickle Moon peaks seen from the Indrahar Pass on the Dhauladhar.

lent views of the Mani Mahesh Kailash and surrounding peaks. Continue to descend. The trail becomes confusing at this point as several other trails cross its path, but you should be able to reach Chhata Kuarsi, the only village in this valley, 8km (5 miles) further on without too much trouble (2223m/7300ft). Chhata Kuarsi is a small but beautiful village, and in its centre a group of houses have balconies that overlook the main square.

On the last day of the trek, make an early start to walk 14km (9 miles) through lovely countryside to Kuarsi Chanaota village (2200m/7220ft). This is a tiring route as you will have to descend and then climb steeply to the ridge in the west, crossing a small pass on the way. The trail then descends steeply through fields and a dense forest until it comes to the village. To reach the road walk 4km (2 miles) further to Machhetar (1900m/6230ft), where there is a rest house and a bus service to Kharamukh.

Drive-Out via Brahmaur

If you have time to spare, the beautiful temple complex at Brahmaur (16km/10 miles) is well worth a day's visit. Otherwise buses and taxis are available to take you to Chamba (48km/30 miles) and Pathankot (122km/76 miles) for trains to Delhi.

COLONEL ROBERTS

Colonel JOM 'Jimmy' Roberts is generally regarded as the father of modern-day organized trekking. From 1937 to 1940, while a young army officer, Roberts was stationed in the Dalhousie Cantonment near Dharamsala. After the Friday evening parade, with like-minded companions, he would trek up towards one of the many passes on the Dhauladhar Range. After spending the weekends trekking and climbing, the party would return to a waiting staff car on Monday morning and report for parade.

Roberts explored many places in Ladakh, Spiti and Nepal, climbing several peaks in the process. Later in life he made Nepal his home and promoted the organized tourism that has now become the norm.

PEAK: MON, TWO-GUN AND OTHERS IN DHAULADHAR

The small range of the Dhauladhar contains many challenging peaks of about 4600m (15000ft). The range can be approached fairly quickly by Himalayan standards (there are no foothills to cross), but the climb to the ridgeline is very steep and acclimatisation is vital. Once on Indrahar Pass it is possible to reach several peaks by their northern approaches.

The route to the summit of Arthur's Seat.

Base Camp

From Mcleodganj climb the steep trail to Triund and stay the night there. Then trek past Laka Got to stay in a large cave. Indrahar Pass can be reached on the next day. There is a small camp-

Two-Gun Peak's rocky and scree slopes present a challenge.

ing ground with a wonderful view to the north of the pass, where you can set up Base Camp.

Standing on the Indrahar Pass, to the immediate left in the northwest stands a group of small peaks called Riflehorn. Next to them is the Two-Gun peak, a small pinnacle. Both can be climbed in a day. The climb is never too difficult but always challenging as you will encounter several sections of scree and rocky sections. Further left rises a sharp peak, Arthur's Seat.

On the right, in the southeast, is the main peak of this range, Mon, a shapely snow peak. From Base Camp descend to the vast depression in the southeast. By traversing this field you will reach the base of Mon Peak. Follow the steep slopes with great care to the final sections. Descend carefully by the same route.

From Base Camp you can attempt several other peaks of similar heights and moderate difficulty: Cairn Camel, Dromedary and others.

CLIMB ESSENTIALS

SUMMIT Two-Gun (4496m/14750ft), Arthur's Seat (4691m/15390ft) and Mon Peak (4610m/15125ft).

PRINCIPAL CAMPS Base Camp 100m (305ft) further down the Ravi Valley side of the Indrahar Pass (4316m/14160ft).

GRADE These peaks offer good rock climbs and ropes and gear are required. Beware of loose rocks.

MAP REFERENCE See sketch-map Trek 16, Dhauladhar.

TREK 17: MANI MAHESH KAILASH CIRCUIT

This is a beautiful trek in a remote area. Chamba Kailash (5656m/18557ft), though not particularly high, is a sacred peak and the Mani Mahesh Lake at its foot is visited by many pilgrims. Hundreds of pilgrims will be around during the Dusherra festival in October and for serious trekkers the trail is best avoided then. The best way to enjoy the area is to circumambulate the mountain by crossing the Chobu Pass on the shoulder of the peak. A guide and a proper map are essential.

Brahmaur to the Chobu Pass

Brahmaur (2220m/7300ft), in the Ravi River Valley, is known for its exquisite temple complex. There is a rough road from Brahmaur eastwards to Hadsar (13km/8 miles) (1980m/6500ft) but it may be best for acclimatisation to walk this distance (the road is scary and the jeeps dilapidated). There is a small rest house about a kilometre before Hadsar, just above the main road. From here proceed along the main valley and follow the broad village trail for 13km (8 miles) to Kugti along the left bank of the Kugti nala with several exhausting ups and downs, until you reach the beautifully located Kugti rest house (2590m/8500ft). The main village is about 1km (⅔ mile) ahead.

The next day descend to the river, cross a bridge over the Kugti nala and enter the Bhujla Valley to the south. There is a steep climb to enter the valley but then the trail climbs gradually along the right bank for 6km (3½ miles). Camp 7km (4 miles) further on, on the vast open ground along the river (2960m/9700ft). The next day follow the nala, gaining height quickly. Several peaks are visible towards the north and the view of Kugti Pass and the peaks on the Ravi–Chenab divide are wonderful. Though small, these peaks are sharp and inviting for climbers. The next camp is 7km (4½ miles) further at the junction where the Kailash nala and Nikora nala meet (3500m/11500ft).

Chobu Pass

The traditional route for locals is to cross the pass from the Bhujla Nala Camp, climbing about 1520m

TREK ESSENTIALS

LENGTH 10 days; 88km (55 miles). Walking from Brahmaur: 3 days to Chobu Pass, 2 days across pass, 2 days walk-out via Mani Mahesh Lake.

ACCESS Train from Delhi to Pathankot. Drive to Chamba, 122km (76 miles) then Brahmaur, 64km (40 miles). A rough road leads to Hadsar, 13km (8 miles), from where the trek begins.

HIGHEST POINT Chobu Pass, 4940m (16200ft). Passes: Chobu.

GRADE Medium.

SEASONS Late June to mid-November.

RESTRICTIONS None.

FURTHER OPTIONS Trek across Kalicho Pass from Kugti into the Chenab Valley.

(5000ft) and descending in a day. But for trekkers it is best to use the small shelter before the pass or camp on one of the many open spaces available on the way. The trail now thins out and a guide is essential for locating the pass. Climb about 600m (2000ft), proceeding more and more towards the right to the walls enclosing the valley (6km/3½ miles). The view of the south face of Kailash is magnificent. There are rough shelters near the walls, or you can camp nearby (4330m/14200ft).

Next day start very early as you are likely to encounter snow as you near the pass, particularly during the pre-monsoon season. Traverse the wall until you reach a prominent gap after 2km (1¼ miles). This is the Chobu Pass (4940m/16200ft).

MANI MAHESH KAILASH CIRCUIT

MANI MAHESH KAILASH CIRCUIT

0 1 2 3 4 5 km
0   3 miles

Chobia
Chobia Nala
Dugi
Kugti
Kao
Paali
Phat
Budhal River
Hadsar
Budhal River
Bhujla
Brahmaur
Dancho
5656m
(18557ft)
Mani Mahesh Lake
Kailash
Sari Got
Chobu Pass
Nala Junction
M A N I
M A H E S H   D H A R
Ravi River
Kuehr
Kala
Holi
Gataunda
Dharadi
N

The south face of Chamba Kailash from the Chobu Pass.

On the other side there is a vast open ground and peaks are visible in all directions.

For the descent from the pass follow your guide carefully. Keep to the right and do not go anywhere near the centre of the gully for the first 200m (650ft). A steep slope on the right of the gully (as you look down the slope) is where the trail is, which leads to the broad valley, and after a while a better trail emerges. Now you are in the western valley and the Kailash peak looks different but equally frightening. Set up camp after 6km (3½ miles) at 4570m (15000ft) or continue to Mani Mahesh Lake, 3 hours and 6km (3½ miles) further on.

Walk-out via Mani Mahesh Lake
Mani Mahesh Lake (4170m/ 13680ft), situated in a small depression high up in the valley, is a place of pilgrimage. Chamba Kailash (also known as Mani Mahesh Kailash) towers above the lake. Many pilgrims visit the lake during the Dusherra festival and *dhabas* (places to eat) and tea stalls spring up along the way. A broad, well-made trail descends very steeply from the lake down into the valley. It winds along the slope for 8km (5 miles) to Danchho (2900m/9515ft), which is the first flat piece of land you will come across. During the pilgrimage season this is a bustling settlement with temporary rest houses. Continue the descent the next day to meet the road 8km (5 miles) further on at Hadsar (1980m/6500ft), where the trail ends. Buses and taxis are available to Brahmaur, Chamba and Pathankot for trains to Delhi.

YOL

The village of Yol in the Kangra Valley is located at the foot of the Dhauladhar Range. Italian Prisoners of War were interned here in an open jail by the British during World War II. An open jail meant the POWs could work in the hills during the day. At the end of the working day the commandant would shout 'To your own locations', which the prisoners shortened to YOL. The village retains the name and a small memorial stands as a reminder of the Italian POWs.

KANGRA VALLEY RAILWAY

BILL AITKEN

The few hill railways which the British built in India are a treat to travel today. The Darjeeling Hill Railway and Shimla Hill Railway are well-known. But one of the gems in the railway's crown is the Kanga Valley Railway, which runs parallel to the Dhauladhar Range and travels through the scenic Kangra region.

The Kangra Valley Railway (KVR) was begun in 1926 and completed in 1929 and cost Rs 296 lakhs, overshooting the estimate by a mere Rs 162 lakhs. It is 164km (102 miles) long and the highest point is 1210m (3870ft) at Ahju. Pathankot is the first stop at 333m (1093ft) and Jogindernagar is the last, 1139m (3737ft) with 30 stations on the way. The KVR has only two tunnels, unlike the Shimla line which has 103.

The Dhauladhar from the Kangra Valley Railway.

The KVR line is remarkable for its scenic beauty and environmental wisdom in following natural contours. There are 971 bridges, some of unique

A railway bridge along the Kangra Valley Railway.

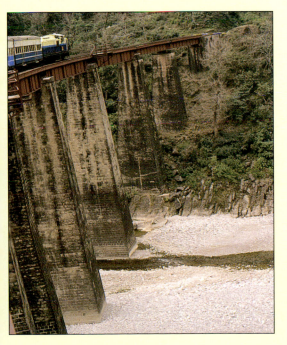

design. The KVR comes closer to the snows than any other railway line in India, running parallel to the Dhauladhar Range only 16km (10 miles) away. The railway's steepest gradient (beyond Baijnath Paprola) is 1 in 19. There are 20 crossing stations and 11 slip sidings in case of backsliding runaway trains. The blue livery of the rolling stock adds to the railway's charm.

Above Jogindernagar lies Shanan Power Station, where the narrow gauge ends. A metre-gauge 'trolley' (a small open car) continues up the mountainside to the reservoir. The KVR locos were the steam ZE and ZF class, now diesel ZDM3. The Nagrota–Jogindernagar section (55km/34 miles) was closed in 1942 and the line uprooted and sent abroad for the war effort. It was relaid and reopened in 1954. The famous steel-arch bridge across Reond nala, opposite Kangra, 60m (197ft) above the river bed, was erected in 1927. Banganga bridge, between Guler and Jawalamukhi, was twice swept away in pre-monsoon storms during construction. Both bridges are legends in Indian railway engineering history.

The Kangra Valley Railway is probably one of the most scenic light railways in the world, its success being to blend successfully the engineering works with the aesthetics of the Kangra Valley. Those who value the more gentle modes of Himalayan transport should set aside a day to jump aboard a train soon.

TREK 18: HAMPTA PASS – CHANDRA TAL

Kullu and Lahaul are adjoining districts, separated by the Rohtang Pass, which remains snowbound from October to June. But the valleys are geographically quite different. The Kullu/Manali valleys are green, with excellent forest cover and heavy rains; Lahaul is in a rain-shadow area, with partial trans-Himalayan barrenness. A trail combining both these areas gives a wonderful walk with two completely different terrains to enjoy.

The road from Delhi–Chandigarh to Kullu/Manali can be covered in a long day's travel. It enters the hilly area from Bilaspur and later travels along the Beas River. As it nears Kullu, the valley opens to a wonderful vista of open fields and apple orchards. Near Manali it gets wilder and rougher. The present-day onslaught of tourists during the season may spoil the ambience of this once sleepy town, but a little further away from the town things are as quiet as before. The trail starts from Preni village (1940m/6370ft).

TREK ESSENTIALS

LENGTH 10 days or 2 weeks; 160km (100 miles). Walking from Manali: 4 days to Chhatru, 4 days to Chandra Tal, 3 days to Baralacha La.

ACCESS Direct flights from Delhi to Bhuntar, 9km (4½ miles) before Kullu. Manali is 41km (25 miles) ahead. Direct buses to Manali from Delhi and Chandigarh.

HIGHEST POINT Baralacha La, 4883m (16020ft). Passes: Hampta, 4268m (14000ft).

GRADE Medium.

SEASONS Late May to end October (not July–mid-September).

RESTRICTIONS None.

FURTHER OPTIONS Join Trek 22 at Darcha (see page 144). During the summer months it is possible to travel to Spiti or Leh by road.

Manali to Chhatru

Drive 20km (12½ miles) south to Preni village, situated on the left bank of the River Beas on the road to Nagar and Jagatsukh. After the bridge on the junction of Duggal and Alain nala, climb a steep ridge to reach Sethan (3000m/9840ft) in about 3 hours (12km/7½ miles). The trail passes through a lovely forest to the Lahauli village of Hampta. The trail alternates between forest and open grounds for 12km (7½ miles) to Chhika.

There are several side streams to cross on the way, but generally each has a small bridge over it. On the way you will pass a place called Bhalu-ka-Gera ('bear's circle', where brown bears are said to hibernate during the winter), and at the right time of the year several species of wild flowers can be seen. Set up camp at Chhika (3360m/11020ft) or stay in the small rest house. Beautiful forested slopes are visible to the east of Chhika, surmountable after 3–4 hours (4km/2 miles) of scrambling. The reward is an excellent view of Deo Tibba and the Indrasan group of peaks.

The trail now continues at almost the same height, along the Hampta nala, passing several side streams and vast meadows. You could cross the Hampta Pass directly but it would be much more pleasant to camp at Ratni Thach (3800m/12,460ft), a lovely meadow reached after 6km (3½ miles). Start early the next day and reach the Hampta Pass (4268m/14000ft) after a 2-km (1¼-mile) climb. The final ridge is a little steep and when snow-bound you will have to cut steps in the ice up the pass. The view from the pass is wonderful. The peaks in Lahaul, particularly in the Kulti Valley and of the Chandrabhaga group, are seen as a huge cluster, with the peak of Mulkila IV raising its head above them. The descent to the Chandra River on the other side is rather steep and follows a long ridge. Once in the valley you will rejoin the

HAMPTA PASS – CHANDRA TAL

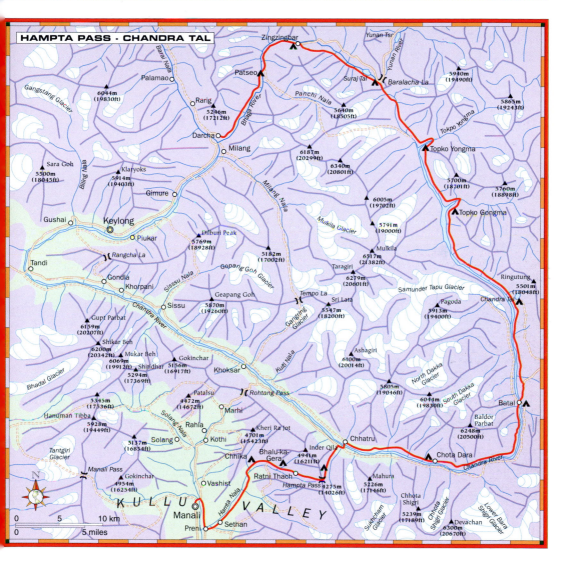

HAMPTA PASS - CHANDRA TAL

road which crosses the bridge across the river to Chhatru, 8km (5 miles) further on (3360m/ 11020ft). However gentle the river appears, do not try to ford the Chandra River – always use a bridge. This deceptive river has swept away a few trekkers trying to take a shortcut. Chhatru has a popular *dhaba* and there is a small rest house where you can spend the night.

Chhatru to Batal and Chandra Tal

For the next two days, the trail follows the right bank of the Chandra River. During the summer months, when the road across the Rohtang Pass is open, you may be able to take a bus to cover this section. Walk 16km (10 miles) to Chota Dara (3517m/11540ft) and a further 16km (10 miles) to Batal (3950m/12960ft). There are lovely views

of the Chota Shigri (literally, 'small glacier') and Bara Shigri ('big glacier'). Several high peaks of Lahaul are visible from this road.

From Batal onwards it can be very windy as the valley opens up here. You can take shelter in the rest house or the *dhaba*. The road, open from mid-August to mid-September, climbs steeply around many hairpin bends to Kunzum La in the east. This road leads to the Spiti Valley. There is a new foot-path leading from Kunzum La that descends to Chandra Tal, but the more direct approach is to walk 16km (10 miles) from Batal, going into the Chandra Valley in the north. Proceed along the left bank of the Chandra by crossing a small bridge near Batal. A wide trail reaches the lake after 16km (10 miles) (4270m/14010ft). Stay for a day, camping on the shores of the lake. The emerald-

The Chandra Tal lake is surrounded by meadows and the snowy peaks of the Samunder Tapu Glacier.

coloured expanse is breathtaking. Situated in a bowl, it offers a view of many peaks, some of them reflected in its serene waters. The huge Samunder Tapu Glacier joins the valley from the west. It is lined with some major peaks on both sides and the Mulkila group at its head.

Chandra Tal to Suraj Tal and Baralacha La
The trail continues along the Chandra on the left bank, crossing several feeder nalas. Make an early start so that you can easily cross these nalas when the water level is low, particularly in mid-summer. The trail to Topko Gongma (*topko*: nala, *gong-ma*: large), 12km (7½ miles) further on (4400m/14435ft) offers excellent views along the way of the Tapu Glacier and its peaks. Next day walk 10km (6 miles) to Topko Yongma ('small nala') (4640m/15220ft). Both these camps are a little before the crossing of the nalas as the latter have to be crossed in the early morning. You may have to make a short detour into the side valleys to find suitable crossing points.

As you approach Baralacha La, 10km (6 miles) further (4883m/16020ft), the scenery gets wilder. This is a historic pass and gives rise to three major rivers from its watershed: Chandra in the southeast, Bhaga in the southwest and the Yunan River in the north. Both sides are lined with mountains and you can even change base camps by driving from one to another. From here you are on a road (again, during summer only) and after visiting Suraj Tal, which gives rise to the Bhaga River, you can proceed to Darcha (44km/27 miles). Otherwise take a short cut to Zingzingbar (4270m/14,010ft), 18km (11 miles). Darcha (3370m/11060ft) can then be reached in a 20-km (12½-mile) walk via Patseo on the last day. Patseo was once a major trading centre between India and Tibet.

Drive-Out
See Trek 22, page 144.

THE CHANDRABHAGA RIVER

The Chandrabhaga River is the lifeline of Lahaul and Kishtwar. It encompasses several valleys and cultures during its journey and is formed by two rivers, the Chandra and the Bhaga.

The Chandra River originates from the Chandra Tal ('lake of the moon'), south of Baralacha La. It flows south and then, going west, cuts across the southern valleys of Lahaul.

The Bhaga River originates west of Baralacha La from Suraj Tal ('lake of the sun') and flows southwards, passing Keylong, the headquarters of Lahaul. At Tandi, south of Keylong, both rivers converge to form the Chandrabhaga, but not for long. Going east, it passes Trilokintah Temple, which represents a sacred mix of Hindu and Buddhist traditions. Beyond this, as it enters Kishtwar territories, it is renamed Chenab and flows through the Muslim states of Kishtwar and Kashmir to merge with the River Indus.

TREK 19: PIN PARVATI PASS

The trans-Himalayan valleys of Spiti were once difficult to gain access to. On one side was the Tibetan plateau and the high passes to the north were closed for most of the year. The British administrators, in search of an alternate route, opened a new pass that led directly into the Spiti Valley from Kullu, a green and fertile land. This high pass was first crossed in August 1884 by Sir Louis Dane. Since then it has been much used by travellers as it halves the distance between the Kullu and Spiti valleys. This route was opened to trekkers in 1993. A guide and a proper map are essential, and the pass is always snow-bound.

Manikaran to Pando Seo Thach

Kullu Valley is a popular tourist destination. The road continues northeast from Kullu for 45km (28 miles) to Manikaran (1697m/5570ft), an expanding settlement with a Sikh *gurudwara* (temple). There are also several hot springs with reputedly medicinal properties. Many hotels and rest houses are available and porters should be arranged here. It is possible to use mules on this trail for the first two days' march.

Manikaran is situated on the banks of the River Parvati, which is lively and in full flow here, rushing down to merge with the Beas River near Bhuntar. The trail to the pass follows the Parvati River upstream. The first day's walk is on the right bank, following a gentle trail through a lovely forest. The trail passes several small villages and tea shops. Near Uchich village are the remains of old silver

Kullu Eiger (5664m/18582ft) from the Parvati valley.

TREK ESSENTIALS

LENGTH 2–3 weeks; 114km (71 miles). Walking from Manikaran: 4 days to Pando Seo Thach, 4 days to Pin Parvati Pass, 3 days to Sagnam.

ACCESS Drive 293km (182 miles) from Delhi to Kullu by road (via Chandigarh and Mandi) or fly to Bhuntar, a small airport nearby. Manikaran is linked to Kullu by an all-weather road (45km/28 miles).

HIGHEST POINT Pin Parvati Pass, 5400m (17715ft). Passes: Pin Parvati.

GRADE Difficult.

SEASONS Late June to mid-October.

RESTRICTIONS It is advisable to stay in large groups and indoors at night in the Manikaran–Pulga area as trouble has been reported here in recent years.

FURTHER OPTIONS Treks across Killung La to upper Khamengar valleys, or visits to various monasteries of Spiti.

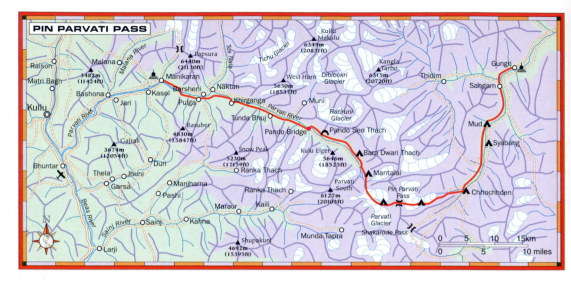

mines, giving this area the name of Rupi ('silver') Valley. Most of the mine shafts were filled in and hidden at the time of the Sikh invasion in 1810 and have never been reopened.

After 12km (7½ miles) and almost a 6-hour walk, the bridge across the Parvati River leads to Pulga (2220m/7285ft). The rest house here is beautiful, built of solid teak wood, and retains its old-world charm. You will need a permit from the Forest Office in Kullu or Bhuntar to stay here, but there are other small hotels and restaurants available nearby. Make sure you look through the entries in the Rest House Register (see box, page 129), which form a fascinating historical record of early trekking.

About 600m (2000ft) above the rest house is an open meadow called Swagani Maidan, which is a delight to walk to for acclimatisation or observing the wildlife. The trail ahead is a 9-km (5½-mile) walk through a lovely forest. There are trails on both banks, so you can either go back and join the trail on the right bank or continue on a wilder trail on the left bank from the rest house.

You will pass the village of Naktan on the right bank and about three nalas have to be crossed before you reach the solid bridge over the Parvati River at Rudranag, beyond which, quite unexpectedly, is the open meadow of Khirganga (2920m/9580ft). There are hot springs here and the entire forest range surrounding this ground is delightful.

The 12-km (7½-mile) walk to Tunda Bhuj is very enjoyable. There are few ups and downs and you will pass the lovely grazing grounds of Mandror and Nihara thaches on the way. During the summer months you are likely to come across several shepherds here. Tunda Bhuj (3400m/11150ft) is situated in a forest of birch trees, and is a beautiful camping ground.

The trail now enters a difficult area. The ground is rocky for about 2km (1¼ miles), the route is somewhat tricky and there is an exposed slab to cross. But thereafter a wide vista opens up: the Thakur Kuan ground. Towards the south is a small but lovely peak, Kullu Eiger (5664m/18582ft), which was climbed in 1996. Its stupendous north face rises 2000m (6562ft). Across the Parvati River a wide valley leads to the Dibibokri Glacier

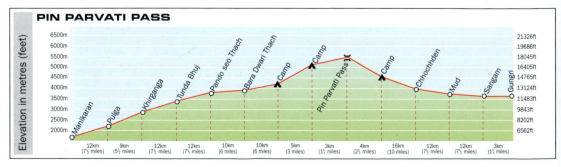

and several high peaks such as Papsura and Dharamsura.

The trail ahead crosses the *thaches* of Doala and Thuli. Here is the first of the Pando Bridges, which uses a huge natural boulder to cross the Dol Par Khol nala. The route is exposed and there is a delicate traverse across a small ledge over the river. The main Pando Bridge is another natural boulder spanning the Parvati River. The enterprising shepherds have built a rocky staircase leading to the bridge and down the other side. Both bridges, named after the Pandava brothers of the epic *Mahabharat,* are masterpieces of local engineering. Once you have crossed the bridges you will reach a wide open ground called Pando Seo Thach (3780m/12400ft) where you can camp, completing a total 12-km (7½-mile) walk for the day.

Pando Seo Thach to Pin Parvati Pass

The fifth day's walk is a pleasure. There are few ascents and descents and after walking for 10km (6 miles) through a broad valley, Bara Dwari Thach (3920m/12860ft) is reached. You can proceed further, but this place is traditionally used as a camping ground as this is the last point in the valley where wood is available for fuel.

Go ahead into a broad valley and then to a moraine ridge seen ahead to its left, 5km (3 miles) on. This is the ridge that dams the Mantalai Lake, considered to be the origin of the Parvati River. There is an open temple here and many traditional cairns and prayer flags. There are small peaks on the Jarayun Dhar on the right. Continue past the lake to a camping ground on your right about 5km (3 miles) ahead (4200m/13780ft). The pass is not at the head of this valley; make a sharp turn towards the east to enter another valley to the Pin Parvati Pass.

To reach the pass, cross the first nala and continue climbing rather steeply. There is a small shepherds' track and at some places further nalas are crossed. About half way, the trail descends the valley to cross over to the opposite ridge. After about 5km (3 miles) the trail crosses an area

strewn with huge boulders. Depending on the season the entire ground from now onwards may be snow-bound and extremely cold. You can see the pass as soon as you have crossed this rocky ground. The original pass was the lowest point on

Approaching Pin Parvati Pass (in the centre of the picture).

the ridge to the right. The pass in current use is at a point a little higher on the ridge than the one marked on the Survey of India map. It is not advisable to cross the pass in the afternoon as the snow will be softer, so camp just after the rocky ground at 5040m (16535ft). You can expect a cold night but the high-altitude views across the valley to the south will compensate for any discomfort.

Next day, start early across the huge open ground leading to the pass in the east, which can be reached in about 4 hours. The prayer flags and cairns on the pass can be seen from a fair distance. This is a traditional pass crossed by shepherds with their flock in summer months. It has a terrific view and you can look towards the peaks and valleys of Spiti. The descent from the pass is steep and on loose, ankle-twisting scree. After about 2 hours, the terrain eases a little and the trail reaches a junction of three valleys. Camp just beyond on a patch of grass on the left bank of the Pin River, reached after 4km (2 miles) of descent (4520m/14830ft). The trail is now in the Spiti Valley.

Fields outside Sagnam village, Spiti.

and the valley is broad and beautiful. The village of Mud in the distance takes about 6 hours to reach and is 12km (7½ miles) away. Mud village lies at the junction of the Killung nala with the Pin and is beautifully positioned, surrounded by fields. There is a small monastery up the hill, which is a wonderful place to camp (3750m/12300ft).

Now the trail leads to Sagnam village (3680m/12075ft) 12km (7½ miles) away. The shortest route is along the left bank, but at two places you have to climb steep scree to cross the landslides. The walk to the village takes about 6 hours. There is a small rest house and many larger houses where trekkers can be accommodated. Sagnam is a large village, strategically located at the junction of the Pin and Khamengar rivers. The green village fields contrast with the jagged peaks surrounding it. The villagers use gas for cooking, and have the latest electric cooking ranges, heaters, television sets and telephones. Daily road transport is available from here onwards.

There is an easier but longer trail on the right bank of the river from Mud which passes through several villages. This trail does not lead to Sagnam but descends directly to Gungri.

Pin Parvati Pass to Sagnam

The terrain is now typically Spitian – barren, but with patches of grass and plenty of scree. Continue on the right bank along the river. After about 6 hours of walking, cross to the left bank, either by a snow-bridge or by fording with ropes. Follow the left bank until you reach a junction of three nalas (16km/10 miles). The name of this camping ground is a real tongue-twister – Chhochhden – but it is a good camping site at 4000m (13120ft). On the way you will notice some ruins on the right bank, where the Bhaba nala joins the valley. This was the Lyungti Khar, the remains of an ancient fort built by the Rajas of Kullu.

The gentle descent continues on the left bank,

Drive-out via Sagnam, Attargo and Kaja

Cross the bridge over the Khamengar River beyond Sagnam village to the Gungri Monastery 4km (2 miles) away. Gungri is one of the five important monasteries in Spiti. A daily bus service is available from here to reach Kaja, the headquarters of Spiti Valley, 16km (10 miles) to the northwest.

The road follows the Khamengar River to Attargo, which is on the other side of the Spiti River. From Kaja you can drive to Manali (209km/130 miles) or Shimla (412km/256 miles).

THE LEGEND OF SHILLA

Shilla, meaning 'a place of monastery', is a small peak in Spiti, on the divide between Lingti and the Shilla nala. It became so famous that any mention of Spiti led to the story of its first ascent by the Survey of India (SOI) and vice versa.

It was first thought to have been climbed in 1860 by an unnamed *khalasi* (pole carrier) of the SOI, who erected a pole on the top. A report of this achievement appeared in *Synoptical Vol. XXXV of the Trigonometrical Survey of India*, published in 1910. It was referred to as peak Parang La No. 2 but the name was later changed to Shilla by the Survey Office. The peak appears as Parang La No. 2 S with a height of 7030m (23064ft) on *SOI Sheet 64 SW*, published in August 1874 (Gya is mentioned as GUA Snowy Peak, 6800m/22309ft, on the same sheet). Shilla retained a dubious altitude record for 47 years until Dr Longstaff climbed Trisul, 7120m (23360ft), in 1907.

The first mountaineers to visit Spiti had their doubts about its height. In 1952 the British–South African team of Snelson and J. de V. Graaff felt that it was a much smaller peak than described and a higher peak (possibly Gya) was observed to the northeast. The British team of Peter Holmes and Trevor Braham felt the same. A letter by Braham in the *Himalayan Journal, Vol. XXVI*, p. 169, established its height at 6111m (20050ft). Now on the latest maps with modern methods of survey, the height of Shilla is firmly established as 6132m (20120ft), losing 897m (2944ft), while Gya has only lost 5½m (18ft) It makes you wonder where the SOI went wrong.

The Indian expedition that climbed Shilla in 1966 did not find a survey pole (hardly surprising after 106 years) and they questioned why the climb done in 1860 took 50 years to be reported. Did the *khalasi* really climb it or is it just a legend?

In Spiti, Shilla is the peak best known to the locals. Almost every lama and villager seems to know of it, however remote their location. Shilla is considered to be a place for the dead leading to heaven, and locals still believe that it is the highest point in Spiti and Ladakh, from where heaven can be seen. No one, the most elderly lama included, seems to be aware of the ascent made by the *khalasi*, to confirm or deny it.

Few villagers in Langja know about the route to Shilla because, according to them, it is still the highest, unclimbed peak. The Shilla legend is here to stay.

The snowy wastes of the impressive Shilla Peak, first thought to have been climbed in 1860.

TREK 20: BHABA PASS – SPITI

A look at the map of Himachal Pradesh shows that the road from Kinnaur makes a 200-km (125-mile) detour to reach the valleys of western Spiti, travelling along the Satluj and Spiti rivers. Spitians from these fertile and populated valleys have always taken a 70-km (44-mile) shortcut by crossing the Bhaba Pass, which descends directly to Wangtu in Kinnaur. Even today many Spitians studying in or with business to conduct in Shimla prefer to take this shortcut instead of unreliable bus connections, encountering road blocks and expensive travel, while the shepherds on both sides cross by similar traditional passes on the ridge.

Sarahan (2165m/7100ft) is a lovely place to stay and the temple of Bhimkali attracts worshippers from all Kinnaur. Moreover, it is a place where you can acclimatise in the comfort of a rest house. The entire Kand Mahadev Range (including the Sorang Valley) is visible from here; a fascinating panorama. From Sarahan, descend to the National Highway at Jyura and drive 65km (40 miles) to Kafnu, a small village off the main road, near the Wangtu Bridge. Mules or porters required for the trek must be hired here in advance before starting the trek.

Make a careful note of the place names here to avoid confusion. The old name was Tari Khango (*tari:* inside, *khango:* gap). On the map the name is Wangar nala. Because of the village it was also called Kafnu nala. But with the new enormous hydro-electric project, the nala is usually referred to as Bhaba nala, as is everything else: the project, the nala and the pass.

TREK ESSENTIALS

LENGTH 2 weeks; 67km (42 miles). Walking from Kafnu: 4 days to Bhaba Pass, 3 days to Sagnam.

ACCESS Trains to Kalka and Shimla from Delhi. Drive 172km (107 miles) via Rampur-Bushahr to Sarahan then 53km (33 miles) to Wangtu, on the main Hindustan–Tibet road, then 12km (7½ miles) to Kafnu

HIGHEST POINT Tari Khango (Bhaba Pass), 4865m (15960ft). Passes: Tari Khango (Bhaba Pass).

GRADE Medium.

FURTHER OPTIONS This trek joins the trail from the Pin Parvati valleys (Trek 19) which can be followed either way.

SEASONS Late June to October.

RESTRICTIONS None, but trekking fees are to be paid in advance at the at the Himachal Pradesh Tourist Office at New Delhi or Shimla; also contact these offices for rates and forms.

The historical significance of the Bhaba Valley lies in its location. Rampur-Bushahr was the seat of an ancient and powerful kingdom of the Rampur Rajas that controlled Spiti. The nearest all-season trail to Spiti was the Bhaba Valley. The valley gave easy and direct access to Spiti whilst avoiding the Kinnauri valleys that border Tibet. In addition, the Bhaba Valley bordered Kullu in the west. The Kullu Rajas (kings) built forts in the Pin Valley, next to the Bhaba Valley, in an attempt to gain control of Spiti. The ruins of one of these forts, Lyungti Khar, can still be seen here. With both borders meeting here, mastery of the valley was vitally important.

The Bhaba Valley lies next to, but not strictly within, the trans-Himalayan terrain and its average rainfall is higher than in other parts of Spiti. As a result you will find a greater diversity of flowers and other wildlife here than in other areas of Spiti. This wealth of flora and fauna has been the subject of a number of studies in recent years. Moreover, the Pin Valley National Park was established

BHABA PASS – SPITI

Elevation in metres (feet)

Kafnu · Mulling · Kara · Phustirang · Bhaba Pass · Chhochhoden · Mud · Sangam · Gungri

6500m (21326ft), 6000m (19686ft), 5500m (18045ft), 5000m (16405ft), 4500m (14765ft), 4000m (13124ft), 3500m (11483ft), 3000m (9843ft), 2500m (8202ft), 2000m (6562ft)

15km (9 miles) · 6km (3⅔ miles) · 6km (3⅔ miles) · 3km (1⅔ miles) · 10km (6 miles) · 12km (7½ miles) · 12km (7½ miles) · 3km (1⅔ miles)

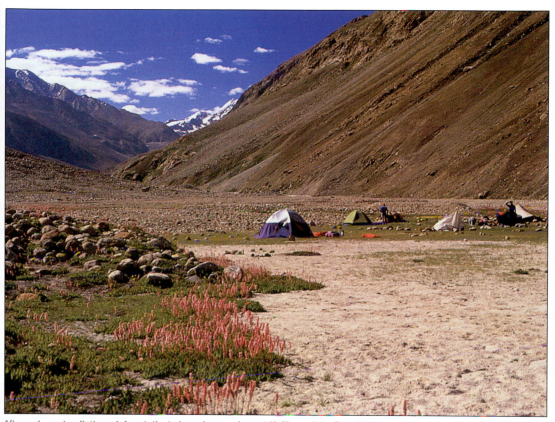

After a pleasant walk through forest, the trek reaches meadows at Mulling and the first night's camp.

in 1990 to protect the ibex which are found here in great numbers.

Kafnu to the Base of the Bhaba Pass

You can use pack-ponies for this trek. The trail leaves the fields of Kafnu, crosses the Bhaba nala and follows the left bank. There are a couple of zigzags as the route meanders through forest and meadow, and it is a 15km (9½ miles) walk to the meadows at Mulling (3280m/1,760ft). Aim to reach this pleasant camping place by mid afternoon, as the trail is fairly wide and well-marked. In season an abundance of alpine flowers and carpet-like meadows surround this camp. The flowers include anemones, gentians and Himalayan blue poppies, while on the Sorgang Dhar a number of impressive ice-falls can be seen.

On the second day a short, level walk leads to a river crossing by way of a natural boulder bridge. Then you gain height gradually, until you reach the meadow at Kara, 6km (3½ miles) further on (3560m/11680ft), where you may be lucky enough to encounter nomadic Gaddi shepherds and their flocks. Gaddi shepherds wear knee-length hand-woven woollen cloaks tied at the waist, and are thought to originate from the earliest settlers in the Himalayan foothills. Their annual migration means that for reasons of safety they clear the mountain trails and mend bridges, from which everyone benefits. Again, this is an excellent campsite, with many species of alpine flowers and good views of a range of unnamed peaks on the border between Kinnaur and Spiti.

PIN PARVATI PASS

Few early Western explorers crossed the Pin Parvati Pass. It is not difficult in fine weather but involves tramping over miles of glacier and camping on it for a night.

The pass was first discovered and crossed from the Spiti side by Sir Louis Dane in 1884, followed by F Skemp in 1906. The first crossing from the Kullu side was made by H Lee Shuttleworth (1921). Colonel JOM Roberts, who was the first mountaineer to explore Spiti, missed its location in 1939 and went another way. It is now crossed by many trekking parties and shepherds.

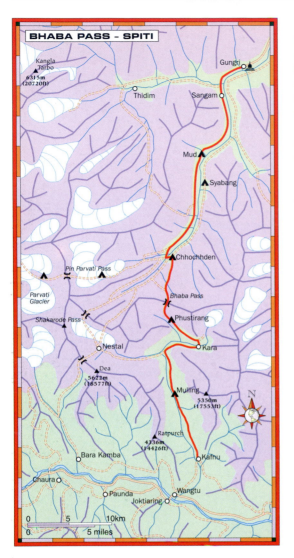

BHABA PASS - SPITI

The third day's steep trek takes you up to the base of the Bhaba Pass. Follow the left bank of the river for 6km (3½ miles) to a level patch of ground known as Phustirang (4200m/13780ft), where several small streams and a small valley (the Bhaba nala) from the Bhaba pass join it. Spend a day resting and acclimatising here.

The view of small peaks in Kinnaur towards the south is wonderful. Particularly attractive is the shapely pinnacle of Hansbeshan Peak (5840m/19161ft), still unclimbed.

Crossing Bhaba Pass to Sagnam

A steep 3-hour, 3km (2 miles) climb leads to the Bhaba Pass (4865m/15960ft), also known as Tari Khango, where you will be rewarded with views of a fine array of peaks. All the peaks towards the Spiti side are visible. A small gap in the distant ridge in the northwest is the Pin Parvati Pass.

It is a long descent to Bara Bulder. The arid, brown slopes of the Pin Valley are in marked contrast to the alpine greenery of the Bhaba Valley. Camp on either side of the river at Chhochhden (4000m/13120ft), 10km (6 miles) further on. Three nalas meet at Chhochhden, which is at the junction of different routes from each of these nalas. One nala descends from the Bhaba Pass. The second one, in the west, leads to the Pin Parvati Pass (see Trek 19, page 127) and to the Kullu valleys. In the southwest the third valley leads to Shakarog Khango (5100m/16730ft) a relatively unknown pass which descends into the Sorang Valley in the south (see Trek 14, page 108).

You are now on the trail from the Pin Parvati Pass to Sagnam village, the largest village in the Pin Valley, from where there is a daily bus to Kaza. The main path is on the left bank, but if the water level is high, and there are no bridges, do not try to ford the nala. The lesser trail on the right bank is reasonably good and will lead to Mud (3750m/12300ft) in some 12km (7½ miles).

Drive-out via Sagnam to Attargo and Kaja

Follow the trail and road as described in Trek 19 (see page 130).

Descent from the Bhaba pass.

HIMACHAL PRADESH DIRECTORY

REGIONAL TRANSPORT

Kinnaur/Spiti: Take the night train to Chandigarh or Kalka. The hill railway travels to Shimla. Direct buses or taxis are available to reach Rekong Peo (the headquarters for Kinnaur) or to go to Kaja (the headquarters for Spiti).

Kullu/Manali: Fly to Bhuntar from Delhi and then drive to Kullu (9km/4½ miles) and Manali (41km/25 miles). Direct overnight bus or taxi from Delhi to Kullu/Manali takes about 18 hours. Train to Chandigarh/Kalka and take a bus or taxi to Kullu/Manali (8 hours/334km). When passes are open you can travel by bus or taxi from Manali to Spiti, Darcha and Leh.

Dhauladhar: Take the night train to Pathankot. There are regular buses and taxis from Dharamsala.

Lahauli ladies in traditional dress.

REST HOUSES/HOTEL LOCATIONS

Barog, Brahmaur, Chamba, Dalhousie, Dharamsala, Kaja, Kalpa, Kasauli, Keylong, Kullu, Manali, Mandi, Manikaran, Naggar, Narkanda, Nichar, Rekong Peo, Rupi, Sangla, Sarahan, Shimla, Solan.

REGIONAL TOURIST OFFICES

Himachal Pradesh Tourism Development Corporation (HPTDC): Ritz Annexe, Shimla 171 00; tel (91-177) 203294, fax (91-177) 203434

HPTDC Office (Delhi):

Chanderlok Building, 36 Janapath, New Delhi 110001; tel (91-11) 3324764, 3325320, fax (91-11) 3731072

LOCAL PLACES OF INTEREST

Shimla: The Mall, Jakoo Hill, Subathu, Kasauli Kufri Ski Resort, Narkanda Hatu Peak.

Spiti: Dankhar, Tabo, Ki, Gungri and Kaja

Monasteries.

Kullu-Manali: Rohtang Pass, Bhrigu Lake, Jawaher Kund, apple orchards at various places, Western Himalayan Mountaineering Institute.

Kinnaur: Monasteries at Chhitkul, Kalpa, Kanam. Rogi Cliffs, Bhimkali Temple at Sarahan.

Lahaul: Keylong, Kardhing Monastery.

Kangra: Graveyard at McLeodganj, Dharamsala, Dalai Lama's Monastery at McLeodganj, temples in Kangra, Sidhhbari and Chamundi Temples.

Chamba: Temples in Chamba and Brahmaur.

TELEPHONE CODES

Chamba 01899, Dharamsala 01892, Kaja 01906, Kalpa 01786, Keylong 01900, Kullu 01902, Manali 01901, Manikaran 01902, Rekong Peo 01786, Sarahan 01799, Shimla 0177.

IMPORTANT PEAKS OBSERVED EN ROUTE

Name	Seen from
Ashagiri	Rohtang Pass
Gepang Goh	Rohtang Pass
Hansbeshan	above Nichar
Hanuman Tibba	Rohtang pass
Jorkanden	Kalpa
Kanamo	Kibbar
Kand Mahadev	Sarahan
Kinnaur Kailash	Kalpa
Kailash	en route to Brahmaur
Ladakhi	Manali
Leo Pargial	Leo village (to Spiti)
Manali	Manali
Manirang	Charang Ghati
Mulkila	Darcha
Parilungbi	Parang La
Rangrik Rang	Charang village
Reo Purgyil	Khab on Spiti road
Shiti Dhar	Manali

7
ZANSKAR-LADAKH

The land is so barren and the passes so high that only the best friends or fiercest enemies would want to visit us.

(Ladakhi proverb)

The people of Ladakh have lived for centuries in barren, inhospitable terrain. But the Ladakh for tourists and the Ladakh for trekkers and climbers are two different worlds. Many people stay at Leh, visit *gompas* and enjoy the barrenness. But if you can manage some treks, there is nothing quite like Tso Moriri. It changes colour every hour with the sun, and the brown hills behind make it resemble something from the pages of a Tolkein novel. Crossing passes is par for the course when trekking in Ladakh, and there are fascinating monasteries at Lamayuru, Diskit and Sumur.

Climbing Chhamser Kangri with Tso Moriri and the Mentok Range in the background.

137

Lama painting a statue of Mahakala at Korzok Monastery.

Ladakh used to be called 'Little Tibet' (present-day Tibet was known as Greater Tibet) and it has a semi-Tibetan landscape and culture. Since Roman times, Leh has been on an important trade route linking the Mediterranean to China. Sometimes called the Central Asia Trade Route, this ancient caravan trail cuts across the Khardung Range to the Saser La. The historic pass of Saser La, which is not open to foreigners at present, is famous for its capricious weather, and is also nicknamed the Skeleton pass on account of the bleached bones to be found there.

Traders came to Leh from all directions: from Tibet in the east, Kullu in the south, Muslims from Balti valleys in the west and caravans from Central Asia in the north. Today, despite the arrival of plane-loads of tourists, Leh has managed to retain most of its charms.

North of Leh is the Khardung Ridge, which runs east from the meeting point of the Shyok and the Indus rivers to meet the Pangong Range. Numerous peaks up to 6200m (20342ft) can be found on this ridge. None of them has been climbed or attempted, because of military security, as well as their relatively low heights. This ridge is crossed by the Khardung La, at about 5400m (17700ft) this is one of the highest motorable passes in the world, leading up to the Eastern Karakoram (Nubra Valley). Some of the highest peaks in the Indian Himalaya are in this region. From the pass, Saser Kangri II is seen to advantage.

The River Indus, originating in western Tibet, flows northwest, enters Ladakh near Demchok and subsequently passes through Rupshu district and Leh. Two famous passes, the Parang La and the Takling La, lead into Rupshu from Spiti.

Rupshu

Rupshu offers wide, barren valleys, the blue waters of Tso Moriri, the attractive nomads (Changpas) and exploratory treks. Southeast of Leh, Rupshu was opened to trekkers and tourists in 1994. It stretches from the Tunglung La to the north to Chumar in the south, Manecham Sumpa in the west and Hanle to the east, encompassing an area of about 15,000km² (5790 sq. miles). This is an exceedingly dry area, even by Tibetan standards. This expanse of high desert is 4500m (14754ft) above sea level and there are only three places where there are permanent dwellings. In 1984, as in 1881, the population comprised about 500 nomads who still live in tents of black hair-cloth.

One of the unique features of Rupshu is Tso (Lake) Moriri, an oval-shaped lake typical of the area nestling between Lungser Kangri and Monto. The southeastern valley of Rupshu has several peaks; the highest of which, Lungser Kangri (6666m/21871ft) was climbed by an Indian team in 1995. Three of the other high peaks, Pologongka, Kula and Chhamser Kangri, were then climbed in quick succession by mountaineers of various nationalities. Many peaks, such as Chakula and Thugje, await their first ascent.

Zanskar

The district lying south of Ladakh takes its name from the river that flows north from Padum in central Zanskar and which, with its many tributaries, finally joins the River Indus just west of Leh. The river forms a terrific gorge and flows through vast plains.

Zanskar has always been the most populated part of Ladakh, with several small villages that maintain close contacts with Kashmir, Lahaul and Kishtwar. It has many *gompas* (monasteries), and trade routes criss-cross the area. To its south lies Kishtwar with its jagged peaks; the Shingo La in the southeast leads to Lahaul while to the northwest is Kargil and the road to Kashmir. Zanskar is one of the more popular areas for trekkers.

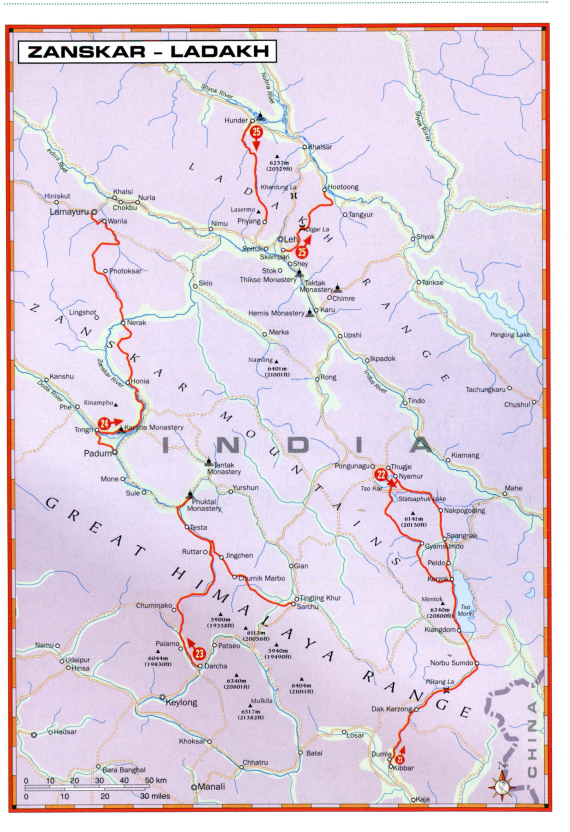

ZANSKAR - LADAKH

TREK 21: PARANG LA TO TSO MORIRI

This remote trail follows the traditional trade route between the people of Spiti, Changthang and Tibet. Beginning in the high altitude meadows of Kibbar, famous for its horses and as snow-leopard country, the trail descends the Kibbar Gorge and then climbs to Parang La. This high-altitude pass is the source of the Pare Chu (river). On both sides of the pass there is an incredible change of scenery as you walk towards the high plateau of the Rupshu through plains at Changthang known for the abundance of wild asses. The trek ends in Korzok, a permanent settlement of the Changpas (nomadic people) on the banks of Tso Moriri.

TREK ESSENTIALS

LENGTH 2 weeks; 92 km (57 miles). Walking from Kibbar: 5 days to Dak Karzong, 5 days to Korzok.

ACCESS Drive from Shimla to Kaja (412km/256 miles) or from Manali to Kaja (209km/130 miles) when Rohtang and Kunzum La passes are open (mid-August–mid-September). Trek starts from Kibbar, 18km (11 miles) from Kaja.

HIGHEST POINT Parang La (5578m/18300ft). Passes: Parang La.

GRADE Strenuous.

SEASONS Late June to end of September.

RESTRICTIONS Permits required but not difficult to obtain.

FURTHER OPTIONS Joins Trek 24 (see page 152).

Reaching Kibbar

Drive 54km (34 miles) from Manali to the Rohtang Pass, from where there are views of the Pir Panjal Range. Lahaul, on the other side of the pass, is at once a stark and forbidding contrast, with its arid

Lamas at Ki Monastery in one of India's highest villages, Kibbar.

landscape and haunting beauty. Drive 126km (78 miles) along the Chandra River to Kunzum La (126km/78 miles), the northern entrance to Spiti.

Descending from the pass, drive along the Spiti River, surrounded by rugged and rocky mountains. Pass the villages of Losar and Rangrik to reach Kaja, the district headquarters (83km/52 miles from Kunzum La Pass). Kibbar village, at 4205m (13800ft) one of the highest inhabited settlements in India, is a short distance away. If you have time, visit the Ki *gompa* about 10km (6 miles) away before beginning the trek.

Kibbar to Parang La and Dak Karzong

The trek follows a gradual path up to the village of Dumla (4510m/14800ft). The first day is an easy 4km (2½ miles) walk but take your time, as these Spitian gorges are renowned for being hard-going.

On day two descend to the gorge bed and start the climb towards the pass, 7km (4½ miles) of steep walk which takes about 5 hours to Thaltak Meadow (4875m/16000ft), where you can camp. The scenery is wild and the gorge is deep. Even at this height the sunlight reflected from the walls of the gorge causes the temperature to soar. Continue to Jagtha (4785m/15700ft), 8km (5 miles), and then 6km (3½ miles) to Bongrojen (5180m/1700ft). This is a long and strenuous day with 7 hours of walking. If not fully acclimatised you should stay at Jagtha, where water is available, for an extra day.

From Bongrojen leave early for the pass. The final 4km (2 miles) is a steep 2-hour climb to the Parang La (5578m/18300ft). The pass lies on the trade route

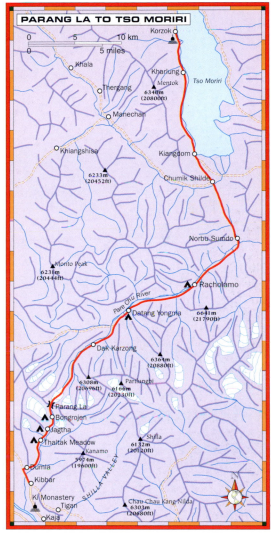

The imposing and historic Dankhar Monastery in Korzok.

between Ladakh and the Spiti Valley, and every August merchants from Kullu, Ladakh, Spiti and Kinnaur hold a trade fair near Kaja.

Generally there is no snow on the Spiti side but you can expect a lot of snow on the Changthang side. There are some great views of the two valleys from the pass. Notice the conical peak of Parilungbi, which dominates the surroundings in the south. This is the first peak in Ladakh visible from Spiti and used to be the landmark for traders crossing the border at Parang La.

As you descend, walk down the left side of the large crevassed glacier to the source of the Pare Chu (cross the river by a snow bridge) in around 2 hours of descent. After the pass the landscape undergoes a dramatic change. From the steep gorges on the Spiti side you now walk across the broad plains of the Pare Chu. Descend 6km (3½ miles) to camp at Dak Karzong (4940m/16200ft) after a total of 5 hours.

Approaching the ruggedly beautiful trading route of Parang La as it passes beneath the peaks of Spiti.

Dak Karzong to Korzok

The route for the next three days is in a fairly open valley with a well-marked trail on the left bank of the Pare Chu (see box).

For the first 5 hours the trek leads 12km (7½ miles) across broad plains to camp at Datang Yongma (4725m/15500ft). The next day, follow the trail to Racholamo (4270m/14000ft) then Norbu Sumdo (4390m/14400ft) and across to Chumik Shilde for 16km (10 miles). Start early as the winds can be strong in the afternoons.

The next day walk across the plains to the southern edge of the oval-shaped Tso Moriri at Kiangdom (4510m/14800ft), named after the *kiangs* (wild Tibetan asses) which roam here freely. The lake breaks into several channels here to create a vast wetland, the breeding ground of several rare species of birds.

The last day of the trek passes along the shore of Tso Moriri. The view of the lake with Lungser Kangri (6666m/21871ft) in the background is unforgettable. The 15km (9 miles) walk is longer than it looks and with the afternoon winds you will be tired when you reach Korzok (4527m/14850ft). Visit the ancient monastery in Korzok (see box, page 155), where the Changpas roam the pastures with their flocks of pashmina goats and still live in yak-skin yurts.

Drive-out via Mahe Bridge

Drive to Leh via Mahe Bridge (213km/133 miles). A taxi will have to be pre-arranged (a costly affair) or you might be able to hitch a lift in one of the trucks that visit Korzok during the summer.

THE PARE CHU

The Pare Chu is a fascinating river that originates just outside the Spiti Valley. The river runs northeast of Parang La to Norbu Sumdo in southeast Ladakh. It flows for about 30km (19 miles) in Ladakh, turns southwards from Chumar and enters Tibetan territory at Lemarle. The river covers another 85km (53 miles) until blocked by the Drongmar Range, then re-enters Indian territory south of Kaurik village. From here it covers another 12km (7½ miles) before it joins the Spiti River near Sumdo. Strategically the Pare Chu makes a complete circle east of the Spiti Valley and provides all access routes to India from Tibet, via small tributaries along narrow valleys; the approach routes are difficult. It is not possible to ford the river at any time of the year as it is very fast-flowing.

PEAK: KANAMO

Spiti contains several small peaks which are enjoyable climbs. One such peak is Kanamo, which stands near the village of Kibbar (reputed to be the highest inhabited village in the world). Its name is related to its surroundings. Kanamo Peak rises above the famous Ki *gompa* (monastery) the holiest in Spiti. *Ka* means 'white' or 'auspicious word of a high priest', while *namo* means 'hostess, a lady'. So the name implies either a 'mountain of good omen' or simply 'white hostess'.

The trail begins from Kibbar village, 18km (11 miles) from Kaja and permission to climb is required in advance from the Indian Mountaineering Foundation, New Delhi.

From Kibbar to Base Camp
Like all the treks and peaks in the trans-

Himalaya areas, a thorough acclimatisation is essential before you start. It is possible to hire a guide and donkeys in the village. From Kibbar village, follow the trail through fields and across several confusing small nalas towards the peak, which is clearly seen in the backdrop of the village to the northeast. Once above the village cross to the foot of the southwest ridge of the peak. Base Camp can be made on the vast open grounds at the foot of the peak.

Southwest Ridge
Next day, follow this long ridge to the summit. There are no technical difficulties en route, and in the autumn season you will encounter very little snow. From the summit there is a wonderful view to the southeast of the deep, narrow gorge of the Shilla nala separating the peak from the Chau Chau Kang Nilda massif ('blue moon in the sky'). This is a sharp, conical peak that you cannot fail to see, and rises from the wide and fertile plateau of the Langja village to the peak's south. The legendary peak of Shilla (see box, page 131) is not visible from this point. To the north you can see several gorges, through which the trail to Parang La passes.

You can return to Base Camp and possibly to Kibbar village the same day.

CLIMB ESSENTIALS

SUMMIT Kanamo, 5974m (19600ft).
PRINCIPAL CAMPS Base Camp: foot of Kanamo (4800m/15750ft), another camp at 5350m (17550ft).
GRADE Easy ridge walk with scree on lower slopes.
MAP REFERENCE Sketch-map Trek 21 (page 141), Parang La.

The route to the summit of Kanamo Peak which rises above the village of Kibbar in Spiti.

TREK 22: SHINGO LA TO PHUKTAL MONASTERY AND PHIRTSE LA

This is one of the most varied and popular treks in the Indian Himalaya. It covers the scenery from the Himalayan greenery of the Kullu Valley to the brown, rugged barrenness of Zanskar. Both have their charm and the views on this trek are unbelievable. However, thorough acclimatisation is essential before embarking on this trek as two high passes are encountered while crossing the trans-Himalayan valleys.

TREK ESSENTIALS

LENGTH 2½ weeks; 135km (84 miles). Walking from Darcha: 3 days to Chuminako, 4 days to Phuktal Monastery, 5 days to Sarchu (trail end) via Phirtse La.

ACCESS Fly or drive to Manali. Drive 115km (71 miles) across Rohtang Pass to Keylong and 30km (19 miles) further to Darcha from where the trail begins.

HIGHEST POINT: Phirtse La, 5275m (17300ft). Passes: Shinkun La (Shingo La) 5090m (16700ft), Phirtse La.

GRADE Strenuous.

SEASONS Late June to end September.

RESTRICTIONS None.

FURTHER OPTIONS Join Trek 23 (see page 147) to Lamayuru via Padum or by road to Kargil.

Darcha to Chuminako

Spend a night at Keylong, the district headquarters, and another night at Darcha (3305m/10840ft) to assist acclimatisation. Darcha was a small camping ground but now has hotels and rest houses. Mules (which can be hired for this trail) will have to be arranged in advance from Manali or Keylong.

From Darcha, the first day's walk of 8km (5 miles) is a gentle start to the trek. Walk up the road that forks and leads into the Sangar Valley after about 2km (1¼ miles). Follow the trail along the left bank of the Sangar nala. Cross a high stone bridge to reach the first day's campsite, a small grassy meadow next to the river at Palamo (3610m/11840ft).

The trail continues along the right bank of the Sangar nala, climbing gradually throughout. The peaks at the head of the Sumdo nala are visible, and the trail reaches the junction of the Sumdo and Sangar nalas. The next camp is 8km (5 miles) further at Sangar Sumdo (3915m/12840ft), just before the rope *jhula* which will ferry you over the next day while the mules swim across.

Climb steeply to enter the upper Sangar Valley. Ramjak (6318m/20729ft), a beautiful, unclimbed peak, comes into view, and several other peaks are visible in the southeast. A gradual ascent leads 6km (3½ miles) to the Ramjak grazing grounds (4360m/14305ft). If tired and not properly acclimatised, camp here, otherwise walk to Chuminako (4665m/15300ft), the next camping ground, at the foot of the pass.

Chuminako to Phuktal Monastery

Start the climb to the pass early. There is a good trail which scrambles over the rocks and scree to a lake halfway, and there is an excellent panorama of many peaks. The Shinkun or Shingo La (5090m/16700ft), on the geographical divide between Lahaul and Zanskar, is reached in about 4 hours and is often very windy. Take a quick look around then begin the 6km (3½ miles) gradual descent on the other side. After about 4 hours you will reach a nala at Lakong (4420m/14500ft)

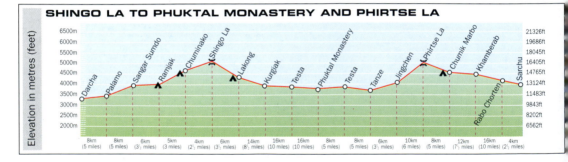

SHINGO LA TO PHUKTAL MONASTERY AND PHIRTSE LA

Elevation in metres (feet)

6500m			21326ft
6000m			19686ft
5500m			18045ft
5000m			16405ft
4500m			14765ft
4000m			13124ft
3500m			11483ft
3000m			9843ft
2500m			8202ft
2000m			6562ft

Darcha, Palamo, Sangar Sumdo, Ramjak, Chuminako, Shingo La, Lakong, Kurgiak, Testa, Phuktal Monastery, Testa, Tanze, Jingchen, Phirtse La, Chumik Marbo, Rabo Chorten, Khamberab, Sarchu

8km (5 miles) 8km (5 miles) 6km (3½ miles) 5km (3 miles) 4km (2½ miles) 6km (3½ miles) 14km (8½ miles) 16km (10 miles) 16km (10 miles) 8km (5 miles) 8km (5 miles) 6km (3½ miles) 10km (6 miles) 8km (5 miles) 12km (7½ miles) 16km (10 miles) 4km (2½ miles)

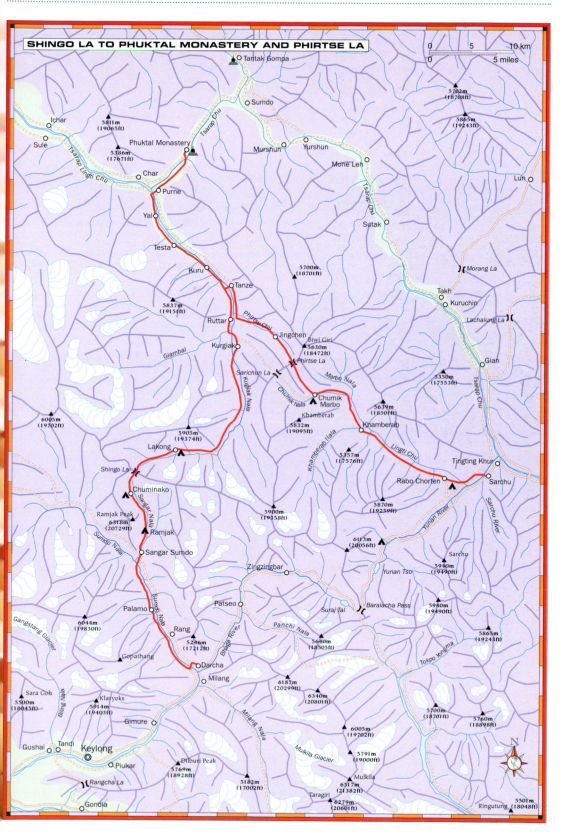

SHINGO LA TO PHUKTAL MONASTERY AND PHIRTSE LA

Phuktal Cave Monastery offers accommodation to trekkers.

where you can camp. Suddenly the trans-Himalayan barrenness semi-desert becomes very apparent.

For the next two days the trail follows beautiful terrain in the Kurgiak River Valley, passing several villages on the way. The first camp is at Kurgiak (4020m/13200ft), 14km (9 miles). Next day continue along the river valley past Tanze and Kuru vil-

On Shinkun Pass and the border between Lahaul and Zanskar.

lages. There are several fields and meadows en route. Camp at Testa (3960m/13000ft) after 16km (10 miles).

Climb to Yal village and descend to the junction of the Kurgiak River and the Tsarap Lingti Chu. Follow the Lingti River on its left bank. Purne is 4km (2 miles) after the junction of the trail from Padum (the headquarters of the Zanskar Valley). Cross a bridge after 4km (2 miles) and after a short climb Phuktal Monastery (3870m/12697ft) will suddenly appear in an impressive profile. Camp below it or stay in the monastery. The lamas will show you a stone carved in the memory of Csoma de Koros (see box, page 46), the Hungarian scholar who lived here for two years.

Phuktal to Phirtse La

The return trek can be made over the Phirtse La. (If you are going to Padum, 20km (12½ miles) away, follow the trail west just beyond Purne.) From Phuktal reverse the route via Purne and Testa to Tanze (3080m/12500ft), 12km (7½ miles). Follow the path to the east and leave the trail by which you entered the valley. Jingchen (4480m/14700ft), where a camp can be made, is 6km (3½ miles) away.

Start early the next day and cover 10km (6 miles) to Phirtse La (5275m/17300ft), climbing gradually to the pass. It will take about 4 hours and the views from the pass are spectacular. The eastern descent is gradual for 8km (5 miles), to the meeting-point of the Marbo and Chumik nalas. Camp at Chumik Marbo (4875m/16000ft). The trail now enters the Lingti plains, a vast, completely flat area with feeder nalas from side valleys joining the Lingti River, which have to be crossed carefully. Enjoy the views before you reach Khamberab (4420m/14500ft) 12km (7½ miles) further on. Next day cross the Lingti plains and cover 16km (10 miles) to Rabo Chorten (4360m/14300ft).

Walk 4km (2 miles) to Sarchu (4420m/13850ft) on the last day, situated on the Leh–Manali highway, where the trek ends.

Drive-out via Leh or Manali

If you have arranged transport in advance, drive to Keylong (107km/66 miles) or Manali (15km/9 miles further on).

TREK 23: LAMAYURU MONASTERY TO PADUM

The ancient Buddhist kingdom of Zanskar, hidden deep in the western reaches of the Great Himalaya Range, has little contact with the outside world. Even the famous Himalayan caravan routes did not pass through since snow makes Zanskar's high passes inaccessible for most months of the year. During the winter months, the locals commute by walking on the frozen Zanskar (Tchaddar) River.

This trek crosses several high passes. The rocky folds of the Zanskari landscape have ever-changing colours, depending on the light. You can see medieval villages, many nestling on the sides of cliffs, irrigated fields of buckwheat and green pea patches or some well-known monasteries such as Lingshet, Karsha and Sani. The trails near the villages are lined with exquisitely carved *mani* stones, inscribed with prayers, and the women in the fields wear the traditional turquoise-and-coral studded headdress, the *perak*.

Lamayuru to Singi La

Lamayuru (3450m/11320ft) is a spectacularly sited monastery on the main road between Leh and Kargil. As you approach Lamayuru, the road climbs 1500m (5000ft) from the banks of the Indus river in 36 hairpin bends known as the Hangroo Loops, in a spectacular feat of engineering by the Indian army. Above the loops is the Lamayuru Monastery.

The first 7km (4½ miles) of the trail pass through the village and climb gently across the mountainside to Prinkiti La (3750m/12300ft) from where it descends a dry, narrow gorge to the village of Shila and continues to Wanla (3245m/10650ft) in 3½ hrs. Camp at Franzila (3200m/10500ft) 6km (3½ miles) further down the trail. Next day follow a wide level path to Franzila village, cross the bridge and climb a ridge until the trail enters a spectacular narrow gorge, with the path being cut into the rocks. If you have hired packhorses this can be difficult for them. The well-defined trail continues to the village of Hanupatta (3780m/12400ft), 15km (9 miles) away. Camp a little beyond the village. This section takes 5–6 hrs.

The third day involves a 6-hour 20km (12½ miles) trek to Photoksar (4235m/13900ft). It begins with a long but fairly gradual ascent to Sir Sir La (4975m/16320ft) and then descends (steeply at first) to the large village of Photoksar.

TREK ESSENTIALS

LENGTH 3 weeks; 187km (116 miles). Walking from Lamayuru: 4 days to Singi La, 4 days to Zangla, 2 days to Padum.

ACCESS Fly or drive to Leh, then a 125km (78 miles) drive leads to Lamayuru Monastery on the main road to Kargil.

HIGHEST POINT Singi La, 5060m (16600ft). Passes: several; highest is Singi La.

GRADE Strenuous.

SEASONS July to September.

RESTRICTIONS None.

FURTHER OPTIONS Combine with Trek 22 (see page 144) to Phuktal Monastery, Shingo La to Darcha.

On day four climb gradually to the top of the Bumiktse La (4200m/13780ft) with wonderful views of the Zanskar Range. Descend gently to the river into a broad valley and climb gradually to the base of Singi La (4600m/15090ft) in approximately 5 hours, 20km (12½ miles).

Singi La to Zangla

The next day starts with a short ascent to the top of Singi La (5060m/16600ft) another vantage point for views of the Zanskar mountains. At Singi La the trail enters the central Zanskar Valley. From the pass an initially steep descent becomes more

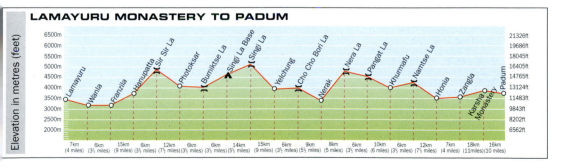

LAMAYURU MONASTERY TO PADUM

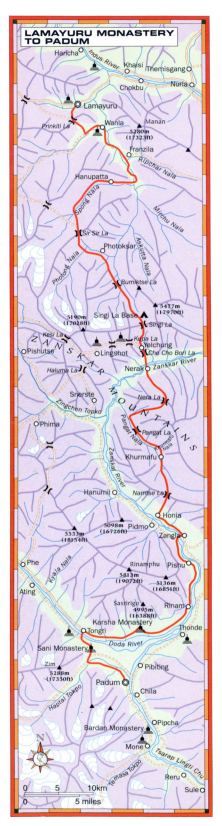

gradual to reach Yelchung (3880m/12730ft), 15km (9 miles) ahead. Two routes lead to Padum from here. The longer one, via Snerste, crosses more to the west and follows the right bank of the Zanskar River, while the shorter one, via Nera La, follows the left bank.

Follow the path to Cho Cho Bori La (4020m/13200ft). After this pass, a rather steep descent leads to the Zanskar River which flows northwards. Cross a bridge over the river and climb 300m (1000ft) to Nerak (3352m/11000ft), 15km (9 miles) further. Camp here, near what is possibly the oldest and broadest tree in Zanskar.

The seventh day is the longest day of the trail. It starts with a steep 2-hour climb of about 8km (5 miles), crossing two or three ridges to reach Nera La (4860m/15966ft). A small traverse leads to another pass, the Pangat La (4570m/15000ft). Suddenly, a magnificent and giant canyon opens up. After a small descent follow the Pangat nala to join the Khurmafu nala and follow the trail south. A total walk of 24km (15 miles) will bring you to the camp grounds of Khurmafu (3810m/12500ft).

The last pass, Namtse La (4430m/14530ft) bars the way to the broad central Zanskar Valley. The climb to the pass is gentle but involves a steep descent to the flat valley and the Zanskar River at Honia (3378m/11080ft) after 18km (11 miles). After a flat walk of 7km (4½ miles) in this beautiful valley you will reach Zangla village (3370m/11050ft), where the locals are very friendly. There are many camping spots nearby.

Zangla to Padum

The last two days are flat walks in the valley and with all the passes already behind, this is a very enjoyable part of the trek.

Cross the long rope bridge across the Zanskar River near Zangla to the right bank. A long walk of 18km (11 miles) brings you to Karsha Monastery (3660m/12000ft), situated on a hill. This is a large monastery which houses several lamas. Camp here. On the last day of the trek, walk 16km (10 miles) to Sani Monastery (3500m/11500ft) and then to Padum

The rope bridge at Zangla swings precariously across the Zanskar River.

Lamayuru Monastery nestles among the rugged mountains that rise up from the banks of the Indus River 1500m (5000ft) below.

(3615m/11858ft), a large town with a road linking it to Kargil (234km/145 miles). There are several houses, lodges and hotels here, and trails lead to Kishtwar (closed at present) and Shingo La. If you are not driving to Kargil (onwards to Srinagar or Leh) then in three more days you can join the Phuktal Monastery trail as follows:

The first day to Reru involves a 16-km (10- mile) walk of approximately 6 hours. The road is under construction and the trail is dusty and monotonous until Bardan *gompa* (3600m/11800ft). Built in the 17th century, this monastery perches like a medieval fortress above the river. It has a giant prayer wheel and its Bhutanese-style assembly hall contains fine old *mandala* (tantric) paintings. Follow the undulating path to Mone, a lovely little village, or continue to Reru where you can camp opposite the village.

The second day's walk to Gyalpoh is difficult, mostly on boulders and across small streams. Descend to the river. The trail cuts across the canyon slope and gets difficult at times. On the opposite bank is the lovely fortified village of Ichar. Continue past some small tea houses to camp at the village of Gyalpoh. This takes approximately 5 hours, 12km (7½ miles). On the third day follow the trail to Purne and Phuktal Monastery in a 10-km (6- mile) walk to join Trek 22.

Walk-out via Darcha

Trek to Darcha (over Shingo La) and drive to Manali (via Keylong and across the Rohtang Pass) as in Trek 22. Or you can drive out via Kargil.

THE TCHADDAR

Literally, 'tchaddar' means a sheet, generally white. Zanskar is a land-locked country with high passes on all sides. Though a moorable road links Padum with Kargil in the west, ethnically the Zanskaris have major links with Leh in the north. The trekking route across the high passes to Lamayuru is blocked due to snow on the heights during the six-month long winter. Due to the severity of the winter, the Zanskar River is frozen too, appearing like a white sheet. Enterprising Zanskaris trek next to the river, passing the gorges and on the frozen river itself, reaching Nimo which is linked to Leh. In recent years this arduous trail has also been followed by Western trekkers.

LEH, A MEETING PLACE FOR CARAVANS

The word that greets you at Leh is *jule*, which is an expression of hello, thank you, *namaste* and goodbye all rolled into one. As you become acquainted with the local people you will hear this word again and again, and it encapsulates the essence of this town as a historic meeting place where many different cultures have come to trade for centuries.

Leh, the capital of Ladakh, is basically a one-street town, with a huge *chorten* or buddhist monument at its entrance. The view of the Stok Kangri Range in the south dominates the Indus Valley.

The Indus is Leh's major river (and of Ladakh), and cuts across the main valley, supplying water to

The town of Leh with its Buddhist *chorten* in the foreground.

what would otherwise be a high desert. The dry, thin air and the barrenness are instantly apparent. During the summer months the people of Leh picnic on the shores of the Indus and during severe winter months, when the river is frozen, trucks drive over it.

To the north of Leh stands the Khardung Range, which separates the town from the East Karakoram Mountains. A road leads to the Khardung Pass (5606m/18392ft), the highest motorable pass in the world, with a wonderful view to the north. Singe Namgyal's Palace, with an ancient monastery, stands on a hill nearby. There are also reminders of less welcome visitors, such as the fort of the ill-fated army of the Dogra general Zorawar Singh which, after capturing Ladakh in the 1840s and building monuments in Leh, proceeded east to Taklakot near Manasarovar Lake in western Tibet. There they were trapped by the winter snows and Zorawar Singh and his army were massacred by Chinese troops.

Leh itself bears signs of the past and scars of the present. You will see a variety of cultures, predominantly Buddhist and Muslim, with several Hindu and Christian families as well. The features of the people vary from Mongolian to Aryan. You can *feel* the Trans-Himalaya.

Leh has long been a meeting place of caravans from Yarkand, Tibet, Kashmir and Kullu. It used to take a month to reach here from Delhi but now you can do it in just two days' road travel or fly direct to Leh. Muslim traders came here from across the Karakoram Pass, which leads to the famous Silk Road. Buddhist monks came from the east, cutting across the Tibetan Plateau and bringing their religion with them. The earliest Western visitors were Christian missionaries such as the Moravian Brethren, some of whom travelled ahead to Central Asia. Hindu traders reached Leh and Ladakh from the southern Kullu and Lahaul valleys. Each culture has left its mark on life in Leh. There is also an obvious Indian Army presence in and around Leh, which has existed since the 1962 war with China.

The Moravian Christian Mission Church (1885) was established by the early Moravian Brethren, who reached Leh by crossing the Mana Pass in Garhwal. Once it housed a huge library. There is a travellers' cemetery here and its most noteworthy resident is the naturalist and geologist Dr Ferdinand Stoliczka, who died in 1874. A popular bird of Ladakh, Stoliczka's Bush-chat, is named after him, and the marble tower on the outskirts of Leh has been erected in his memory.

Today, as always, many cultures mix on the streets of Leh. There is a German Mission that helps farmers while the Indian Army has introduced several new varieties of crops to the region and the town has been made far greener by their efforts. The Institute of Ladakh Studies is located in the town and has recorded much of Leh's history. In 1995 the Japanese built a *shanti stupa* (peace monument) that towers above the town.

The historic Moravian Christian Mission Church in Leh.

There are several comfortable hotels, taxis and agents to cater for trekkers and tourists. Many large houses line the horizon and there are excellent schools.

The inhabitants of Leh make the most of modern-day transport and migrate to the Indian plains by the plane-load during the severe winter months.

Leh is home to Muslims, Christians, Hindus, and Buddhists who worship at the Thikse Monastery (below).

TREK 24: TSO MORIRI TO TSO KAR (RUPSHU)

The trans-Himalayan villagers were traders covering large distances, but they rarely carried their loads themselves, unlike their counterparts in Garhwal. These villagers rode horses and their loads were carried on pack animals. This trail crosses several passes in the Rupshu area, which is a spectacular district in southeast Ladakh. It starts at Korzok, the only major village in the Rupshu and, after circling the historic Tso Kar (Salt Lake), meets the road. This is an easy trail passing through very beautiful riding and trekking country.

From Leh, the road travels east to Upshi (46km/28 miles) on the Manali Highway. After passing Chumathang, the road crosses a bridge at Mahe, where permits will be inspected. Turning west and then south, a sandy road crosses the small pass of Namshang La from where you can see Tazangkuru Lake. The descent towards Tso Moriri crosses many streams and finally you drive along the lake's western shore to Korzok (31km/19 miles). Visit the monastery and spend a day here to acclimatise. Horses, *khotas* (load-carrying donkeys) and a guide can be arranged here.

TREK ESSENTIALS

LENGTH 2 weeks; 130km (81miles). Walking from Korzok: 4 days to Thugje, 4 days to Korzok.
ACCESS Fly to Leh, then drive 213km (132 miles) to Korzok via Mahe.
HIGHEST POINT Kanyur La (5410m/17750ft). Passes: several; the highest after Kanyur La is Yalegaon, 5400m (17715ft).
GRADE Easy.
SEASONS Mid-June to mid-September.
RESTRICTIONS Permits required but readily obtainable.
FURTHER OPTIONS Join Trek 21 (page 140) across Parang La.

Korzok to Thugje

A long ridge containing the peaks of the Mentok range runs behind Korzok (4527m/14850ft). A gap in the ridge leads to Korzokphule, a vast open ground used by the villagers for grazing and for some meagre cultivation. The trail begins by crossing this open ground. Slowly turning southwards, the trail climbs to a prominent ridge and Yalegaon

Pass (5400m/17715ft). Some maps mark this as Lamlung Pass. There are several easy peaks near the pass. Descend the Lam Lungpa river from the pass to Gyamsumdo (5100m/16730ft). The total walk is 18km (11 miles). The trail crosses the same terrain the next day as you climb to Gyamsu (5400m/17715ft) and cross Kanyur La (5410m/17750ft). One of the common features of this area is the afternoon hailstorm, generated by the heat of the Rupshu plain. This is usually a short but often severe phenomenon. From the second pass descend to meet the Spanglung Sarpa nala and camp after 16km (10 miles) in the wide-open plain of Razang Kuru, (4915m/16125ft) by the stream which drains the vast snowfields on the high ridges to the east. On these ridges the snow is permanent and the area is nicknamed 'Rupshu ice-cap' by the pilots who fly over it.

On the third day you enter a wonderful country where you are likely to come across some wild *skyangs* (wild donkeys) roaming the slopes. Cross the small pass of Rang La (4980m/16340ft) and traverse a valley after a short descent. The path

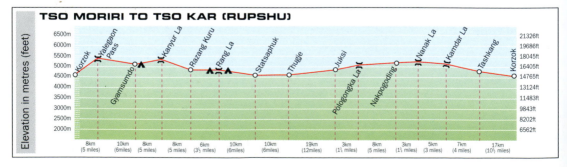

TSO MORIRI TO TSO KAR (RUPSHU)

climbs the next ridge to the small depression of Statsaphuk (4600m/15090ft), from where the vast plains of the Statsaphuk Lake, Tso Kar and Pologongka Peak are visible. The descent to the first lake is gentle and the next night is spent camping on the grass, a rare thing in barren Rupshu. Now you are in completely flat countryside. The trail cuts between the two lakes and crosses this vast plain. You will come across some salt deposits – Tso Kar once produced salt for most of Ladakh. You will also cross a road which traverses the plain from Pologongka to Debring (on the Leh–Manali road).

Continue to the northern edge of the plain to reach Thugje village after 10km (6 miles) (4600m/15090ft). This is a nomad village with hardly any proper houses. The Changpas camp here during the summer months and scatter all around the plain with their pashmina goats. A small but ancient monastery overlooks Thugje. As you climb up the gentle trail along a long *mani* wall you will see a vast panorama, particularly of Tso Kar with white salt deposits all around it. Tso Kar is also the home of rare black-necked cranes, which were first spotted in Ladakh by the well-known Indian ornithologist, Dr Salim Ali.

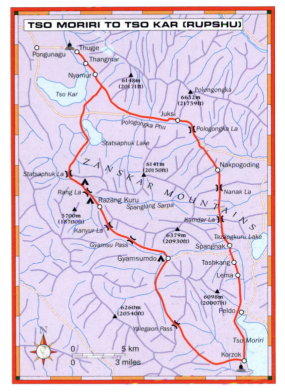

Thugje to Korzok

From Thugje retrace the route south to a prominent depression in the east, the Pologongka La, a traditional pass that you can now drive over. After a flat walk of 19km (12 miles), camp at Juksi (4940m/16210ft) where water is available. The camping ground is right next to the road and you may meet jeep-safari travellers, now frequently found in this area. Opposite the camp rises the huge massif of Pologongka Peak (6632m/21760ft), the recently climbed, second highest peak in Rupshu. Next day continue to Pologongka La (5060m/16600ft). The road descends steeply in a zigzag, the trail leaves it to the south and crosses the high ridge on the horizon, on the other side of which is the plain of Nakpogoding ('place of black rocks'), with a nala of the same name crossing it in the middle. Camp next to the Nakpogoding nala.

The trail now traverses the open slopes and crosses several ridges, the small depression of Nanak La (5240m/17190ft) and later, after a vast meadow, the Kamdar La (5120m/16799ft). There is a wonderful view of the Tazangkuru from this pass and in the distance you will see the emerald

Changpa nomads tending their pashmina goats in Thugje, near Rupshu.

PEAK: MENTOK II

This is a lovely peak on a long ridge running south from the Korzok village. To its east lies Tso Moriri and to the west is the Phirste Phu Valley. In July and August the entire Korzokphule valley is green with flowers giving the peak its name; Mentok means flower in Tibetan. On some old maps this peak is known as Mata.

Getting to Base Camp

From Korzok walk with mules and khotas (load-carrying donkeys) into the vast Korzokphule Valley behind Korzok village to the immediate west. Keep generally to the left once you enter this valley. After about 6km (3½ miles), set up Base Camp at the foot of the steep slopes at 4600m (15100ft). A broad trail leads to the base.

Climb the steep slopes, zigzagging on a shepherds' trail to reach the col between Mentok I and II. While Peak I requires some delicate climbing, Peak II is a fairly simple climb going up steep scree slopes. From early June to mid-July the upper slopes may be snow-bound creating tiring snow plods.

The route to the summit of Mentok II from the second camp, on the col.

CLIMB ESSENTIALS

SUMMIT Mentok II, 6172m (20250ft)
PRINCIPAL CAMPS Base camp: foot of Mentok II (4600m/15100ft). Two more camps on the western slopes at 5250m (17220ft) and 5800m (19030ft).
GRADE Easy snow-plod.
MAP REFERENCE See sketch-map for Tso Kar–Tso Moriri (Rupshu) (Trek 24) on page 153.

Steps may need to be cut with an ice axe on the steeper sections. The first camp is set up on a small flat piece of ground on the steep eastern slopes, at 5250m (17220 ft). The second camp is on the col, to the north of Peak II, at 5800m (19030 ft).

From the summit there are excellent views of the Chhamser Kangri and Lungser Kangri peaks to the east across the Tso Moriri. To the west are the rolling hills of Rupshu. You can traverse this ridge and descend from various points.

waters of Tso Moriri which appears deceptively close, as if you can reach the lake by evening, but it is still two days away. The trail descends steeply to the camp at Tashkang (4800m/15750ft) after 15km (9 miles).

On the last day take a short cut to the western shore of Tso Moriri. This walk is enjoyable especially as it takes you past some Changpa camps. However, each camp is guarded by ferocious dogs, so make sure that the owner is present and welcomes you before you go anywhere near it.

The Changpas have an interesting legend about how the name of Tso Moriri originated. A female nun (*chomo*) was riding a yak along the lakeside. She tried to stop the yak by pulling on the reins and shouting 'Ri Ri', the traditional call to halt a yak. The yak failed to stop and pulled her into the lake, and hence the name of Tso Moriri. An old gazetteer gives a more mundane explanation, stating 'Moriri' as mountain, therefore Tso Moriri translates as mountain lake.

In the evening walk leisurely along the road by the side of the lake and reach Korzok after 17km (10½ miles) to complete the trek.

Drive-out via Leh
Drive back to Leh – transport must be pre-arranged, as there are no local buses or taxis.

The salt plains of Tso Kar from Thugje Monastery.

THE VILLAGE OF KORZOK

Korzok is a small village and most of its inhabitants are nomadic shepherds. During the summer months they camp at various places in their *rabos* (small tents) and look after their flock. Their sheep produce pashmina, one of the most expensive types of wool. The recent boom in its value has led to their prosperity, though this is not evident in their lifestyle.

The name 'Korzok' means the middle of the body (where the soul resides) or the middle of a mountain (where it is). The village has a superb location, overlooking Tso Moriri. The monastery at Korzok is very old and thought to have been built about 500 years ago. Lying on the route between Spiti and Ladakh, the monastery was visited by almost all the early explorers and today it is a popular tourist destination. People as far away as Hanle in the south and the Indus Valley in the north have followed the teaching of this monastery's gurus. In 1995 a lama-incarnate arrived from Darjeeling to head the congregation. The young lama-incarnate, known locally as a *tulku*, was then a six-year-old boy.

There is a small palace next to the monastery and the erstwhile 'king' and 'queen' of the Rupshu district work at the rest house and at the Nyoma weaving centre.

PEAK: CHHAMSER KANGRI

This is the third highest peak of Ladakh but not too difficult. Permission to climb is required from the Indian Mountaineering Foundation, New Delhi. Proper acclimatisation is essential and you will need to spend at least five days after arriving in Leh to acclimatise. To reach the summit, follow the Kurchyu nala up to the western face.

Korzok to Base Camp

Drive from Leh to Korzok on Tso Moriri as in Trek 24 (see page 155). Porters and mules are available in the village. In a day-long trek, walk along the lake to the eastern shore. After a climb, you will reach a grassy slope called Kurchyu (4915m/16125ft). Water is available here and you can establish Base Camp.

Western Slopes

Climb the slopes above Base Camp to a large plateau to set up another camp at Rugyado Phu (5720m/18770ft). Cross over to the south on this slope and, after a long walk, another higher plateau is reached to set up Camp 1 at 6160m (20210ft). The ascent is never difficult but with increasing altitude the thin air makes it hard work. The afternoon heat in Ladakh is also very dehydrating.

Southern Ridge

On the summit day follow the southern ridge, reaching it from the last camp by following the western steep slopes. Some snow or scree covered grounds will be tricky. Once on the ridge, follow the long and rising slopes to the summit.

There is a wonderful view from the top, looking east to the Indus, while on the west is Tso Moriri. You can make a fast descent from the summit, reaching Korzok in about three days.

CLIMB ESSENTIALS

SUMMIT Chhamser Kangri (6622m/21725ft).
PRINCIPAL CAMPS Base Camp: Kurchyu (4915m/16125ft). Two more camps on the western slopes at Rugyado Phu (5720m/18770ft) and Camp 1 (6160m/20210ft).
GRADE Some steep snow but no crevasses.
MAP REFERENCE See sketch-map of Rupshu/Tso Moriri.

The route to the summit of Chhamser Kangri Peak across its western face from Tso Moriri.

PEAK: LUNGSER KANGRI

The route to Lungser Kangri Peak. Tso Moriri is in the foreground.

This is the highest peak in Ladakh but easy to climb and quite popular with climbers. Permission to do so is required from the IMF. Proper acclimatisation is a necessity, and you must spend at least five days after arrival in Leh to acclimatise.

Korzok to Base Camp

Drive from Leh to Korzok by Tso Moriri (see trek 24). Mules (or pack-horses) are available in the village. In a day-long trek follow the shores of the lake to the eastern shore. After a climb you will reach a grassy slope called Kurchyu. Water is available here. Continue to another prominent nala named after the peak, the Lungser nala, which drains into Tso Moriri, to establish Base Camp (4915/16125ft).

Camp 1 and Camp 2

Follow the Lungser nala which at first rises gently and leads to a bowl. Take a path on the left hand side to reach an open plateau. Camp here (6160m/20210ft) as some water is available. The next day keep going ahead to a small lake. It is possible to camp here but it is better to descend about 300m (1000ft) to a nala to camp (6240m/20570ft). If you camp at the lake or above, you will have reclimb these slopes, after a tiring day to the summit, on your return.

East to the Summit

On the summit day proceed to the prominent col to the east, climbing steeply at first. Turn south on the ridge, which in a series of slopes climbs to the peak. The final peak is very tiring and deceptive, as the false summits rise in waves for a long distance. The extreme southern edge is the top. A view of the Hanle plateau is your reward with a sight of Tso Moriri to the west.

Descend quickly as the distance is long. Reach the last camp and rest. Next day you can return to Korzok, if desired, in a long day's trek.

CLIMB ESSENTIALS

SUMMIT Lungser Kangri, 6666m (21870ft).
PRINCIPAL CAMPS Base Camp: above the lake at Kurchyu (4915m/16125ft). Two more camps at 6160m (20210ft) and 6240m (20470ft).
GRADE Tiring traverse on summit ridge; some crevasses.
MAP REFERENCE See sketch-map of Rupshu/Tso Moriri (Trek 24) page 152.

TREK 25: THE NUBRA VALLEY

The prominent Khardung Ridge runs north of Leh. The traditional pass of Khardung La across the ridge is now a road with heavy traffic, which carries supplies to the remote but fertile Nubra and Shyok valleys. These valleys were only recently opened to trekkers, so most parts of these valleys remain unexplored and unknown: still a mystery to the outside world. An easy broad valley leads across the Digar La, which crosses the main Ladakh Range. The return is via the Lasermo La from Hunder which re-crosses the Ladakh range to Leh in the south.

Leh, literally, 'a meeting place for caravans', is the capital of Ladakh. Once remote, it is now a popular tourist destination, with several hotels and daily flights linking it to Delhi, Srinagar, Jammu and Chandigarh. Spend at least 2 nights here for acclimatisation before trekking, particularly if you have arrived by plane.

The Indus flows through the centre of the Leh valley, and there are several famous *gompas* (monasteries) here. The trek described begins at Skampari.

TREK ESSENTIALS

LENGTH 2 weeks; 124km (77½ miles). Walking from Skampari: 5 days to Khalsar, 5 days from Hunder to Phyang (return route).
ACCESS Fly or drive to Leh, thentake a bus to Skampari.
HIGHEST POINT Digar La, 5420m (17780ft); Passes: Digar La, Lasermo La, 5400m (17710ft).
GRADE Easy.
SEASONS July to September.
RESTRICTIONS Groups of a minimum of 4 persons are required for the trek.
FURTHER OPTIONS Visits to the unknown parts of the Nubra Valley and its monasteries can be combined with this trek.

Skampari to Khalsar

The first day's trek is a gradual climb on a fairly broad trail to Sabu village and monastery, 9km (6 miles) (3480m/11420ft). Continue along the trail for about a kilometre to camp at the ruins of Sabu Zong – Zong means 'fort' in Ladakhi.

On the second day, continue climbing through pastures along the Sabu nala. Grand views, particularly of the Stok Kangri range, towards the Indus valley open up. Finally, level ground is reached at Digar Polu (south), 8km (5 miles), (4500m/

14760ft). Three kilometres (1¾ miles) further on, where two nalas meet, there is an open camping ground (4830m/15850ft). From here, the next day's climb to the pass is easier.

Start early the next day and continue climbing along the Sabu nala to a prominent fork in the valleys. Follow the valley to the northeast and, after a traverse along the slopes, Digar La, 9km (6 miles), 5 hrs, (5420m/17780ft), is reached. From the top the most beautiful views of the Karakoram Mountains, particularly the Arganglas and Saser Kangri massifs, are visible. Cross small plateaus to camp at the northern base of the pass at Digar Polu (north), (4600m/15,090ft), 9km (6 miles).

Continue to descend along the Lungtung Phu River to the large village of Digar, 12km (8 miles) (4035m/13240ft), from where you can visit the little monastery above the village as well as the historic village of Khyumru which is located across the river. There is a school at Digar and you can meet the friendly villagers as they go about their daily chores.

The last day of the trek from Digar is a fairly hot stretch as you walk in the open above the Shyok River and passing far above the village of Aghyam. Camp at Hootoong (3200m/10,500ft). The village is on the banks of the Shyok River and a new motor

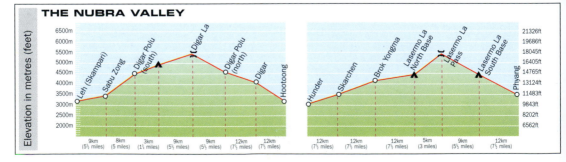

THE NUBRA VALLEY

Elevation in metres (feet)

Leh (Skampari) – Sabu Zong – Digar Polu (south) – Digar La – Digar Polu (north) – Digar – Hootoong

9km (5½ miles) · 8km (5 miles) · 3km (1¾ miles) · 9km (5½ miles) · 9km (5½ miles) · 12km (7½ miles) · 12km (7½ miles)

Hunder – Skarchen – Brok Yongma – Lasermo La North Base – Lasermo La Pass – Lasermo La South Base – Phyang

12km (7½ miles) · 12km (7½ miles) · 12km (7½ miles) · 5km (3 miles) · 9km (5½ miles) · 12km (7½ miles)

6500m · 6000m · 5500m · 5000m · 4500m · 4000m · 3500m · 3000m · 2500m · 2000m

21326ft · 19686ft · 18045ft · 16405ft · 14765ft · 13124ft · 11483ft · 9843ft · 8202ft · 6562ft

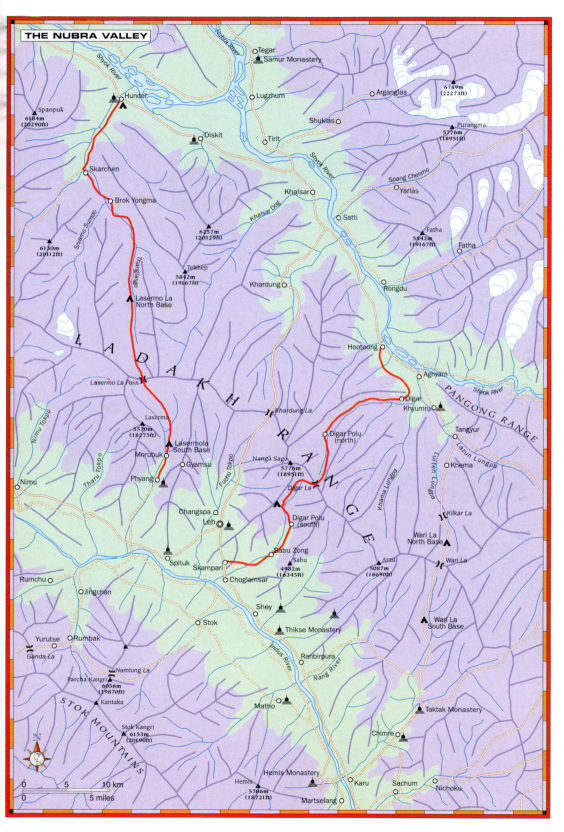

The Nubra Valley near the remote village of Panamik.

Nubra and the Shyok rivers the fertile and green Nubra Valley can be visited as far as the remote village of Panamik, which has many beautiful monasteries. The Shyok Valley in the west has a lovely fortified monastery next to the road at Hunder. You could drive from Khalsar back to Leh (95km/59 miles) across the Khardung La (5602m/18380ft) with spectacular views. But better still is to return across the Khardung Ridge in a 4-day trek, as described below.

road (under construction) from Leh across Wari La joins the trail here.

From Hootoong, you can walk to the roadhead at Khalsar in 3 to 4 hours, and take a bus or truck to Hunder (29km/18 miles), but, a better option, which must be arranged in advance, is to raft down the fast-flowing Shyok River to the camp at Hunder.

From Khalsar, near the meeting point of the

The view from the roof of Sumur Monastery.

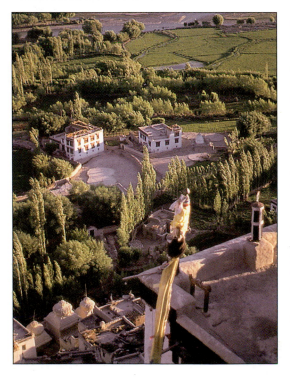

Hunder to Phyang

A pleasant alternative after reaching the Nubra Valley is to walk back to Leh across the Lasermo La (5400m/17710ft) from Hunder, the last point open to trekkers in the Shyok Valley. Turn south from here and follow the broad valley for 12km (7½ miles), with a trail along the river to a bridge. After the bridge a gentle climb brings you to a narrow and impressive gorge leading to a long plateau, beyond which is the small hamlet of Skarchen (3500m/11480ft) at the confluence of two streams.

Next day continue gradually for 12km (7½ miles) up the beautiful, flower-filled summer pastures of Hunder Dok and follow the Thanglasgo River to camp at Brok Yogma (4200m/13780ft). The next day the gentle climb follows a stream through more flower-carpeted pastures to camp at the base of Lasermo La (4500m/14760ft), 12km (7½ miles).

Climb to the snowline and moraine to the Lasermo La (5400m/17710ft). There are excellent views of the Karakoram Mountains behind and the valleys on both sides. If there is snow on the pass (it is easier to cross after mid-August) the pack animals will have to be unloaded. Descend into the Phyang Valley to camp (4500m/14760ft), 14km (8½ miles).

Walk-out via Phyang

The easiest way out is to descend steeply to Morubuk, walk to Phyang (12km/7½ miles) and hitch a lift to Leh. For those with more time and energy, two further passes in this valley can be crossed, both gradual. Walk along the ridge to the pastures of Gyamsu, 12km (7½ miles), and then either drive back to Leh, or continue walking to Leh where the trek ends at Changspa village, a 20-km (12½-mile), 7-hour walk in total.

ZANSKAR-LADAKH DIRECTORY

REGIONAL TRANSPORT
The quickest way to Ladakh is to fly to Leh from Delhi. Daily flights connect Leh with Delhi, Chandigarh, Srinagar and Jammu. By road it takes at least a 4-day journey to reach Leh: via Manali by the Manali–Leh highway (generally open July to October). At present it is not advisable to travel on the road from Srinagar to Leh.

REST HOUSE/HOTEL LOCATIONS
Alchi, Diskit, Kargil, Korzok, Lamayuru, Leh, Padum, Panamik, Stok, Tegar, Thikse.

REGIONAL TOURIST OFFICES
Tourist Reception Centre, Srinagar (Jammu & Kashmir State) 191 001, tel (91-194) 452-690, fax (91-194) 479-548
J & K Tourist Office, 201/203 Kanishka Shopping Plaza, 19 Ashoka Road, New Delhi 110 001, tel (91-11) 334-5373, fax (91-11) 336-7881
J & K Tourist Office, Vir Marg, Jammu, tel (91-191) 548172 fax(91-191) 548-358
J & K Tourist Office, Main Road, Leh, Ladakh, tel (91-1982) 52297 fax (91-1982) 52095

RESTRICTIONS
Zanskar is open to trekkers and climbers without any restrictions. The eastern parts of Ladakh such as Pangong Lake are open with permits for visitors. The southeastern areas of the Rupshu Valley allow unrestricted travel. This has given access to a large number of peaks and treks, including Lungser Kangri, Chhamser Kangri and Kula. However, you will still need a formal permit from Leh to visit the area. The Nubra Valley up to Sasoma is open to foreigners (in groups of four) with permits. Tourists are allowed free access to Diskit and Hunder, from where they can trek south across the Khardung Range. Areas such as the Siachen Glacier and Rimo are highly restricted.

LOCAL PLACES OF INTEREST
Leh: Namgyal Palace, Zorawar Fort, Shanti Stupa, Stoliczka memorial, Moravian Church, Spituk Monastery.
Around Leh: Stok Palace and Museum, Stakna, Thikse, Shey, Hemis and Matho monasteries, Khardung La.
Ladakh: Likir, Lamayuru and Alchi monasteries, Dahanu Aryan village.
Long drives from Leh: Lakes Pangong and Tso Moriri.
Nubra Valley: Diskit, Sumur and Hunder monasteries, Panamik Hot Springs, Bactrian camels near Diskit.
Zanskar: Karsha, Sani, Ringdom and Phuktal monasteries.

TELEPHONE CODES
Jammu 0191, Kargil 01985, Leh 01982, Padum 01983, Srinagar 0194.

IMPORTANT PEAKS SEEN EN ROUTE

Name of peak	Seen from
Saser Kangri Group	Khardung La
Stok Kangri	Leh
Lungser Kangri	Rupshu Valley
Chhamser Kangri	Korzok
Parilungbi	Parang La
Monto	Tso Moriri trail
Ramjak	Shingo La

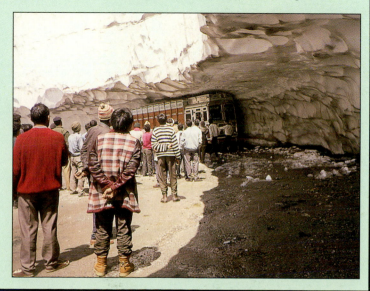
Traffic jam, a common hazard on the Manali–Leh Road, near the Rohtang Pass.

PROTECTING THE HIMALAYA

Whoever thought that the mighty mountains that form formidable frontiers would need protection? Now sustainable development and carrying capacity are some of the buzzwords doing the rounds in politically correct circles; there is an increasing awareness of the subject, and a substantial amount of funds is being made available for preserving the environment as a heritage for the future.

The Himalaya gets visitors in such volume that in several places, roads and campsites have become part of the landscape, wildlife has been chased away into areas away from their natural habitats, and the food-chain and ecosystem have been seriously disrupted. Poachers and hunters have shrunk the numbers of animals such as the musk and the hunting deer, tahr, goral and snow leopards. According to the Wildlife (Protection) Act of 1972, within all the National Parks, six of the fifteen indigenous species of mammals and seven of the eighty observed species of birds are considered endangered. It is hoped that areas like Hemkund, Har-ki-Dun, Gangotri and portions of the Zanskar Valley (amongst the main popular trekking destinations) have not reached the point of no return.

Yaks graze in Dzongri's serene valley below Kangchenjunga Peak.

Considering that over 2 million tourists and possibly an equal number of pilgrims visit various areas in the Himalaya, and that the infrastructure to cater to their needs is poor, the impact on the environment is enormous and uncontrolled. Mules, ponies and cattle are allowed to overgraze. Non-biodegradable rubbish such as gas cylinders, carbon tetrachloride bottles and even first aid medicines is accumulating, and the fragile ecosystem of the high ranges cannot cope with the destruction. The result? Landslides, permanent loss of important medicinal herbs, extinction of insect, bird and animal species, many of which are found nowhere else in the world, floods in the plains, erosion on the slopes, and an increase in human misery in the long term. A major basic resource, water, is overused and depleted.

Many of the Himalayan regions earn a lot of revenue through tourism. Local workers, once dependent on subsistence farming, have now become entrepreneurs. There are probably very few families whose income is not affected, directly or indirectly, by tourism. Although an increasing number of tourists indicates a faster rate of destruction, India actively promotes the expansion of the tourism industry for the economic benefits it can bring. There has been an unplanned use of the resources without study of the long-term consequences, and it is only now that desperate measures are being taken to save whatever possible.

There are essentially four players in the business of environmental preservation, the primary and most important one being the indigenous population. It has the maximum to lose, and it should be educated about the long-term losses and shown that its economic progress need not be at the expense of the environment. The second is the government/administrative authority who needs to implement new rules. The third are the non-government organizations (NGOs), who can give technical guidance and act as a link between the people and the government and also help spread awareness amongst the people. And lastly the cause of it all, the tourists themselves, who need to be educated and monitored to ensure that they leave the area as it was when they arrived.

In the early 1960s, the Indo-Tibetan borders were sealed and the locals of the various Himalayan regions could no longer follow their traditional occupation: trade. That period coincided with the rise of trekking in the region, and the community did well – fortunately with no immediate serious damage to the surroundings. However, land degradation, deforestation and pollution present an increasing threat. A start towards preserving the areas been made, but progress is slow and the efforts need to be accelerated. In many areas nature parks and biosphere reserves have been established, and eco-tourism is

A carpet of flowers in the Kurgiak Valley of Zanskar. Undisturbed for centuries, will it survive the onslaught of more and more trekkers?

being encouraged to address the problems.

Mountaineering and trekking associations, nature conservationists and tourism boards need to regularly hold workshops, training programmes, clean-ups and tree plantation drives. The aims must be to:

- Train managers for sustainable tourism.
- Provide training and awareness in conservation, and techniques for field and office staff of the trekking agencies.
- Help co-ordinate trekking staff and local community people, especially from the trekking regions, and promote environmentally friendly trekking.
- Raise awareness of issues such as health and hygiene and explain their importance.
- Familiarize participants with cultural and natural heritage and its relation to the trekking business.
- Make participants realize the importance of alternative fuel with regard to the environment.
- Enlighten participants about recycling of disposable items and their impact on trekking.

Human needs have to be balanced with the environment on a sustainable basis by ensuring maximum community participation through a process in which people are both the principal actors and beneficiaries. Tourists themselves also have to be educated on what effect they have on the place they have chosen to visit, and this is no mean task.

The crucial factor in the above activities is the involvement of the indigenous population, for whom the environment can be a steady and long-term source of income if the community is sufficiently edu-

cated in sustainable exploitation. As was demonstrated in the Chipko movement in Tehri (Garhwal Himalaya) when Sunderlal Bahuguna inspired the local women to physically hold on to the trees to prevent the contractors from cutting them, it is the people's convictions that can work the most wonders.

GANGOTRI GLACIER

The Gangotri Glacier is perhaps the most visited place in the Indian Himalaya. The Gangotri temple has been visited by thousands of pilgrims for generations and a road now reaches it. About 20km away is the snout of the main glacier at Gaumukh, and many expeditions and trekkers have visited its upper reaches and side valleys. In the past, porters would carry the party's equipment and food, and use wood and the area's other scarce resources. Then the Bhojbasa (literally, 'place of birch trees') was suddenly devoid of birch trees and shrubs. To feed the pilgrims, tea stalls and dhabas sprang up near Gaumukh and used yet more of the precious local resources. As a result, this area sustained a worse human impact than anywhere else in the Himalayan environment.

In response to the worsening situation, the Himalayan Environment Trust (HET), under the patronage of Sir Edmund Hillary, started the 'The Gangotri Conservation Project', one of the first of its kind in the Indian Himalaya. Porters were employed to clean the base camp sites, toilets were erected, and an incinerator was installed near the temple. HET also helped to draw up strict rules and a Code of Conduct for visitors. Funded by the international community, the project has received contributions from various sources.

MINIMAL IMPACT TREKKING

As the fastest growing industry in the world, tourism has touched every part of the globe, and the Himalaya is no exception. Its extraordinary growth has led its detractors to conclude that tourism has ruined many a fine coastline, destroyed unique wilderness areas and wildlife habitats such as Tso Moriri, polluted the air and water, uprooted communities, undermined traditional ways of life, and corrupted local cultures.

Major parts of the Indian Himalaya have been closed to visitors in the past owing to the inner line restrictions, which prohibit visitors beyond a certain point near the Tibetan border, and as a result these remained well-preserved. The necessary presence of defence forces of various sizes took its toll on the environment, but overall the areas stayed unspoiled and culturally intact. Ladakh Valley was then opened in the early 1970s to Indian and foreign visitors, and many have now visited the area. Again in the early 1990s several more areas were opened to visitors.

TSO MORIRI LAKE

As a result of 'inner line' restrictions, Tso Moriri lake and southeast Ladakh were under wraps for almost 35 years, and even before that time its difficult terrain limited access. Thus, people at the only village on its shore, Korzok, had very little contact with outsiders and lived a traditional existence. As restrictions were lifted, roads were built and it was possible to travel through this area by jeep. Rupshu arrived at a crossroad in its history. Suddenly this part of Ladakh became very popular with jeep-safari travellers and casual visitors as well as serious trekkers and mountaineers.

The area's main attractions were its beauty and its previous remoteness. Whilst remote, the area was not completely unknown. Several early travellers had visited Korzok, for it lay on the main trail joining Shimla and Spiti with Ladakh. Many people visited the lake, but did not have a major impact on the environment of the area.

At first I was a bit apprehensive about visiting Tso Moriri. It was first opened to tourist trekkers in 1994, and soon afterwards articles appeared in the press about the environmental degradation taking place in

An unspoilt meadow in the Bhilangana Valley in Garhwal.

southeast Ladakh's remote lake. The main culprits were fumes from taxis, piles of rubbish and crass commercialism. It seemed as if merely breathing the air would mean polluting it, and environmentalists recommended a total ban on visitors.

During our stay at Korzok we expected the worst sort of destruction as described by the prophets of environmental doom. But we encountered nothing more than the occasional jeep arriving with tourists. They camped near the village and visited the monastery and lake. There was no sight of the litter and fumes we had read about.

The Changpa faces lit up at the sight of tourists, for tourists mean prosperity. However, the villagers themselves were using several commercial products whose packaging was carelessly discarded. Perhaps, more than the tourists, it was the villagers who needed to be educated in matters of cleanliness and pollution, and how to use the products, including bottles and aluminium foil.

In many ways, though, the Changpas were benefiting from their interaction with modern civilization. It was changing their lifestyle, not necessarily for the worse as feared. Until only a few years ago the Changpas used the lake both to dump their rubbish and wash themselves in every morning. The quality of their houses and clothes had improved, medical facilities for both men and goats were now available, and transport enabled them to sell their wool at a better price. Some progressive measures for the future were also proposed by the authorities. No houses were allowed to be built within 700m of the lake, and the existing rest house, which was within that radius, was to be moved. Many researchers were working in this unique area. The advent of civilization and the new road had allowed tourists to enjoy the beauty of the area, and the locals to benefit.

Towards the end of the trek we spent a few hours in a nomad camp on the shores of Tso Moriri lake, observing their lifestyle and enjoying their hospitality. Nothing had changed for them as they milked the goats in the strong Rupshu wind. Children were playing, *goor goor* tea (salty tea) was served inside their comfortable *rabos* (tents), horses were grazing and a ferocious dog was constantly barking outside. In the distance, the peaks we had recently climbed rose above the deep, blue waters of Tso Moriri around which the *nangpas* (brahmany ducks) nonchalantly fluttered. I wouldn't exchange this serenity for all the dollars tourists might bring. Perhaps environmentalists are right after all. Some things must be fiercely preserved.

RESPONSIBLE TREKKING

This brings us to the conflicting interests of tourism and trekking in the remote Indian valleys. As Aamir Ali says in his famous article ('Ladakh, 1979', *Himalayan Journal*, Vol. 37, page 113), 'The old dilemma: protect Ladakh completely from outside influence as if it was a museum? Unacceptable. Allow free access to every tripper and carpet-bagger? Surely not. Where is the golden mean?'

With this debate in mind, it is the duty of all trekkers to take every care to preserve the natural environment and leave no trace of their visit. The rules are simple and should be the daily trekking habit for every visitor:

- Plan your trip carefully with the environment in mind.
- Leave the plastic and foil culture at home – wrap your food and toilet accessories in biodegradable packing and take any non-biodegradable rubbish back with you to the roadhead.
- Dig a deep hole at every campsite to bury biodegradable leftovers such as vegetable and fruit peelings.
- Carry a bundle of match sticks to burn all toilet paper and other wrappings.
- Toilet trenches should always be dug. Each member of the group should carry a small shovel to ensure all faeces are buried under the soil at least 50m from any water source.
- Ensure that you have enough kerosene for the entire trek. Discourage use of wood fires.
- Set a good example by clearing away the existing rubbish.
- Giving away sweets and pens encourages begging in the village children. Play games or share your meal with them instead.
- Plan food with local availability in mind. Try, for example, *tsampa* (a local bread made from roasted millet flour). Carry and cook your own staple foods such as rice, lentils and vegetables.
- Sharing food with others is part of Indian culture, and it is polite and friendly to share food with people on trains and treks.
- Touch money and food with your right hand. Do not drink water from another person's bottle. Food should be respected and never thrown away. Food that is not spoiled can be offered to villagers.
- Washing and bathing should be done from a bucket of water away from the river so as to not pollute the villages down river. No nude bathing please.

- Try to wear loose, long cotton trousers and top. Villagers dislike exposed hands and legs, less still a low neckline. Please respect their feelings.
- While in the villages never touch anything with your feet. No person should be touched by one's foot. Always remove footwear when entering a temple, monastery or shrine or even a house.
- Try not to show affection towards your companions publicly as this, too, is frowned upon.
- Always ask for permission before taking a photo as some people do not wish to have their picture taken. Remember to send copies if you have promised to do so. These mementos are cherished.
- Take care of your valuables, and do not flaunt your expensive belongings.

There is great debate in India about modern trekking and its impact on the environment. Trekking in such a vast and remote area is not only about observing mountains and wildlife. It is about people and places, history and landscapes. Both tourists and those who promote and provide for them affect the places they visit and the lives of local people. But as long as we strive to balance the preservation of the environment and ancient cultures with the enjoyment of visitors, trekkers and mountaineers, there is hope. One cannot keep 'change' out of the lives of people by banning all visitors. On the other hand, visitors to the Indian Himalaya could start a tiny cartwheel rolling that precipitates and speeds the kind of change that will exacerbate the destruction of the environment. The impact is both positive and negative depending on the choices made. It is imperative to appreciate the true 'value' of such areas and not merely to know the 'price' of visiting them.

Trekkers resting on a pass in Kinnaur.

MOUNTAIN PHOTOGRAPHY

In conjunction with a meticulously kept journal, a collection of photographs is the best way of recording your impressions of the Himalaya – for capturing those precious moments of scenic splendour and remembering the many people encountered along the way. Few travel these days without a camera, but attitudes to photography vary from the casual to the complete obsessive. As you will be carrying your camera equipment for many weeks or months during a season trekking in the Himalaya, careful consideration should be given to both the type of camera chosen and the film stock used.

PRINT PHOTOGRAPHY

If all you require at the end of your trip is a set of prints to pass round amongst your family and friends, then using one of the middle speed (100–200ASA) print films and having it processed by a normal commercial service should be adequate. In this case, a compact auto-focus camera with a zoom lens and built-in flash is ideal. There are hundreds to choose from, but for mountain and general outdoor use go for a waterproof or 'splash-proof' model, as these tend to have rubber seals that also serve to keep dust at bay.

If you go for the print option it is not really worth carrying a heavy professional SLR system unless you are prepared to pay for expensive specialist processing and printing. However beautifully you may monitor your exposures – to capture particular features of a landscape, for example, or detail in a wonderful shadowy forest – using the sophisticated exposure meter on a modern SLR, all this will be lost when you come to have the film processed and printed by a standard service. The modern machines used by these print-processing services simply take an average exposure value for the print. In practical terms this means that any scenes containing a high degree of contrast will be disappointing, with either sky detail washed out or foreground shadow lost completely.

SLIDE PHOTOGRAPHY

If you think you may want to give the odd slide show, reproduce some of your images for framing or even consider publishing the odd shot you should opt for colour slides. The total contrast capable of being accurately rendered by a slide film is over ten times that which a print can reproduce. In a mountain environment, where scenes often include snow slopes in bright sunshine and valleys in deep shadow, the benefits of reversal or slide films are enormous. As this type of film is developed by a set process, any subtle exposure variations made with the camera are faithfully reproduced in the final transparency.

By 'bracketing', ie. making one exposure at the value indicated by your camera's meter, and then another either side of it by up to one f-stop, you can be sure of capturing the effect you want. For example, if the meter indicates an exposure of 1/250 sec @ f8, also shoot 1/250 @ f5.6 and 1/250 @ f11. Many modern cameras have the facility to do this automatically.

A couple of other factors should be considered for slide photography. The exposure meters of most SLR cameras are calibrated for print film, and slide emulsions tend to be more sensitive. As a rule of thumb I always underexpose slide film by 1/3 or 2/3 of a stop – that is, I shoot 50ASA film at 64 or 80ASA. This is only a very minor adjustment, but it does allow the film to produce maximum colour saturation. Every camera's meter is slightly different, so if you are taking your photography seriously, shoot a roll of your chosen film at home and bracket each exposure by up to two whole stops and observe the results. This will also give you a good idea of how the film handles over- and under-exposure.

Choice of Film and Lenses

The choice of film is always a matter provoking debate. The faster the film (the more sensitive to light), the less capable it is of reproducing either colour saturation or contrast. Slower films are richer, sharper and have greater latitude. They also require more light to create an image, and in low-light conditions this can be problematic as your shutter-speeds decrease, introducing the possibility of camera-shake blurring the picture. The longer the focal length of the lens, the more pronounced this effect becomes, and for sharp hand-held exposures your shutter speed should be a value higher than the focal length of your lens in mm. Don't shoot slower than 1/125 sec with a 135mm lens. High in the Himalaya the light is often intense, and this problem only really occurs at dawn and dusk, but enthusiasts will want to be capturing just these times of day and thus the choice of lens is crucial.

The speed of film you choose will affect the type of lens you need. Let us assume that you want perfectly exposed, pin-sharp slides with rich colour saturation. Fuji's Velvia is an obvious choice, but it's only rated at 50ASA, and by the time you've put a polarising filter on your camera you've effectively reduced this to 18ASA. Most zoom lenses have maximum apertures in the f3.5–f5.6 range, and in low light, shooting slow film, you would be struggling with shutter-speeds of 1/4sec or slower, which is way too slow for hand-held exposures. To allow yourself flexibility in these light levels, you should really use a faster lens (ie one capable of transmitting more light). Professional photographers always choose this option and use lenses with maximum apertures of f2, f1.8 or even f1.4 (and even then often in conjunction with a tripod). It is possible to buy faster-than-average zoom lenses, but they are prohibitively expensive.

Almost 99 per cent of pictures taken with a zoom tend to be at one or other end of its range, where a zoom lens is at its least efficient. I would always argue for carrying two or three fast lenses with fixed focal lengths akin to the extent of a zoom. Use a 28mm f2.8, a 50mm f1.4 and a 90mm f2 rather than a 28–80mm f5.6 zoom. You may have to think about your photography a little more, but your results will be vastly improved.

BATTERIES AND CAMERA CARE
Another key point to consider when choosing a camera for the Himalaya is the type of battery required. Modern auto-focus, power-wind cameras of all types rely totally on battery power to function. There is actually a strong argument for using vintage mechanical cameras. Alkaline cells perform very poorly in low temperatures, though a camera that runs on lithium cells performs better and will be happily snapping away before dawn at 5000m (16405ft) when the thermometer is showing -25°C. All batteries drain more quickly at low temperatures, so keep them warm in your tent over night.

Dust, water and physical violence are the enemies of both photographic film and the delicate mechanisms inside every camera. Use a modern padded camera case, preferably one with a dust-gusset. Carry a blower-brush and lens tissues and use them meticulously. Clean the back of the camera every time you open it to change a film – the slightest specks of dust on the pressure-plate inside will give you skies bisected by perfect tram-lines. Heat and humidity both ruin any kind of film, so carry yours in a proper waterproof bag – especially the exposed rolls.

The majestic Shivling Peak rises above the Gangotri Glacier in the evening light.

TECHNIQUE
However many books you read, seminars you attend or friends you discuss it with, you'll only ever define your own photographic style and find out what pleases you by travelling with your camera, pointing it at the world and contemplating the results. Mountain landscape photography requires a certain element of technical accomplishment, but most of it is the result of the vision of the photographer.

One essential point to remember is that the definitive mountain photograph does not depend on form and composition, but on light. Mountain light. In the rarefied air of the high Himalaya nature puts on a daily light show that often defies language to describe it. Most of the time it defies the photographer to capture it as well, but there are two 'magic hours', around sunrise and sunset, when colour and contrast and shadow combine to bring the contours of any vista alive. Those seeking further inspiration should start by looking at Galen Rowell's superlative essay on the subject of mountain photography, *Mountain Light*.

Photographing People
Perhaps the most contentious and potentially negative aspect of travelling with a camera, in the Himalaya and the world at large, is the insatiable appetite of the average traveller for pictures of 'exotic' people. If you cannot spare the time and effort to befriend and talk to people on the trail do not be surprised if they don't consent to being photographed. Successful portraiture is a dynamic, intense process, which demands input from both sides of the camera and a sympathetic, compassionate eye on the part of the photographer. The essential ingredient is time.

HEALTH AND SAFETY

A complex and as yet not fully understood set of physical and biochemical changes occurs as the human body is exposed to the decreased levels of oxygen available in the air breathed at high altitude. The general term used to describe these changes is **acclimatisation**.

ACUTE MOUNTAIN SICKNESS

The symptoms of Acute Mountain Sickness (**AMS**), brought on when a person ascends too fast for adequate acclimatisation to take place, are simply due to the collection of fluid between the cells of the body, or edema. This primarily occurs in two potentially dangerous areas – the lungs (high-altitude pulmonary edema or **HAPE**) and the brain (high-altitude cerebral edema or **HACE**). Initial symptoms may be mild, and are not a reason to panic or disrupt an itinerary. Shortness of breath and a dry, hacking cough are early signs of HAPE, whilst headaches (especially on waking in the morning), loss of appetite and nausea are indicative of HACE.

Other, less serious, signs of inadequate acclimatisation are peripheral edema (swollen fingers, toes or face) and **Chaine-Stokes respiration** at night (a sleeping person stops breathing for half a minute or so, and then takes several deep breaths before slowly tailing off again). The latter is more alarming for any person sharing the tent – it is not dangerous, and the urge to shake the victim awake should be resisted. These conditions may develop together.

Religious adherence to three simple rules will prevent any drama or crisis due to mountain sickness:

· Learn and recognise the symptoms of AMS and do not be afraid to communicate them to your companions.
· Do not continue to ascend while suffering any of the symptoms.
· Do not remain at the same altitude if your symptoms are worsening, even if it means descending at night.

Various medical preparations are available to treat AMS, though none should properly be used prophylactically (as a preventative). Parties travelling to high (ie over 5000m/16405ft) and remote areas where descent or evacuation may be difficult or impossible should perhaps contemplate carrying a hyperbaric chamber such as a Gammov Bag. These are expensive, heavy to carry and need to be used discriminatingly, but in serious cases they can undoubtedly save lives. Their main benefit is that a debilitated victim, placed in one for several hours, may then be capable of walking down rather than being stretchered. For a traumatised party in extremis, this can be crucial. However, Gammov bags should not be used to prolong time spent at altitude by those not acclimatising naturally.

BASIC MOUNTAIN FIRST AID

'First Aid' refers to the initial management of an injured person before they are taken to a doctor or hospital. In many of the remote Himalayan areas, a doctor or hospital could be over a week's walk away. Knowing the basics of first aid, and managing an injury correctly in the first instance can often mean the difference between life and death, and prevent the later development of life threatening complications.

In the event of an accident in which immediate action is taken to save a life, the priorities are **ABC**:

A – AIRWAY B – BREATHING C – CIRCULATION

AIRWAY
Establish an open airway.

Listen for breathing sounds and if there are none, lift the chin and jaw upwards, and tilt the head back.

If there is an obvious foreign body blocking the airway, such as vomit or food, remove it.

With any victim who has fallen from a height or received a head injury, be aware that they may have broken their neck, and if at all possible do not attempt to move the patient. Keep the neck straight. In any situation where the airway is obstructed, however, the airway MUST take first priority.

BREATHING
Breathing patient
If, after clearing the airway, the victim is breathing, turn them on their side into the **recovery position**. The lower leg should be straight and the the upper one bent at the knee to act as stabiliser. Ensure that the airway remains open by continuing to extend the head, and tilt the jaw.

Non-breathing patient
Start mouth-to-mouth resuscitation: pinch the nose and blow into the victim's mouth. Form a tight seal with your own lips and watch their chest rise as you exhale. Perform two effective breaths before checking the pulse.

CIRCULATION
If the victim continues not to breath after two rescue breaths then check the pulse in their neck. If there is no pulse, start Cardio Pulmonary Resuscitation (**CPR**). CPR is performed by placing the heel of your hand,

with your other hand on top, on the middle of the victims chest, 2 fingers distance above the bottom of the sternum (chest bone). Press down to a depth of 4cm (1½in), at a rate of 100 per minute. After every 15 compressions give 2 rescue breaths, and continue at a rate of 15:2.

Continue until the victim shows signs of life, until you are exhausted or until skilled assistance arrives.

Bleeding

If there is an obvious site of major bleeding, attempt to stop the flow of blood by applying firm pressure over the site directly for at least 10 minutes, without releasing pressure. Maintain pressure during evacuation as much as possible by applying a firm bandage and dressing. Do not remove during evacuation.

If the bleeding is from a limb, then a tourniquet can be applied above the site of bleeding, taking great care not to over-tighten and stop the flow of blood to the limb entirely.

Remember that not all bleeding sites are visible and the patient may be bleeding heavily inside their chest, abdomen or limb. Always remember ABC (see above).

Hypothermia

Do not forget that an injured person in extreme conditions will become hypothermic very quickly.

Remove wet clothes if possible, shelter from wind and rain and cover with emergency blankets, sleeping bag etc. Lie with the victim if all else fails.

A person is not considered dead until WARMED AND DEAD. With a hypothermic person always continue resuscitation attempts (if possible) until the person is warmed.

Drowning

The priorities for a person who has been pulled from water are the same as for any unconscious patient – ABC (see above). Remember that they will also be hypothermic.

Choking

If the patient is conscious, bend them over forwards and carry out firm back blows. Encourage them to cough. If the back blows fail, then attempt abdominal thrusts ('Heimlich manoeuvre') by standing behind the patient and placing both arms around the upper part of the abdomen. Clenching one fist and holding this with your other hand, pull sharply backwards and inwards. This will hopefully produce a sudden expulsion, causing the foreign body to be ejected from the airway.

If the patient is unconscious, then ABC (see above) are first priorities. An abdominal thrust can be tried by straddling the victim and pushing down into the upper abdomen with your two clenched hands.

Fractured Limbs

Any suspected fractured bone should be splinted as comfortably as possible using whatever means are available. Examples are tree bark, pieces cut from closed-cell mattresses ('Karrimats'), Thermarests, pieces of wood, walking sticks etc.

If the bone is sticking out of the skin then cover with a dressing and evacuate. If evacuation is delayed then consider starting antibiotics such as penicillin to prevent infection.

Straightening a badly deformed limb will help relieve pain and stop internal bleeding.

Dislocations

If a joint is obviously dislocated then it may be worth attempting to reduce it (put it back in place), as this will help with relief of pain. Give adequate pain relief, splint the limb involved afterwards as comfortably as possible and evacuate.

If a limb below a dislocation is white, pulseless and painful then this may mean that a major blood vessel to the limb is compressed. The limb is at risk of gangrene and the joint must be put back in place immediately if possible.

Lacerations and Cuts

The basic rule of thumb is that any cut older than 6 hours should not be sutured (stitched). If a wound is dirty and old, clean it thoroughly with antiseptic (povidone iodine is best) and cover with a clean dressing.

Freshly cleaned recent cuts can be sutured or closed if less than 6 hours old. Consider using paper or 'butterfly' sutures.

If there are signs of infection such as pain, redness and pus, then start antibiotics, such as penicillin, amoxycillin.

Dehydration

If you suspect that a person is dehydrated then if possible give Oral Rehydration Salts (ORS). This should be given in small sips every 10 minutes to prevent vomiting.

If there is no ORS available, it can be made by warming 1 litre of water and dissolving 8 teaspoons of sugar + 1 teaspoon of salt.

If the patient is unable to take oral fluids then intravenous fluids should be started. Evacuation will be necessary.

Confirming Death

A person is only deemed dead when there are no signs of life:

· No breathing
· No pulse
· Pupils are fixed (do not move when a light is shined) and dilated
· Hypothermia has been excluded

Bibliography

SELECT BIBLIOGRAPHY OF BOOKS RELATED TO THE INDIAN HIMALAYA

General

Aitken, Bill: *Riding the Ranges*, Penguin, New Delhi (1998).

Aitkinson, E.T.: *The Himalayan Gazetteer*, Govt. of India, Allahabad (1882).

Ali, Aamir: *Environmental Protection of the Himalaya*, Himalayan Club (1988)

Bauer, Paul: *Kangchenjunga Challenge*, William Kimber, London (1955).

Bauer, Paul: *Himalayan Quest*, Nicholson & Watson, London (1938).

Braham, T.: *Himalayan Odyssey*, George, Allen & Unwin, London (1974).

Bruce, C.G.: *Twenty Years in the Himalaya*, Arnold, London (1910).

Chamoli, S.P.: *The Great Himalayan Traverse*, Vikas, New Delhi (1994).

Gibson, J.T.M.: *As I Saw It*, Mukul Prakashan, Delhi (1976).

Hunt, John: *Life is Meeting*, Hodder & Stoughton, London (1978).

Kapadia, Geeta: *The Himalaya in My Sketchbook*, Indus Publishing, New Delhi (1996).

Kapadia, Harish: *A Passage to Himalaya*, Oxford University Press, Mumbai (Bombay) (2001).

Kapadia, Harish: *High Himalaya Unknown Valleys*, Indus Publishing, New Delhi (1993).

Kapadia, Harish: *Meeting the Mountains*, Indus Publishing, New Delhi (1998).

Kohli, Captain M.S.: *Mountaineering in India*, Vikas, New Delhi (1989).

Kohli, Harish: *Across the Frozen Himalaya*, Indus, New Delhi (2000).

Longstaff, T.G.: *This My Voyage*, John Murray, London (1950).

Mason, Kenneth: *Abode of Snow*, Rupert Hart Davis, London (1955).

Mehta, Soli (with Kapadia, Harish): *Exploring the Hidden Himalaya*, Hodder & Stoughton (1990), second edition, Indus, New Delhi (1998).

Mumm, A.L.: *Five Months in the Himalaya*, Arnold, London (1909).

Neate, Jill: *High Asia*, Unwin Hayman, London (1989).

Noyce, Wilfrid: *Mountains and Men*, Geoffrey Bles, London (1954).

Rizvi, J.: *Trans-Himalayan Caravans*, Oxford, Delhi (2000).

Sircar, Joydeep: *Himalayan Handbook*, Private, Calcutta (1979).

Walker, Derek: *The Pundits*, University Press of Kentucky, Kentucky (1990).

Wilson, Andrew: *The Abode of Snow*, Ratna Pustak Bhandar (reprint 1979), first published London (1885).

Himalayan Journal: Volumes 1 (1928) - 57 (2001).

Indian Mountaineer: Nos.1 (1978) - 36 (2001).

Sikkim and Assam

Bajpai, C.R.: *China's Shadow over Sikkim*, Lancer Publishers, New Delhi (1999).

Brown, Percy: *Tours in Sikkim*, W. Newman, Calcutta (1934).

Cooke, C.R.: *Dust and Snow*, Private, London (1988).

Freshfield, D.W.: *Round Kangchenjunga*, Arnold, London (1903).

Kapadia, Harish: *Across Peaks and Passes in Darjeeling and Sikkim Himalaya*, Indus, New Delhi (2001).

Kumar, Col N.: *Kanchenjunga*, Vision Books, New Delhi (1978).

Singh, Hukam: *Kangchenjunga Ascent from East*, The Offsetters, New Delhi (1994).

Waddell, A.: *Among the Himalayas*, Constable, London (1899).

Kumaun and Garhwal

Aitken, Bill: *The Nanda Devi Affair*, Penguin, New Delhi (1994).

Babicz, Jan: *Peaks and Passes of the Garhwal Himalaya*, Alpinistyczay Klub, Spot (1990).

Boardman, Peter: *The Shining Mountain*, Hodder & Stoughton, London (1978).

Bonington, C.J.S.: *Changabang*, Heinemann, London (1975).

Calvert, H.: *Smythe's Mountains*, Gollancz, London (1985).

Gansser, A. & Arnold, H.: *The Throne of the Gods*, Macmillan, London (1939).

Gill, Major H.S.: *Kamet and Abi Gamin: A Gunner's Odyssey*, Lancer International, New Delhi (1989).

Kapadia, Harish: *Across Peaks and Passes in Garhwal Himalaya*, Indus, New Delhi (1999).

Kapadia, Harish: *Across Peaks and Passes in Kumaun Himalaya*, Indus, New Delhi (1999).

Kumar, Colonel N.: *Nilkantha*, Vision Books, New Delhi (1965).

Languepin, J.J.: *Nanda Devi 1951*, Arthaud, Paris (1952).

Murray, W.H.: *The Scottish Himalayan Expedition*, J.M. Dent & Son, London (1957).

Patel, J.: *The Garhwal Kumaon Himalayas*, Himalayan Club, Bombay (1985).

Randhawa, M.S.: *The Kumaon Himalayas*, Oxford and I.B.H., New Delhi (1970).

Roskelley, J.: *Nanda Devi – The Tragic Expedition*, Stackpole Books, Harrisburg (1987).

Saunders, Victor: *No Place to Fall*, Hodder & Sharma, K.P.: *Garhwal & Kumaon*, Ciceron Press,

Cumbria (1998).
Stoughton, London (1994).
Smythe, F.S.: *Valley of Flowers*, Hodder & Stoughton,
London (1938).
Smythe, F.S.: *Kamet Conquered*, Gollancz, London
(1932).
Shipton, Eric: *Nanda Devi*, Hodder & Stoughton
(1936).
Shipton, Eric: *That Untravelled World*, Hodder &
Stoughton, London (1969).
Tilman, H.W.: *Ascent of Nanda Devi*, University Press,
Cambridge (1937).
Venables, Stephen: *A Slender Thread*, Hutchinson
London (2000).
Weir, Thomas: *The Ultimate Mountains*, Cassell,
London (1953).

Kinnaur
Kapadia, Harish: *Across Peaks and Passes in
Himachal Pradesh*, Indus, New Delhi (1999).
Kumar, K.I.: *Kinner Kailash Expedition*, Vision Books,
New Delhi (1979).
Mamgain, M.D. (Ed): *Kinnaur District Gazetteer*.
Himachal Pradesh Government (1971)
Pallis, Marco: *Peaks and Lamas*, Cassell, London
(1939).
Sanan, Deepak (with Swadi, Dhanu): *Exploring
Kinnaur & Spiti*, Indus, New Delhi (1998).

Spiti
Holmes, Peter: *Mountains and a Monastery*, Geoffrey
Bles, London (1958).
Kapadia, Harish: *Spiti, Adventures in the Trans-
Himalaya*, Indus Publishing, New Delhi (1996).
Khosla, G.D.: *Himalayan Circuit*, Macmillan, London
(1956).

Kullu and Lahaul
Bruce, C.G.: *Kulu and Lahoul*, Arnold, London
(1914).
Bruce, C.G.: *Himalayan Wanderer*, Maclehose,
London (1934).
Chaudhry, Minakshi: *Exploring Pangi Himalaya*, Indus,
New Delhi (1998).
Chetwode, Penelope: *Kullu*, Allied Publishing, Delhi
(1984).
Gill, M.S.: *Himalayan Wonderland*, Vikas, Delhi
(1972).
Harcourt, A.F.P.: *The Himalayan Districts of Kooloo,
Lahoul and Spiti*, Vivek (reprint) (1972).
Khosla, G.D.: *Himalayan Circuit*, Macmillan, London
(1956).
Noble, Christina: *Over the High Passes*, Collins,
London (1987).
Noble, Christina: *At Home in the Himalayas*, Collins,
London (1991).
Randhawa, M.S.: *Travels in the Western Himalayas*,
Thomson Press, Delhi (1974).
Scarr, Josephine: *Four Miles High*, Gollancz, London

(1966).
Sharma, M.M.: *Through the Valley of the Gods*, Vision
Books, New Delhi (1977).

Kishtwar
Kolb, Fritz: *Himalayan Venture*, Lutterworth Press,
London (1959).
Venables, S.: *Painted Mountains*, Hodder &
Stoughton, London (1986).

Kashmir, Zanskar and Ladakh
Cunningham, A.: *Ladakh*, Sagar, New Delhi, reprint
(1977), (first published 1853).
Deacock, Antonia: *No Purdah in Padam*, Harrap,
London (1960).
Gazetteer of Kashmir and Ladakh, Govt. publication,
Calcutta (1890).
Harvey, Andrew: *A Journey in Ladakh*, Jonathan Cape,
London (1983).
Jackson, John A.: *Sonamarg Climbing and Trekking
Guide*, Govt. of Jammu & Kashmir, Srinagar (1976).
Kapadia, Harish: *Across Peaks and Passes in Ladakh,
Zanskar and East Karakoram*, Indus, New Delhi
(1999).
Kaul, S. And Kaul, H.N.: *Ladakh Through the Ages*,
Indus Publishing, New Delhi (1992).
Mason, Kenneth: *Routes in the Western Himalaya
and Kashmir*, G.O.I. Press, Calcutta (1929).
Névé, Dr E.F.: *Beyond Pir Panjal*, Church Missionary
Society, London (1915).
Noyce, C.W.F.: *A Climber's Guide to Sonamarg*,
Himalayan Club, New Delhi (1945).
Peissel, Michel: *Zanskar, the Hidden Kingdom*,
Collins and Harvill, London (1979).
Pierre, Bernard: *A Mountain Called Nun Kun*, Hodder
& Stoughton, London (1955).
Rizvi, J.: *Ladakh, Cross-road of High Asia*, Oxford
University, Delhi (1983).
Workman, W.H. and F.B.: *Peaks and Glaciers of Nun
Kun*, Constable, London (1909).
Younghusband, F.: *Kashmir*, Murray, London (1909).

Eastern Karakoram
Hillary, Peter: *Rimo*, Hodder & Stoughton, London
(1988).
Khanna, Y.C.: *Saser Kangri*, I.T.B.P., New Delhi
(1980).
Khullar, Brig. D.K.: *A Mountain of Happiness*,
Interprint, New Delhi (1995).
Saunders, Victor: *Elusive Summits*, Hodder &
Stoughton, London (1990).
Shipton, Eric: *That Untravelled World*, Hodder &
Stoughton, London (1969).
Venables, S.: *Painted Mountains*, Hodder &
Stoughton, London (1986).
Workman, F. and W.: *Two Summers in the Ice-wilds of
Eastern Karakoram*, T. Fisher Unwin, London (1912).
Young, Peter: *Himalayan Holiday*, Herbert Jenkins,
London (1943).

Glossary

achaar = spicy pickle
angrez = foreigner, from mis-pronunciation of English
bazaar = market place
Bhagwat Gita = Hindu religious verse
bharal = Tibetan blue sheep
chai = tea
chang = home-brewed alcoholic drink, like beer
chatti or *dharamshala* = pilgrim shelter
chorten = Tibetan word for stupa
chu = small river
chuli = cooking hearth
dahi = yoghurt or curds
dalbhat = staple food of lentils

cooked as watery soup with boiled rice
dhaba = road-side eating place
dhar = ridge
dhura = pass
gad = small river
gaon = village
garam = hot
ghat = river bank
ghati = pass
gompa = Buddhist monastery
gurudwara = Sikh place of worship
jule = greeting
jutta = shoes
kangri = mountain
khachar = mules
khana = meal

kharak = grazing ground
khola = river
khota = load carrying donkey
kund = small lake
la = pass
lama = Buddhist monk
lungpa = small river
Mahabharat = Hindu epic
mandala = Buddhist religious form of painting
mandir = temple
mela = trade fair
nala = small river
namaste = greetings
pani = water
parikrama = pilgrim route around sacred mountain or temple

pashmina = cashmere wool
prayag = meeting point of rivers
puja = religious ceremony
Purana, Ramayan = Hindu epics
rasta = road
rimpoche = revered high-ranking lama or 'precious one'
rishi or *sadhu* = sage
sangam = meeting place of rivers
Shiva = Hindu God
skyang = wild donkey
tal = lake
thangka = Tibetan sacred painting, usually on canvas
tso = lake
yatri = pilgrim

Index

Lt. Nawang Kapadia (1975–2000)

AUTHOR'S ACKNOWLEDGEMENTS

I must express my thanks to several companions who have explored the mountain trails, described in this book, with me over the years. Their camaraderie has made these Himalayan treks hugely enjoyable, and in fact one of the main reasons I go trekking is to be with them in the Himalaya. I wish to thank, in particular, Jagdish Nanavati who methodically introduced me to the sport, Vijay Kothari who has shared most of the treks mentioned here and the Himalayan Club which has provided reference material over the years. On most of these treks Harsinh and his fellow villagers from the village of Harkot, Kumaun, have accompanied me; carrying luggage, cooking and looking after my well-being, and most of the time pampering me! Their working enthusiasm, beyond the call of duty, made things very pleasant often under trying circumstances.

Yangdu Goba and Motup Goba of Rimo Expeditions were helpful with providing and checking information about the Sikkim and Ladakh areas. Sheela Jaywant, Huzefa Electricwala and my wife Geeta Kapadia helped with the proofs and finer points. I am thankful to the contributors of additional material and photographs as mentioned below. Their time, energy and insight have made this an enjoyable book to write – as enjoyable as any Himalayan trek!

I wish to dedicate this book to my son Lt. Nawang Kapadia (1975–2000). He shared my passion for trekking and love of nature, and he gave his life defending the Himalaya.

CONTRIBUTORS
Additional text contributors:
Bill Aitken (Kangra Valley Railway, page 123); Dr Natalie Hawkrigg (Health and Safety, pages 168–9); Sheela Jaywant (Protecting the Himalaya, pages 164–5); J.C. Nanavati (The Art of Trekking, page 30); Steve Razzetti (Mountain Photography, pages 166–7).

Additional photographic contributors
Romesh Bhattacharjee pages 154, 157; Marion Mantkelow 123 (2), 126; Huzefa Electricwala page 49; Yangdu Goba page 162.